Reinhold Niebuhr in the 1960s

Reinhold Niebuhr in the 1960s

Christian Realism for a Secular Age

RONALD H. STONE

FORTRESS PRESS
MINNEAPOLIS

REINHOLD NIEBUHR IN THE 1960S

Christian Realism for a Secular Age

Cover image: Dr. Reinhold Niebuhr speaking at the Union Theological Seminary. (Photo by Walter Sanders/The LIFE Picture Collection/Getty Images)

Cover design: Laurie Ingram

Print ISBN: 978-1-5064-4624-0

eBook ISBN: 978-1-5064-4625-7

The paper used in this publication meets the minimum requirements of American National Standard for Information Sciences — Permanence of Paper for Printed Library Materials, ANSI Z329.48-1984.

Manufactured in the U.S.A.

To
Alan Jay Stone
faithful younger brother

Contents

Preface

Reinhold Niebuhr retired in the spring of 1960. In his final address at Union Theological Seminary he advised students to find their integrity in remaining honest in their ministries. He urged them to seek to increase the church's relevance to the horrible problems of nuclear armaments in a revolutionary world. They were held responsible to help resolve the race issue and to free African Americans from oppression. Reinhold remained one more year on Morningside Heights to serve in the Columbia University seminar on war and peace directed by Professor William Fox. Then he spent terms at Harvard and Princeton universities lecturing on democracy.

The decade began in the election of John F. Kennedy, promising a younger, newer generation from World War II that he would boldly lead. Kennedy was Niebuhr's third choice for president that year, but he supported and endorsed him. Many of his advisors and cabinet were devotees of Niebuhr or at least well read in his philosophy. The president's biographer-advisor would claim that Niebuhr was the most influential theologian of the century in America, and a vice president would assert that no other preacher was as influential as Niebuhr. The next president would award him the Freedom Medal of Honor. Niebuhr's influence was at its maximum during the Kennedy presidency and the early years of the Johnson presidency. Church membership and attendance reached its height during the 1950s, and young theologians drawn to the church by the relevance of Martin Luther King Jr.'s work and the thought of Paul Tillich and Reinhold Niebuhr were crowding the nation's seminaries.

By the end of the decade, Reinhold Niebuhr's contribution was under attack from within the walls of Union Theological Seminary and in the pages of his own journal, *Christianity and Crisis*. The decade had killed its leaders, Martin Luther King Jr., John and Robert Kennedy, and driven President Johnson out of office. Students occupied the offices of their academies. Many who hoped for a new day of democracy were disillusioned and engaged in rioting or dropping out. Utopianism gave way to disillusionment. Cities, particularly black neighborhoods, burned, and the purposefulness of a Kennedy seemed to be lost. The promising civil rights movement was in disarray, and militant leadership within the black community in its divisiveness had even killed Malcolm X. The Federal Bureau of Investigation turned to killing militant black leaders and corrupting student radicals. Even pacifists were regarded by the establishment as dangerous, and they were falsely persecuted. The decade was colored by the threat of nuclear apocalypse.

None of the three biographies by Charles Brown, Richard Fox, or June Bingham focuses on Reinhold Niebuhr's work in the 1960s. My own previous writing on Niebuhr has not adequately analyzed the important work of this decade. It was a turbulent decade and Niebuhr commented on most of its events. But more than commenting, he produced several important works in this decade on politics, international relations, and racial relations. The primary purpose of this work is to correct my own deficiencies; in these pages, I turn toward this late Niebuhr, and perhaps provide fuller analysis than the other works on his thought and life in the decade.

The turbulence and utopianism of the decade produced a torrent of works criticizing Niebuhr's work and his developed position of Christian realism. His reputation as a guide for the century suffered abuse in the closing decades of the century. However, in the twenty-first century his work on political theory and his guidance for American foreign policy took on a renewed importance. His skepticism about militantly exporting American democracy was confirmed by the debacle of the US invasion of Iraq and the continuing war. His writing about the limited responsibility for US leadership made sense as other powers rose to share world leadership. The echo of Niebuhr's thought in the Nobel Prize address by President Barack Obama and the "soft diplomacy" emphasis of Hillary Clinton made sense of a moral or Christian realism on the world scene. His hope that Soviet Communism would collapse was confirmed at the end of the twentieth century and moderate realism seemed the way forward.

His essays and books of the 1960s reveal more attention to the crisis in race relations than his publications of the 1950s. By the end of the decade his increased militancy was obvious to those who read his contributions to the subject. Even as sharp a critic as James Cone has avowed that his militancy approached that of Malcolm X in some of his later writings.

Furthermore, his insistence that Christian realism committed to domestic reform as well as international responsibility brushed aside neo-conservative claims that he was akin to an Edmund Burke conservative. Recognizing the idealist-realist combination in the history of American policy, he made clear his own distance from cynicism or realpolitik.

One of the further, more subtle differences from earlier periods of his thought is the decrease in theological vocabulary in his writing. The theological convictions are evident, and so this study includes brief analysis of his earlier theological writing. But the demise after his ill health of his more church-oriented journal, *Christianity and Crisis*, and his inability to control it after his resignation from the board, meant that he was writing more for secular journals. He now admitted he was working more on international relations than theology and that his vocation had been to teach social ethics/political theory in a Protestant seminary.

My own reading of Niebuhr started in 1959 before moving to New York City and Union Theological Seminary. Personal study with him started in 1963 when I attended his brilliant lectures on the theory of democracy at Barnard College. Democracy was a historically contingent development in the West that could gain some other adherents, but it was not a universal solution to the problems of government. Study with him followed while pursuing a PhD in religion and international politics at Columbia University, and continued throughout my career as a professor in colleges, universities and seminaries, and beyond. I wrote this book in retirement because his story of the 1960s needs to be told. Significant in this story is to show how he continued to be a great teacher through the trauma of many aliments following his strokes. Near the close of the decade, as his last student-assistant and then junior colleague, we worked together on projects and in friendship. Others shared his friendship and colleagueship, and I have tried to tell this part of history primarily through letters he wrote.

I am in debt to Mark C. Russell of the Barbour Library of the Pittsburgh Theological Seminary for his capacity to locate and provide Niebuhr essays from obscure journals and books. I thank Michael Gibson, Paul Lutter, and Allyce Amidon of Fortress Press for taking the risk of guiding this book to publication. May I also thank half a century of students from Morningside College, Vassar College, Columbia University, Union Theological Seminary, Pacific Lutheran University, Pittsburgh Theological Seminary, the University of Pittsburgh, and the Osher Program at Carnegie Mellon University, who have challenged and questioned me about Niebuhr. Two professors at my alma mater deserve special appreciation for asking me to teach my first class in international relations, Albert Sellen, PhD, and my first class in ethics, Joseph Uemura, PhD. Challenges to my appreciation of Niebuhr came through feminist theologian Susan Nelson, process theologian Marjorie Suchocki, liberation sociologist Gonzalo Castillo, and black theologian James Cone. My lifetime colleague Walter Wiest joined in my honoring and teaching of Niebuhr.

Ursula, Christopher, and Elizabeth Niebuhr Sifton all contributed to my understanding of Reinhold and this book is in debt to all of them. A special relationship with Charles Brown over forty years of Niebuhr interpretation has provided me with many manuscripts and a multitude of ideas. My early teachers of Niebuhr, the late Roger L. Shinn and John C. Bennett, began this project with me in the 1960s, and they continued to fashion my interpretation as long as they lived.

1.

Introduction

> It is as difficult in our day as in the day of Jeremiah to preach "the Word of the Lord," for that runs counter to the complacency of men and of nations. It is sharper than a "two-edged sword." It must hurt before it can heal.

Niebuhr was thrust into the ministry of the Evangelical Synod by his father's death in April 1914. He assumed the temporary role of preacher in his father's pulpit, having completed seminary that spring. He was ordained two months later. His father's friend commissioned Reinhold and symbolically placed his father's mantle upon the young man's shoulders, as the prophet Elijah's mantle had been placed on his successor's shoulders. Elisha followed Elijah in the work of arguing for religious ethical integrity and criticizing kings when they failed. Both the prophets had been experts in international relations as well as religious piety. Reinhold's father, Gustav, had encouraged him to further study at Yale University. That fall, he took his leave of the church and went off to Yale. He took with him his father's commitments to biblical theology, the social gospel, German progressive scholarship, understanding institutional building, and the ecumenical church. The father had also taught him Greek and gifted him with a personal faith, trust, and commitment to faith as undergirding personal vocation and the meaningfulness of human history.

He continued preaching and serving a small church while at Yale. There he deepened his scholarship and became committed to the general philosophy of William James, whose learning combined pragmatism, piety, and an understanding of the varieties of religious experience. The pragmatic tendency to evaluate ideas by their social usefulness remained with Niebuhr. He judged the church by its relevant usefulness in his first book, *Does Civilization Need Religion?*

His early ministry in Detroit immediately invested him in issues of war and peace as World War I (1914–18) involved his German-speaking congregation. The pain of industrialization dominated Detroit and affected his ministry. Race riots exploded before he left Detroit, and his response in the church and society won him the chairmanship on the Commission on Race Relations involving him in African American struggles and Detroit politics. These three issues would continue in his writing and teaching as he left Detroit in 1928 for a teaching and journalistic position in New York City at Union Seminary and *The World Tomorrow*, a socialist/pacifist journal. By the time he left Detroit, he was a well-regarded writer and leader on all three of the social issues of his ministry. The importance of his writing to his New York call needs to be recognized. His teaching ability was not known, and he had not served as an employed editor before. He was known as a preacher/speaker, but it was the writing that won him the respect of national leaders and his patron Sherwood Eddy. Before leaving Detroit, he pulled together from his diary a book, *Leaves from the Notebook of a Tamed Cynic*, a vision of ministry that combined personal piety and social responsibility of the church and its ministry. Later embarrassed by some of its youthful naïveté, he refused to permit its republication until 1957 when he succumbed to the demand for a further publication. The other book from Detroit utilized the untranslated German works of Max Weber and Ernst Troeltsch to examine the social witness of the churches, with the title *Does Civilization Need Religion?* His answer was affirmative when the church acts to relieve human suffering and is relevant to the interpretation of the times.

His first academic appointment (1928–30) was overwhelmed by the Depression and the trajectory of the world toward its worst conflagration, World War II. By 1932, his groundbreaking *Moral Man and Immoral Society* sought solutions to the Depression and the spiraling down of Europe. His politics were now frankly socialist in the way of Paul Tillich's *The Socialist Decision*. H. Richard Niebuhr had translated Tillich's *The Religious Situation*, familiarizing Reinhold with Tillich's work. Tillich's desperate situation led to Niebuhr participating in a rescue operation of Tillich before Hitler could kill him. The Niebuhr-Tillich support for the Jews and for combating Hitler led them both deeply into political action, including involvement with the underground in Germany. Tillich's religious symbolism and his theology influenced Niebuhr in his *An Interpretation of Christian Ethics* and his

Gifford lectures, *The Nature and Destiny of Man* (published in two volumes, 1939 and 1941). Niebuhr had moved to the right in his theology and left in his politics since his ministry in Detroit. Gradually by 1940, his politics had moved back to the left-middle supporting Franklin D. Roosevelt. His theology became the most important in America. Because the politics and thought of the 1960s presuppose his earlier theology, two brief chapters on this wartime theology are included before analyzing his new work in the 1960s. Gradually the contribution of Tillich in the 1950s and Niebuhr's brother Helmut would come to have equal or greater recognition in shaping the American theological outlook. Reinhold helped financially assist Helmut's study of Troeltsch in Germany. Helmut's translation of Tillich's *The Religious Situation* had won Tillich the recognition in America that made it possible for Reinhold to solicit the support of Columbia University and Union to support his transition to America.

The decade of the 1940s saw workers win gains though the war, the Roosevelt administration, and strong unionization. His strategy of joining his ethics to the union movement seemed to be succeeding. Niebuhr's wartime book, *The Children of Light and the Children of Darkness*, defended democracy with a realist political philosophy forecasting his further work in political philosophy. He gained fame as a critic of isolationism and pacifism, calling the United States to assume world responsibility. The second half of the decade focused on the contest with Communism, in which he advocated intellectual competition, foreign aid, patience for the long struggle, and military resistance where needed and prudent. His continual criticism of the American illusion of moral progress led many to regard him as a pessimist. However, as an ethicist he hoped for social progress and labored for it institutionally and intellectually. His church and speaking trips to Europe were complemented in this decade by flying to England in a bomber to speak to troops. On this trip, he ended up under a table with Edward R. Murrow during a German bombing raid. He traveled after the war to inspect the de-Nazification of German educational institutions. His last government trip to Europe was as a delegate to the founding conference of UNESCO. At home, he was called to counsel with the State Department Planning Staff.

The Republican domination of the 1950s led his friend Paul Tillich to withdraw from direct political activity after heavy wartime broadcasts for the Voice of America and his attempt to influence Roosevelt in the previous decade. Niebuhr continued his opposition to the Republicans, John Foster Dulles's policies, and the spirit and actions of the anticommunist right wing. His book written before his 1952 stroke, *The Irony of American History*, was particularly well received by historians, political scientists, and others interested in the American character's role in politics and international relations. The stroke and complicating illnesses forced him to reduce his schedule of whirlwind travel and speaking. He recovered enough to continue teaching, and his production of published essays diminished only slightly.

He advised the candidate and more particularly his supporters in the Democratic Party in the campaigns of Adlai Stevenson. Stevenson's son told one reputable source that Stevenson wanted to choose Niebuhr for his secretary of state before his stroke. He had hoped for the nomination of Hubert H. Humphrey for the 1960 presidential contest, but he settled for John F. Kennedy with reservations.

The chronological evolution of Niebuhr is essential to understanding him because major motifs in his mind changed throughout the twentieth century. This book argues that the theological, political thought of his last decade is of great importance to contemporary thought. Also, his work on race relations became more important than at previous periods, though many of his important social action projects for the empowerment of the blacks were decades earlier. The thought of the last decade is not the Niebuhr of the 1920s, 30s, 40s, or 50s, and it deserves more interpretation than it has previously received.

Most of the other studies of Niebuhr have either slighted or misrepresented the thought and politics of Niebuhr in his mature years. It is important not to assume Niebuhr's position to be that of the 1932 book, *Moral Man and Immoral Society*. At the time, he was leaving pacifism, evaluating strategies of nonviolence, hoping to visit Gandhi in India, and struggling with Marxist interpretations of society and the American economy. This is not the mature Niebuhr. The neoconservatives in foreign policy have tried to claim his authority without grasping his reluctance to export democracy with the American military. Others have blamed him for the thought that led to the Vietnam War, ignoring his own position in the 1960s. His understanding of the needed cooperation among nations and the partnership with the Russians in avoiding nuclear war was missed. His position on race relations is not generally known, as that came to maturity in the 1960s. I have spoken to academic audiences where his limitations in the 1960s due to severe strokes were neither understood nor even known.

Niebuhr devoted most of his work in the 1960s to international relations, race relations, politics, and political philosophy to guide the American empire into wise, mature policies. In addition to publishing works on politics he wrote a lot on race relations as he became more militant in criticizing the oppression. Though I read *The Structure of Nations and Empires*, his 1959 book, in the early 1960s, I am starting this book with an analysis of it. He had been on a sabbatical with a grant from the Rockefeller Foundation as a Visiting Scholar at the Institute for Advanced Study in Princeton in 1958 to study patterns of empires and the rivalry between the Soviet Union and the United States. That issue is still very much with us. His books and late lectures on democracy and imperial responsibility have not received much attention. This study is an attempt to overcome that oversight.

In 1963, political philosophers in Great Britain asked: "Is political philosophy dead, and if so, who killed it?" Five years later, Isaiah Berlin answered that as long as there was political argument and different views of justice, sovereignty, ethics, and preferred models of political organization, political philosophy was a perennial human question. He moved right into Niebuhr's territory by asserting that behind the different answers to political philosophy was the model of human life presupposed by the thinkers. Throughout this period Niebuhr was producing political philosophy, and though he often drew upon his older arguments, he produced a rather complete political philosophy that still holds up remarkably well and provides foundations for political thought in the twenty-first century.

Perhaps the central reason for this book is that the walks I took with Reinhold through the 1960s were the most important education I ever received. I have mentioned them in previous writing, but I have never attempted to describe in detail the marvelous adventure with "Reinie" that characterized the later years of my doctoral studies in ethics, political philosophy, international relations, and philosophy of religion. These walks and his letters need to be interpreted to get a fuller picture of Reinhold than we have. He often referred to the best education in Horace Mann's metaphor: "The student sitting on one end of the log and the teacher on the other." We did not have the log between us, but we were among the trees of Riverside Drive in all seasons.

Because this book emphasizes his later studies of politics, it begins with the 1959 book on empire that underlies his thinking and publications of the 1960s. These years are the decade of his most intensive work in international relations and political philosophy, but these subjects presuppose his theology, more than many interpreters understand. America's foreign policy moved from Kennedy's realistic Cold War policies through President Johnson's crusade in Vietnam to Richard Nixon's cynical Cold War policies during the later 1960s. The student radicals shifted from the idealistic belief that a demonstration could change foreign policy to cynically dropping out. They arose in moralism and enthusiasm and ended in violence and despair. Drugs, sexual experimentation, para-religions, Oriental mysticism, dropping out, and new communal living forms of life all enticed and betrayed them. Politics of the establishment seemed disgusting to them, whereas the truth is that politics always has a disgusting element. Some dreamed of revolution, but most of them had not used a gun, and they did not know how, in most cases, to make or deliver a bomb. David R. Williams tells the story and sees it partially as a revolt against Niebuhr who disdained both the nonpolitical and the moralistic.[1]

His appreciation of the despairing anger of African Americans grew during the 1960s. The essay published in *Social Action*,[2] "The Negro Minority and Its Fate in a Self-Righteous Nation," was the best piece he published among many on the issue. He lived near African Americans, but he was not one of them. It became fashion among interpreters of Niebuhr of late to suggest that he failed to respond adequately to the black revolution. The better scholars like James Cone reveal the ambiguity of their criticisms. Cone comes to write about Niebuhr as sounding like Malcolm X in his fury over racial oppression.[3] I think the reader of most of Niebuhr's essays on race in the 1960s will understand that he became the best white-churchman interpreter of the crisis in race relations and oppression.

One hoped-for contribution of this book on Niebuhr is the evidence that he was heroic in overcoming pain to continue his fight for justice. He experienced his first strokes at nearly sixty years of age in 1952. Suffering from spastic paralysis, he endured further strokes in the 1960s. His health was limited by a prostate operation, depression from his limitations, paralysis, stroke-related weakness, a broken tailbone, head injuries from falls, and frequent attacks from old-age illnesses until the final pneumonia. In this book the details of these reactions are left primarily to his descriptions of pain and illness in his own letters. His work in the 1960s is the work of a traumatized, semi-paralyzed teacher who overcame severe limitations to produce more work than most professors complete in good health.

1. David R. Williams, *Searching for God in the Sixties* (Newark: University of Delaware Press, 2011).

2. Charles C. Brown, ed., *A Reinhold Niebuhr Reader* (Philadelphia: Trinity Press International, 1992), 118–23.

3. James Cone, *The Cross and the Lynching Tree* (Maryknoll, NY: Orbis, 2011), 57.

2.

Cold War Empires

> We do not know whether we will survive or whether the great powers will destroy each other in their fateful struggle on the abyss of nuclear annihilation. But we hope that we have the wisdom and responsibility to escape this fate, in which case we could have a more universal community.

Reinhold Niebuhr had a long background of political participation. His severe stroke in 1952 paralyzed his left side, ending his traveling-speaking career and denying him the energy to sustain his role in several religious and political organizations he had founded. His influence was felt through his writing, and by the late 1950s his literary output had returned to his pre-stroke production level. The most significant book of this decade of his life was published in 1959, and I read it before I knew Niebuhr. It was read and absorbed by some in the 1960s, particularly by those drawn into his circle of influence by the earlier volumes: *Moral Man and Immoral Society, The Children of Light and the Children of Darkness, The Nature and Destiny of Man,* and *The Irony of American History.*

This volume, *The Structure of Nations and Empires*, provided the background for my conversations with Niebuhr. It was his philosophy of international politics for competition and coexistence with the Soviet Union. It was intended to advise foreign policy thinkers like those he associated with in the Council on Foreign Relations. Niebuhr appreciated the difficulty of democratic foreign policy. The general populace could not be expected to understand foreign policy. They were much better at domestic policy, where their immediate interests were felt strongly. A governing elite was responsible for foreign policy, and the role of the president in setting the direction of policy was immense.

Reinhold Niebuhr's sabbatical as a visiting scholar at the Institute for Advanced Study in Princeton was sponsored by the Rockefeller Foundation. Robert Oppenheimer directed the Institute following George Kennan. It's hard to imagine a more establishment position for a professor nearing retirement. The study of 1958 combined with some previous essays produced the volume *The Structure of Nations and Empires*, and the class he introduced at the seminary was titled "Moral Issues in International Politics." It established the primary direction for his work in the 1960s in political philosophy and international relations.

He worried that overreliance on the United Nations and American moralism produced policies based on illusion. The United Nations was aiding previous empires to disintegrate. However, empires remained in China, India, Russia, and the United States. Previous empires in Mexico and Brazil were still dominating polyglot populations. European empires were slowly being dissolved and sometimes with imperial resistance. The superpowers of Russia and the United States competed for influence in the dissolving European empires. Niebuhr admitted he had an eye on contemporary struggles and suggested he was attempting to provide a political philosophy to guide the United States through the Cold War.

Quickly in the second chapter he reveals his distaste for the liberal theory of international relations guiding President Eisenhower and Secretary Dulles's team. Both leaders, to his mind, assumed the autonomy of the nation-state, obscured intermediate forms of dominance, and hoped for universal community through the United Nations reinforced by collective security. The reality was the centrality of the two superpowers' competition.

The decade of the 60s was a period of war. It was not total war, but a season of war. Thomas Hobbes had remarked that as a rainy season is not all rain, neither is a season of war all war. But the Cold War characterized the decade and wars broke out in the Congo, Indo-China, and the Dominican Republic. Cold War tensions were felt particularly in Berlin and Cuba, and the threat of nuclear war dominated the times.

Niebuhr saw the times as characterized by the three revolutions John H. Hertz identified.[1] First, the dissolution of the World War II alliance produced the worldwide rivalry between the Soviet Union and the United States. The competition was fueled by the repudiation by Communism of the capitalist economic system that dominated the world. Politically the alliance led by the democratic states aimed to curtail the growth of the Communist system. The interjection of nuclear weapons

1. John H. Hertz, *International Politics in the Atomic Age* (New York: Columbia University Press, 1962), 11.

into the ideological and economic battle created a second new factor. Third, the former colonies of Europe were trying out new forms of government under an explosion of new nationalisms. It was a world in a threefold revolution. From Niebuhr's perspective, the United States needed to maintain minimum order through balancing Russian power while avoiding war. The major instruments for maintaining this order were deterrence and diplomacy. The Cold War reduced the significance of the United Nations and magnified the relevance of the two major empires upon which stability rested.

IMPERIALISM

Niebuhr understood the United States as an empire. It had displaced the indigenous nations, conquered and annexed part of the Mexican empire, absorbing some of its people, and had taken territories from the British, Spanish, French, and Russian empires. Through the Spanish-American war in his childhood, it had expanded its power across the oceans. As he grew to maturity, its economic outreach expanded its power, and the two world wars had married its economic power to its military power. His Augustinian theology led him to understand that Christianity had come to maturity in an empire. Appreciation of Charles Cochrane's book *Christianity and Classical Culture* in his discussion circles encouraged him to think of empire as the context for much of his own thought. He also regarded the Soviet Union as an empire, and it never occurred to him to think of the United States as the sole empire. Empires had preceded nation-states, and he thought of them as an intermediary form in the present between nation-states and the unrealized world community.

The concept of empire came to bear heavy weight in political philosophy in the last stage of his career. *The Structure of Nations and Empires*, his most formal work in international relations, does not provide an all-embracing system or a complete model for thinking about the subject, but it analyzes the phenomenon of empire in many of its expressions. It argued that there are discernible patterns by which strong nations relate to weaker nations, and it made an effort to isolate discernible patterns of imperialism.[2] The practical efforts of Niebuhr came through as he related the struggle between the Soviet Union and the United States to perennial and contingent aspects of imperial competition.[3] He noted that the

2. Reinhold Niebuhr, *The Structure of Nations and Empires* (New York: Charles Scribner's Sons, 1959), 1.

3. Niebuhr, *Structure of Nations*, 2.

term was difficult to use in contemporary political discourse.[4] He used it to refer to a pattern of hegemony exercised by one nation over another.[5] For *Structures of Nations and Empires*, it was a recurring pattern within the international system and one of the most important characteristics of the Cold War.[6] Despite the liberal and/or Marxist critique of imperialism, the respective empires exercised hegemonic control by military force, economics, and diplomacy over other members of their alliances.

Niebuhr's understanding of imperialism relates to his understanding of power, and it contains a note of inevitability. Stronger nations tend to impose their will upon weaker nations. The conflict among motives often gives the stronger nations a sense of universality to their claims that the weaker nations regard as hypocrisy, but actually the claims reflect the mixture of motives that usually characterize imperialism. The motivations of missionary, economic, and political are usually present and mixed in imperial ventures. The missionary implies the export of an ideology that the imperial empire may regard as universal. The economic motivation does not necessarily mean that the whole empire profits but indicates that important interests in the empire can profit from imperial actions.[7]

Political motivations can be as broad as self-defense or the seeking of prestige or the maximization of power.[8] National strength for Niebuhr almost inevitably leads toward imperialism and its rationalization.[9] The moral ambiguity of imperialism reflects the domination inherent in the political process even though it accentuates it because of the cross-cultural domination.[10]

His survey of the forms of imperialism showed that their claims for universality were overstated and the legacy of European imperialism had beneficial aspects as well as harmful accents. He thought that though empires were never as beneficial as their ideological supporters claimed, they were only seldom as evil as their nationalist critics supposed. Both of the major rivals in the Cold War had historic critical postures toward imperialism and consequently reflected contradictions from that ideology in actual practice.[11] Rivalry between the two empires was unavoid-

4. Niebuhr, *Structure of Nations*, 3.

5. Niebuhr, *Structure of Nations*, 206.

6. Niebuhr repeatedly attacked the theory that capitalism was the cause of imperialism. *Structure of Nations*, 23; *Christian Realism and Political Problems* (New York: Charles Scribner's Sons, 1953), 57.

7. Niebuhr, *Structure of Nations*, 202–3.

8. Niebuhr, *Structure of Nations*.

9. Niebuhr, *Structure of Nations*, 215; see also 25, 216, 295, and 298.

10. Niebuhr, *Structure of Nations*, 10–32.

11. Niebuhr, *Structure of Nations*, 11.

able, but Niebuhr hoped to provide a perspective on the Cold War that would free the American public from fanatically regarding the Soviet Union as a unique, unalloyed evil. The new empire did have unprecedented features, but he believed an emphasis on the "perennial and constant factors" of the rivalry would encourage the wisdom needed for a long period of competitive coexistence.

Niebuhr's attitude toward American imperialism had shifted. Prior to World War II, he had seen the developments toward American imperialism and had warned against it. He had particularly feared that a combination of American military might with its economic power would be dangerous to world peace. Noting the British Labour Party's opposition to imperialism, he had hoped for such a position developing in the United States.[12] During World War II, he had adjusted to the realities of the United States's new power and, rejecting isolation, hoped for responsible use of power. Eventually for him, imperialism came to mean the "exercise of the responsibilities of power."[13]

NIEBUHR BEFORE RETIREMENT

Finishing his sabbatical at Princeton, the Niebuhrs returned to their apartment on 122nd street in the Union Theological Seminary quadrangle. Reinhold was unable to assist in the arrangements for his mother, Lydia, to move from McCormick Theological Seminary to Richard Niebuhr's residence after the death of their sister, Hulda, in Chicago. Richard undertook the responsibility to shelter their mother as Reinhold had in earlier years before his marriage. Reinhold's left-arm paralysis and frequent pain reminded him of his vulnerability and mortality. But he was in no hurry to retire. Writing his friend Bishop Scarlett, he noted his dread at the approaching mandatory retirement from Union at the age of sixty-eight. He had no hobbies; his life was one of work. Through pain and paralysis, he continued to write essays; the outpouring of his last two years of teaching was not far below his earlier years.

Niebuhr's journal, *Christianity and Crisis*, described the context of his times. He kept up regular writing on Russia and developments in the Soviet Union. His editorials stressed the superior achievements of Russia in military technology. He also believed Russia's rapid economic developments were attractive to the poor nations. Its rise from a backward society toward a developed power of educational sophistication

12. Reinhold Niebuhr, "Perils of American Power," *Atlantic Monthly*, January 1932, 90–91.

13. Reinhold Niebuhr, "Mr. Khrushchev and Post Stalin Russia," *Christianity and Crisis* 19, no. 3 (Mar. 2, 1959): 18.

was closer to their needs than the riches of the North Atlantic world. He suggested that the competition between the USSR and the United States would last for decades. He did not expect much progress on the division of Germany or disarmament.

The journal recorded the pressures of science, technology, and economics to increasingly secularize society. Edward Farley argued that social institutions were by their nature secular, others would[14] decry the secularization of the public schools. Niebuhr himself was somewhat secularized in that he reserved the messages of grace and faith and theology for the church while urging Christians to live fully in the secular world. He wrote in two voices: *Christianity and Crisis* sounded his more theological reflections and *The New Leader* his more political reflections. Sometimes, however, the essays just bore different titles in his various publication ventures.

The rapprochement between Roman Catholics and Protestants was an important third theme in *Christianity and Crisis*. Catholicism had won acceptance and Protestants were forced to share power. The election campaign by John F. Kennedy beginning in 1959 was an example of this, and it won the support of Reinhold Niebuhr. Niebuhr's friends Robert McAfee Brown and John C. Bennett developed into leaders in this new cooperation with Catholicism.[15]

A fourth emphasis of the journal, not regarded as a national trend, supported the shifting of economic resources to the aid of the poor. The trajectory required the strengthening of governmental resources to regulate control of corporations toward purposes of the public good. An example of the emphasis was the publication, almost in full, of Senator Adlai Stevenson's speech of 1959 to the Institute of Life Insurance. Niebuhr had endorsed Stevenson twice in his presidential campaigns, and Stevenson had mentioned privately that Niebuhr had been his choice for secretary of state.

The speech centered on the need for governmental intervention and guidance for steel manufacturers and their unionized employees. However, moving beyond the impending steel strike Stevenson called on business and governmental leadership to define a national purpose to overcome poverty and to release the God-given potential of all Americans. Bennett's comments praised the emphasis on increased public spending on education. Niebuhr focused on the need of government to secure the public interest in intervention when labor and business

14. Edward Farley, "Another View of Secularism," *Christianity and Crisis* 19, no. 5 (Mar. 30, 1959): 43–44.

15. John C. Bennett, "Protestant-Roman Catholic Dialogue," *Christianity and Crisis* 19, no. 2 (June 8, 1959): 2.

were spiraling into threatening the common welfare. Stevenson's speech stressed many of the leading public causes that the journal pursued during the Cold War. The public welfare aspects of democratic capitalism remained a Niebuhr priority during the Cold War.[16]

Another note of emphasis in *Christianity and Crisis* as the decade of the 1960s opened was its expansion of essays on other nations on the world scene. Essays on India were written by both Indians and Americans. Africa received more attention than previously. Niebuhr wrote an essay-editorial against apartheid in 1960 and suggested World Council of Churches action against the apartheid-centered Dutch Reformed Church of South Africa. Alan Paton added a Christian critique from South Africa to the policies of the journal. Essays on China appeared more often than earlier, and US policy refusing to recognize the government in Beijing was derided.

Another change in emphasis mentioned by Niebuhr was that the journal, twenty years after its founding, would give more emphasis to cultural issues.[17] There was a crisis in the culture as well as in politics.

INTERNATIONAL POLITICS

Hans J. Morgenthau, the great political philosopher and expert in international relations at the University of Chicago, paid tribute to Niebuhr in *Christianity and Crisis*.[18] He focused on two questions: Does the new factor of nuclear weapons override the perennial perceptions of how international relations work in the competition among empires, and, can the moral failures of human judgment and the ambiguities of international politics be overcome sufficiently to speak rationally of the moral reality of international politics? He left both questions unanswered. Niebuhr's answer to both would have been: Yes and No. Morgenthau thought the questions could be illuminated as Reinhold Niebuhr had, but he insisted they could not be resolved.

Niebuhr's publishing of *The Structure of Nations and Empires* in 1959 marked an emphasis in his published work. Rather than publishing on other of his themes, particularly race and economics, he pounded on the themes of the book. He reiterated the rivalry with the Soviet Union for

16. Adlai Stevenson, "The Survival of the Free Society," *Christianity and Crisis* 19, no. 23 (Jan. 11, 1960): 204–8.

17. Reinhold Niebuhr, "Why Christianity and Crisis?" *Christianity and Crisis* 20, no. 1 (Feb. 8, 1960): 2.

18. Hans J. Morgenthau, "The Intellectual and Moral Dilemma of History," *Christianity and Crisis* 20, no. 1 (Feb. 8, 1960): 3–7.

the allegiances of the Global South. He emphasized how difficult the competition would be, given Russian technological superiority in rockets and missiles. He would praise the equity in the Russian educational system. Its rise from Czarist poverty to Soviet economic development might be a lure to the poor world to follow centralized forms of government for development. He insisted on the West's development of economic and military strength to counter the Russians while at the same time praising initiatives for peace like the Khrushchev visit to the United States.[19] Out of a dozen editorials for his journal, eight were on international relations, two on the threatened steel strike, one on racial justice, and one on the Pope's Council.[20]

Niebuhr's fall essay for *The Christian Century* brought together themes he had already written about in other journals and in his new book. The three major issues for "The Test of Christian Faith Today" were race relations, economic justice, and the catastrophic threat of the Cold War. If we survived, the race issue was the most clear and urgent. Protestantism had failed in the United States and compounded the failure in South Africa. Quoting both Jesus on love and Paul on "one blood," he insisted that the moral issue was straightforward for the church. The economic issues were now subject to secular answers.

The steel industry conflict would be resolved by the balances of power rather than by Christian moral concerns. He even suggested that perhaps there was a new relevance to Luther's "two realms." Following his reading of Brunner's *The Divine Imperative*, he felt that maybe the church's greatest relevance was in the "soft kernel" of personal relations. But now, secularization of the reforms of the welfare state was proceeding without relevant church input.

At least in this essay, Niebuhr seemed blind to the input of the African American church on the issue of racial justice. He should never have referred to "development which has practically excluded the church from the problem of racial justice." Niebuhr knew better. He wanted to get on to his central issue: "the tragedy of the Cold War." He wrote: "Neither side wants war but there is no certain protection against miscalculation and misadventure."[21]

The nuclear terror held in some balance prevented either side from rationally beginning a war. There was no chance of success in a nuclear

19. Reinhold Niebuhr, "Coexistence under a Nuclear Stalemate," *Christianity and Crisis* 19, no. 15 (Sept. 21, 1959): 121–22.

20. Reinhold Niebuhr, "Index to volume XIX," *Christianity and Crisis* 19, no. 23 (Jan. 11, 1960): 216.

21. Reinhold Niebuhr, "The Test of the Christian Faith Today," *The Christian Century* 76, no. 43 (Oct. 28, 1959): 1241.

war. The tragedy of total terror had not been anticipated in philosophies. The biblical images of Christ and anti-Christ illustrated that good and evil grow together but provided no answers. Niebuhr had hopes of the claims of coexistence allowing both superpowers to live together in the absence of war. Competing civilizations had learned in the past to live and let live. He referred to Islam and Western Christianity and also to Protestantism and Catholicism after the Thirty Years War. No simple answers were available. Probably his optimism of tolerance between Western Christianity and Islam was overly emphasized and unhistorical.

The Christian frame of meaning could encourage humility and recognition of the relativism of our answers before the majesty of God. The injunction to love our enemy could lead us to engage in acts of peacemaking. Patience and humility were needed along with resolution. But he ended on a somber note:

> That witness must prompt humble awareness that Western Civilization as we know it, as well as the Communist adversary, may be melted in the crucible of historic destiny.[22]

Norman K. Gottwald responded to Niebuhr with a stinging critique, suggesting Niebuhr had abandoned Christian ethics and dismissed the Lordship of Christ.[23] Niebuhr's response wondered if Gottwald was advocating an abandonment of the deterrent? If so, he thought he should say so.[24]

Though he had turned toward international politics, he made two attempts to define Protestant social ethics in this last year of teaching at Union. The stronger essay was published in the *Union Seminary Quarterly Review.* He spelled out in two dozen paragraphs his perspective. The New Testament is far removed from the secular, technical questions of the late twentieth century. The Sermon on the Mount and Christ's sacrifice on the cross touch on ultimate perspectives more than social realities. A social ethic involves compromise and toleration more than the absolutes of ultimate perspectives. Luther divided the realm of grace from the realm of society. Calvin related the two more closely. Calvinism became coopted in the United States by Social Darwinism and bourgeois culture. A more creative Calvinism was found in the English seventeenth-century revolutionary movement. Prosperity,

22. Niebuhr, "The Test of the Christian Faith Today," 1243.

23. Norman K. Gottwald, "Niebuhr on Nuclear War," *The Christian Century* 76, no. 45 (Nov. 11, 1959): 1311–12.

24. Reinhold Niebuhr, "Niebuhr to Gottwald," *The Christian Century* 57, no. 50 (Dec. 16, 1959): 477.

government, and war have revealed the ambiguities of formulating an adequate Protestant social ethic. The contemporary ecumenical community is developing a more adequate social ethic, utilizing pragmatism and the social principles of responsibility, order, equality, liberty, and tolerance.

Theologically, the biblical sense of divine providence and the dual perspective on humanity as image of God and sinner are necessary. This modern ethic avoids utopianism and abstract fanaticism. The passion for justice expresses the love commandment for the neighbor. This social ethic seeks wisdom in empiricism, social thought, science, and the culture of the day.[25] The statement distanced itself from biblical obscurantism or the Barthian escape to eschatology, which he had criticized in two other 1959 essays. He wanted decisions to be taken with the risks in view and the decision makers to be informed.

25. Reinhold Niebuhr, "The Problem of a Protestant Social Ethic," *Union Seminary Quarterly Review* 15, no. 1 (Nov. 1959): 1–11.

3.

Human Nature

Man has always been his most vexing problem. How should he think of himself?

My introduction to Reinhold Niebuhr was through reading his *The Nature and Destiny of Man* during the summer of 1959. I had just finished leading the Iowa Methodist Student Movement through its race relations project and attending its government seminar in New York City and Washington, DC. Now I had chosen to serve a Methodist Community Church on the banks of the Missouri River Valley in Salix, Iowa. My district superintendent presented me with his copies of the two-volume work. He had attended Union Theological Seminary where I expected to study, and he had known Niebuhr as professor and leader of the Fellowship of Christian Socialists. My own decision for ministerial studies was founded in enthusiasm for the civil rights movement of Dr. Martin Luther King Jr. and the church's promises of social reform. I had worked on a Native American reservation and taken some risks for civil rights, so socially I was prepared for Union Theological Seminary and its realistic version of the social gospel. I think my district superintendent thought I needed more intellectual preparation, hence his gift to me for my summer reading. I would read a chapter each morning before heading out to call on the Protestants of the Missouri Valley near my little village. Neither he nor I knew how formative my developing encounters with Niebuhr would be.

Niebuhr's 1939–41 books were anchored in the minds of his readers in the 1960s. His writing was moving away from this biblical theology, as his secular readers and fans refused to accept it. Still, in the church, he was understood as this heavy biblical theologian who read the Scripture through a Reformation perspective qualified by the disciplines of biblical criticism. He was always more complicated than that, as he attempted to synthesize the Renaissance and the Reformation in terms of Enlightenment and modern philosophy.

The first volume read: "Man has always been his most vexing problem."[1] The opening pages explored the unsatisfactory perspectives that strayed into idealism or materialism. For him, human nature was spirit rooted in its animal nature. He focused mostly on Platonic, Aristotelian, and Stoic perspectives before showing that the classical Greek tragedies were closer to the main Christian perspective. Zeus as the god of order is supreme, but the life of the gods and humans is shaped by the struggle between the Dionysian and the Olympian forces.

Like John Calvin, Niebuhr's view of man combines the biblical views with the analysis of humanity. God and humanity are understood together. Avoiding overreliance on rationality, he turns to biblical symbols. Humanity is best understood as made in the image of God on whom we depend. Humanity is also sinful, as it turns away from God to pursue its own egoism. The distinctive contribution of Niebuhr's view is that humanity transcends its animal nature and is radically free. Both sin and greatness reside in the transcendence of humanity over its naturalistic origins. Niebuhr settles for the paradox of humanity's fall and its partial transcendence of nature. In quick strokes, he concludes the chapter that summarizes alternative views. The modern views of humanity lose the capacity to protect individuality and human freedom. The optimistic views of modernity are defeated by the history of oppression and war. The pessimistic views end in cutting the nerve of social reform. Humanity's freedom and individuality are best protected in thought and practice if humanity is understood in its relationship to God. There is in this chapter a move akin to Paul Tillich's method of correlation. Both in thought and European politics the question of the preservation of human freedom, dignity, and individuality was asked. Niebuhr's answer was: neither classical thought nor modern life succeeded in understanding humanity. He presented a brief argument that humanity was best understood and protected in Christian theology.

VITALITY AND FORM

The second chapter poses the problem of the relation of human vitalities to the human shaping of those vitalities. For Niebuhr, the classical Chris-

1. Reinhold Niebuhr, *The Nature and Destiny of Man*, vol. 1, *Human Nature* (New York: Charles Scribner's Sons, 1941), 1.

tian answer was that vitality and form are united in God and dialectically in tension in human life. Modern thought foundered in trying to interpret human life by overreliance on either pole as a dominant form of interpretation. Marx, Freud, and Nietzsche were existentialist protests that called attention to the rationalist pretensions of bourgeois society or Hegelian philosophy. The conclusions are that four untenable interpretations are characteristic of modern culture: (1) The destructive fury of fascism; (2) The false harmonies of liberalism; (3) The discounting of rationalistic illusions with a hope in revolution; (4) No solution to the conflict of vitality and order and accommodation to the adjustments of Freud.[2] The chapter is probably the best he wrote on those three thinkers, but in its breadth, it also rushes too quickly from Aristotle to Schopenhauer. He used some of Paul Tillich's thought, but Tillich remained critical of his cross-comparisons without the context of various schools of thought. Niebuhr's own reading of Kierkegaard on anxiety was a turning point in the chapter, though only in reference to a footnote indicating that the Freudian analysis would benefit from Søren Kierkegaard's *Der Begriff der Angst*.[3]

By the time of the publication in 1941, it was clear that neither romanticism nor idealism had preserved the dignity of the individual. The chapter on "Individuality in Modern Culture"[4] probably had a surplus of philosophical argument in showing that the individual of modern culture freed from medieval bonds and church discipline had lost itself in the iron cage of industrialism. Then the swallowing of individuality by fascism, Nazism, and Communism drove the masses into the self-destructive World War. Neither the ideas of modern humanity nor its politics kept humanity from losing individuality in thought and destruction. Niebuhr believed that the significance of a free spirit was best understood in subordination to the freedom of God.

EASY CONSCIENCE

Niebuhr claimed those who were attacking the church's dogma of original sin supported an easy conscience for modern humanity. Both Hegel and Marx agreed in recognizing humanity's essential virtue. Either through reason or revolution, this goodness could be released. Humanity held on to its good opinion of itself through war and economic oppression. Institutions were perceived to have been corrupted and their

2. Niebuhr, *Nature and Destiny*, 53.
3. Niebuhr, *Nature and Destiny*, 44.
4. Niebuhr, *Nature and Destiny*, 59–92.

displacement would free humanity to its essential worth. Nature and reason or their combination was seen as possibly restoring humanity to its harmony. Social reform or education was regarded in modernity as the means of restoring humanity to its essential goodness. Even his colleague at Columbia, John Dewey, repeated the mistakes of his predecessors in believing reformed education or cooperative intellectual inquiry could free humanity from its collective disasters.

Even the post-Niebuhrian philosopher John Rawls projected his own ideals of a disinterested social organism choosing equal justice as its norm. Of course, no such disinterested collection of human individuals could ever be found, and no one is prevented from objecting out of their own egoism. Essentially, Rawls's innocence position is mythical like the garden of Eden.

Neither rational prudence nor rational necessity can contain the spiritual drive of humanity to increase its power.[5] Humanity's transcendence over nature in freedom suggests the need to vanquish the human condition and to strive for domination or to lose oneself in sloth. The easy conscience of modern philosophy is false, and the faculty member could have learned it through watching faculty meetings. Similarly, the political philosopher could have seen it by participating in actual politics.

The first four chapters set the stage for the affirmations of the Christian view of humanity in the remaining six chapters. Niebuhr utilized a negative method of correlation. He challenged other anthropologies and showed them to be irrelevant or dangerous; he presented a more detailed version of the Christian view. He believed deeply that human learning was dialogical, that is, it moved from presuppositions to research to conclusions in dialogue with presuppositions and challenges to other ideas. If he had exposed the weaknesses of alternative modern versions, then to him the Christian view deserved consideration. That which he described as the Christian view or biblical view was, of course, his view. His concept was a thoroughly critical view, and only incidentally that of popular preaching, believing, or theologizing.

Only in the exposition of the Christian view could his work be regarded as thorough. In the previous four chapters his work had depended upon generalizations. He threw comparisons of generalizations or types of thought against each other. Some of this method he had acquired from his teacher at Yale, Douglas C. Macintosh. This work through generalizations was a characteristic of New York City intellectuals in the 1930s, and he was a master of it. Irving Howe described the distinctive tone of these writers. They were not specialists, but gen-

5. Niebuhr, *Nature and Destiny*, 122.

eralists. Their thought reigned over many subjects and fields, pressing "toward some encompassing moral or social observation." Daniel Bell described them as "specialists in generalization."[6]

THE CHRISTIAN VIEW OF HUMANITY

Niebuhr argues that the greatness of humanity and its squalor are best understood by relating time to eternity. As humanity transcends itself and reflects upon humanity, it needs perspective from beyond itself that locates meaning in history. Prophetic religion relates to a vision and clues of meaning within history. As humanity transcends itself, so God transcends history.

This meaning is found both in personal experience and in the interpretation of social and historical experience in religious traditions. Or to put it in contemporary language, the real spirituality of individuals depends on the social interpretation of religious traditions. He writes of those insights and organized systems of thought as personal and general revelation. The religious experience of dependence is real in both forms. Feelings of "unqualified dependence" and conscience in both echoed interpretation of the social tradition as reflecting descriptions of experience in biblical traditions. In support of these claims, he exegetes biblical references from the New and Old Testaments. This dialectic from personal-social interpretation to contemporary reality is characteristic of Niebuhr in these chapters. Three forms of religious experience—dependence, judgment, and quest for forgiveness—are correlated with the answers of Creator, Judge, and Redeemer covering Niebuhr's rather meager, simplified doctrine of God.

He completes the chapter by explicating his interpretation of sin as the human willingness in its freedom to exalt itself. Humans forget they are dependent creatures and in pride think they are divine. The prophets criticized Israel's pretensions to become divine and also recognized that its destroyers also suffer from pride. His evidence is taken from the prophets and the Psalms. Biblical faith interprets destruction as a revelation of God's wrath against the pride of humanity. Though he is particularly exegeting texts supporting his interpretation, he wrote: "The problem has its peculiar and poignant relevance to the historical situation of our own day."[7]

Here as elsewhere in his theology, the answer of the Bible to human

6. Quoted in Damon Linker, "Pleasures of Dispute," *New York Times Book Review*, Jan. 10, 2016, 17.

7. Niebuhr, *Nature and Destiny*, 140.

guilt is not to make humanity moral but to recognize that ultimate reality overcomes sin by absorbing and forgiving it. The biblical issue is not primarily to know God and certainly not to find union with God, but to accept divine forgiveness. Here he separates his interpretation, which he regards as the early Reformation's interpretation, from Roman Catholic or some Anglican interpretations of Christian faith. The nature of both humanity and God is love, but the biblical search is how God and humanity can be reconciled from the human attempts to escape its finitude.

There are pages in the chapter that would lead to the conclusion that he is writing about the religious national prides of Nazism, Shinto, and fascism. But other paragraphs, near the end of the chapter, focus on Christology or how this prideful human assertion can be overcome only through forgiveness, which perceives the meaning of Christ as the forgiveness that overcomes human alienation. The warning against sin as pride is universal and is relevant to both human nature and international politics.

IMAGE OF GOD

Through the biblical symbol of the image of God, the sixth chapter argues that humanity, though a dependent creature, has a spiritual dimension. The narrative winds through biblical interpretation, historical and theological arguments, and contemporary existentialism, with regard to Heidegger, Max Scheler, and Kierkegaard, to the Niebuhrian conclusion that the spirit, which includes reason, transcends its human nature and in that transcendence is tempted to idolatry. Chapters like this, which put everyone in dialogue, prompted Tillich to complain that Niebuhr failed to relate ideas to their temporal context and that he too easily mixed philosophical and religious concepts.[8] Therefore, I am sympathetic to Tillich's complaint. Also, contemporary ecological theology requires that human nature be examined in deeper naturalistic, scientific categories.

Humanity as the image of God was the bedrock of Niebuhr's attitude toward religion. Religion's task, Niebuhr avers, was to provide a vision of meaning. That meaning was the explication of humanity as good, but finite. He did not think we could arrive at adequate understanding of ourselves only through reason. Humanity needed revelation, which

8. Paul Tillich, in *A Prophetic Voice in Our Time*, ed. Harold R. Landon (Greenwich, NY: Seabury, 1962), 33–34.

came through interpretation of individual experience in the categories of the social-historical development of religion.

> The problem of meaning, which is the basic problem of religion, transcends the ordinary rational problem of tracing the relation of things to each other as the freedom of man's spirit transcends his rational faculties.[9]

Christianity has been subject to many interpretations and therefore to dilution of its true genius. However, Niebuhr found its best guide in existentialism. In the 1960s at Union, students would be urged to read deeply in existentialism in its secular and theological interpretations, and much of the best Protestant preaching in New York City was based on Niebuhr or Tillich's existentialism. While Niebuhr read Sartre, Camus, Heidegger, Bultmann, and Tillich, he utilized Kierkegaard the most in his theology.

> Kierkegaard has interpreted the true meaning of human selfhood more accurately than any modern, and possibly than any previous Christian theologian.[10]

Basic human character depends upon the self developing its consciousness of its self. In the process, it transcends itself, but then can return to its concreteness in the temporal. The temporal self is a synthesis of the particular and its self-reflection. Niebuhr, of course, was reading Kierkegaard in German, synthesizing his reflections in Niebuhr's American reality to present this fresh work to his readers. In the doctrine of the self, he was drawing upon *The Sickness unto Death*. It was Niebuhr's turn of Kierkegaard into social existentialism that was so important. Later assaults on the existentialist narrative by linguistic philosophy and postmodernism would render Niebuhr's synthesis less popular, but in New York in the 1940s to the 1960s it was enriching and practical.

HUMAN SIN

Chapters 7–10 of *Human Nature* presents the predominant thesis of the book. Intellectually they are un-American chapters. They challenge the easy moralism of bourgeois life and the optimism grounded in the mythology of progressivism of the young Republic. First heard in post–World War I Presbyterian-influenced Scotland, they were not as shocking there as in sectarian-influenced America. The shock of the

9. Niebuhr, *Nature and Destiny*, 164.
10. Niebuhr, *Nature and Destiny*, 170–71.

twentieth century as a continually war-oriented America had not been realized yet. Scotland had already lost much of a generation of its young men and it was leaning toward another war.

Though his first volume is titled *Human Nature*, Niebuhr writes of humanity as "Man." However, his reflection is more inclined to the powerful oppressor than to the oppressed. To be more specific, his analysis was based on the sin of the dominant race or class rather than on the sin of victims.

The human being of spirit and nature was understood as insecure. In this anxiety over insecurity the temptation was to rebel in pride to exalt oneself. The rebellion he labeled as the "religious dimension of sin."[11] The social expression of sin was injustice. Here for the first time in the book he noted the sin of sensuality, which covered the alternative escape of freedom. This was the attempt to escape the human problem by surrendering to some form of subservience or addiction. His whole analysis is much more focused on pride. The chapters could have used more description of the classical sevenfold analysis of sin, but he was pursuing the problems of pride.

Sin was the inevitable search for security over the perils of human freedom. Humanity sought security through dominating other lives, natural and human. Following Kierkegaard and using Heidegger, humanity had the wrong and mistaken response to anxiety out of insecurity. Pursued both by animals and other humans, they responded with forceful domination. The limits of humanity attracted responses of pride and sensuality with concomitant adjustments of fight or flight, distorting human existence. Niebuhr read the Christian tradition as emphasizing pride more than sensuality (later sloth) and the latter being somehow derived from pride.

His specification[12] of pride into four forms—(a) pride of power, of both those seeking power and defending it, (b) intellectual pride and false ideology, (c) moral pride, and (d) spiritual pride—seemed to cover the characteristics of dogmatic religions, self-righteousness, militarism, and intellectual pretension of the 1939 culture he lectured in and the present. It still is revelatory of the ideologies of militant-radical Islam versus dogmatic, democratic Christianity in which we live. The exposure of the sinful para-religious movements of those times and our times still cuts deeper than most of our secular political science or religious-political rhetoric.

Christianity was for Niebuhr a complex system of meaning in which

11. Niebuhr, *Nature and Destiny*, 179.
12. Niebuhr, *Nature and Destiny*, 186–207.

God is understood as the source and end of finitude in which humanity lives for a while. In it, pride could be exposed and humility encouraged, and humanity could in trust live with its vulnerabilities. Of course, religions became prideful and humanity deceived itself with false systems of meaning like nationalism, Communism, Nazism, and fascism. These systems were full of deceptions that promised securities and knowledge that could not be realized.

He compared the anxiety of human freedom to a sailor climbing a mast. The person is anxious to achieve the goal of the crow's nest above and threatened by the meaningless abyss into which one falls if the grip on the rope is not tight. Niebuhr's writing on collective egoism is an extension of *Moral Man and Immoral Society* (1932). His overcoming of his earlier Marxism made the contrast of self and society less extreme. In 1932 it had been a personal problem, contrasting his fading Christian pacifism with the requirements of socialist change. However, the collective egoism of groups and nations was still more extreme than individual self-love, which was more subject to social correction and restraints of conscience.

The egotism of groups was most exaggerated in nation-states and empires. Lecturing in 1939 and publishing in 1941, he had material at hand in fascism, Communism, and Nazism. In all three, the states became gods or claimed the role of gods. Pride had evolved from tribal polytheism to imperial religions.

His argument places special burdens on the elite and the powerful. He regards the best of biblical ethics as anti-aristocratic. He resists, though, the translation of the anti-aristocratic tendencies into a "simple political interpretation."[13] Self-righteousness appears among the poor as well as the powerful, but the powerful sin against the poor or the white against the black more grievously than the reverse. Years later, these insights of criticism are directed against Christian social radicals and Christian oligarchs, but his political critique was against the practices of the powerful.

Taking Adam as representative of humanity, Niebuhr followed Kierkegaard's Augustinian reading of Paul as representing the human in anxious unbelief as responsible for human sin even though sin was presupposed. Nazis were responsible and deserved punishment even if their context predisposed them to pursue ignorant idolatry to destroy civilization.

The final chapter of the book focuses on the goodness of the essence of humanity. Human experience discloses that the species has a memory of innocence. In expressions of the state of nature or of an unsullied con-

13. Niebuhr, *Nature and Destiny*, 225.

science, the goodness of humanity is informed. Something of the image of God remains. Niebuhr rejects "total depravity." He portrays humanity as ambiguous, but with a myth of innocence expressed in perfectionism. He has a place for utopian thought, but he rejects it as policy. If we were at our best we would live lives of faith, hope, and love, but in reality we achieve much less. The chapter affirms the need of overcoming both Renaissance optimism and Reformation pessimism, and it suggests that is the issue of the volume to follow.

Critics of Niebuhr's "unrelieved pessimism" write as if they never read the last chapter of the book, but critics reflecting modern optimism could never be satisfied with the last chapter. Even divine grace is forgiveness and not pure power to produce the perfect life. The chapter is about the good essence of humanity, but wherever it steps into history it is about sinful existence. The human hope that some form of social organization would free humanity from violating its conscience formed in the freedom of the self is an illusion. Both love and justice reflect the goodness of human nature and the freedom of the human spirit. They require attempts to live them out as the essence of humanity. But, they are not fulfilled other than ambiguously in human society and culture. So the uneasy conscience is part of human life.

4.

Human Destiny

> All historic schemes and structures of justice must take the contingencies of nature and history and the fact of sin into consideration.

The first chapter of the second volume of *The Nature and Destiny of Man* merges partial answers to the meaning of history from a variety of religions, philosophies, and literatures to illustrate that most cultures did not expect messianic answers to the ambiguities of history. He found in the prophetic traditions of Israel and particularly in Amos a message of God's condemnation of the nation's historical existence. He had learned of the relevance of Amos in Samuel Press's class at Eden Theological Seminary in St. Louis, and he would return to it in 1968 to express his criticism of President Richard Nixon. All nations failed to achieve justice. Prophetic judgment only hints at a hope that messianic expectations and apocalyptic literature developed further.

History is morally too ambiguous for the expectations of messianic rulers who could unite power and righteousness. Instead, history from the Old Testament is a struggle of human will to take and use power. Power corrupts, and so messianic promises are illusions and apocalyptic hopes point toward fulfillment but without historical realization.

Within this very biblical theology, Niebuhr follows his oft-repeated advice to "take the Bible seriously, but not literally." He relies on the liberal scholarship of his day, dismissing the last optimistic chapter of Amos as an addition of a later author. For Niebuhr, this literature leaves the relationship of divine judgment to divine will mysterious, as its answers are unsatisfactory. All strong nations fall into the sin of pride, and they are defeated. They are judged, and the messianic hopes are deepened.[1]

Throughout the book Niebuhr balanced the freedom of humanity against the necessities of nature. Astronomy and biology suggest there are developments in nature that exhibit more anomalies and freedom than Niebuhr perceived. Even regarding human nature, he probably assumed more givens than contemporary thinkers assume. Differences between the male and female of the species may be more affected by social changes than he assumed.

Niebuhr's second chapter, "The Disclosure and the Fulfillment of the Meaning of Life and History," was more beyond the capacity of college students than the first chapter. A dozen years later I would hear him reflect on his deathbed its Pauline center.

> Who shall separate us from the love of Christ? Shall tribulation or distress, or persecution, or nakedness, or peril, or sword . . . ? Nay in all these things, we are more than conquerors through him that loved us. For I am persuaded, that neither death nor life, nor things present, nor things to come, nor height, nor depth, nor any other creature shall be able to separate us from the love of God which is Christ Jesus our Lord.[2]

This expected Christ or Messiah's meaning was transformed by Jesus in the memory of the early church to express both human finitude and transcendence. The suffering of humanity in its awful history became the suffering of God, and its forgiveness is symbolized by Christ. Meaning and therefore power could be found by identification and adoption into the community. Christ's suffering expressed the character of suffering history and his victory expressed the religious transcendence of that history.

Beyond his interpretation of Jesus and his ethic and Paul's essential agreement he sorted out the meaning of atonement. He moved through Kierkegaard on several points of interpretation to disagree with Karl Barth and to note his agreement with Emil Brunner. Looking back on the chapter from a perspective of three-quarters of a century, it is fascinating how perfectly he expressed the life of power and creativity under conditions of terrible suffering that began only a dozen years after he wrote the chapter. He accepted the Messiah's reinterpretation and found the meaning of history in God's suffering to be forgiveness.

The third chapter, "The Possibilities and Limits of History," is on

1. Reinhold Niebuhr, *The Nature and Destiny of Man*, 2 vols. (New York: Charles Scribner's Sons, 1941), 2:31.

2. Niebuhr, *Nature and Destiny*, 2:52.

the character of "sacrificial love." This radical love is perceived by faith in Jesus's acceptance of the cross. Religiously, "self-sacrificial love" is a human possibility. But historically mutual love, brotherhood, and justice are the relevant possibilities. The relativities of historical achievement are expressed by faith in sacrificial love. That love is the nature of the divine and therefore beyond history. By the time these lectures were published, Dietrich Bonhoeffer, Niebuhr's student and friend, was well into his journey into sacrificial love as he risked his existence by assisting Jews to escape Nazism and entered into anti-Hitler sabotage. Sacrificial love in faith is relevant to history, but scarce in ordinary history. It transcends and is in history as God is in Christ. It is the height of Christian ethics, which cannot escape history but works within it. Niebuhr in the chapter continually calls on Christians in faith to act in actual history and to refuse the escapes of mystical experience or knowledge. Love, "agape," promises no success in history, but it may impel historical action. Sentimental versions of Christianity or liberalism that promise success through nonviolence are illusory, though "sacrificial love" translated through brotherhood and the struggle for justice may choose nonviolence as the most likely social strategy. But it also calls for resistance to tyranny, nonviolent or violent.

Chapter 4 continues to rely on modern biblical scholars and on his own extensive exegesis. It could be called biblical theology. On subjects like the meaning of grace, he accepts an interpretation of biblical texts as authoritative. However, his writing also ranges over the history of Western thought and into modern psychology. He regards the reception of grace through faith as both power of a relatively new life and forgiveness. Humans do not obtain the power of Christ in its totality, but they receive some. He interprets his theology as Pauline in that sin remains in the converted, as Paul confesses. The history of the Christian life of grace is victory and failure for all Christians. Religious pride is a terrible danger, and so the continuing incompleteness of human life needs recognition.

The fifth chapter follows Adolf von Harnack in arguing that the Pauline doctrine of justification by faith while still a sinner was mostly forgotten until Augustine four centuries later. But even Augustine allowed for perfection in those that loved God. In other less careful hands the church could become the perfect City of God and its political head the "Vicar of Christ." Human self-esteem resisted the idea that even believers and priests were sinners. Society's fantasies kept hoping that one more reform would perfect society. The prophetic critique of history and Jesus's warnings to the religious righteous should have guarded against these prideful assertions, but human self-assertion overcame their warnings. Victories for the Hellenic spirit portraying Christ as a way for humanity to eternity and/or perfection triumphed in the Eastern church and to a large degree in the Roman church.

Niebuhr noted that the fine distinctions of theologians and philosophers seemed needlessly sharp to the nonprofessional. Yet, the distinctions were necessary to refine theology and to protect against heresies that would split the church. A more faithful and more rigorous church would have never permitted Nazism or Communism to emerge on Christian ground. The theology of sin Niebuhr represented recognized people as saved in principle, but not in fact. It laid the ground for his Christian Realism and political expression in an embattled democracy. The second half of the book assumes the meaning of history to be Christ's atoning action. It illustrates this about the Renaissance and Reformation, identifying Niebuhr's perspective as their synthesis. Then two chapters analyze toleration and justice through the lens of Christian Realism. The final chapter repeats the argument of the book in terms of religious symbols of the historical end and historical fulfillment.

Niebuhr celebrates the Renaissance affirmation of human possibilities and the rebirth of learning. He notes the Christian and particularly Franciscan contributions to the movement. His criticism of the enthusiasm is in regard to its translation of Christian eschatological expectations into illusions of human moral progress. Too many trajectories from the Renaissance trusted in human fulfillment but forgot the themes of divine judgment.

Niebuhr placed his short study of sectarian Protestantism within the story of the Renaissance. He believed the sectarian perspective of utopianism was closer to the Renaissance than to the more orthodox Protestantism. Their ideal societies were an illusion, but they came to have great influence in the United States. The Renaissance optimism also triumphed in the new world and almost completely obscured the less optimistic Reformation impulses.

In one paragraph, Niebuhr compared the optimism of bourgeois culture to the youth who, sensing an awakening mind and the achievement of great responsibilities, expects fulfillment of his dreams. Neither the youth nor the culture recognized that each new achievement presented its own set of problems.[3] Many of Niebuhr's students, of course, were those youth, and youthful resistance to the critique of optimism was inevitable.

3. Niebuhr, *Nature and Destiny*, 2:182.

It was the Reformation that emphasized the resistance of sin more than the other schools of thought. Niebuhr's intention was to combine the Renaissance sense of possibilities with the Reformation's conviction that fulfillment was in God's judgment and forgiveness and not simply in saving history. Neither Lutheran social defeatism nor Calvinist biblical authority and moralism provided the answers. However, their sense that the doctrine of atonement was central to explaining human history was correct. Grace implies that history has meaning but not fulfillment. Atonement is the beginning of wisdom about human life and its possibilities and limitations.

The two penultimate chapters of the book explore the search for truth and justice. Humanity is under obligation to pursue these goals, but they cannot be realized in history. Niebuhr is speaking about the truth concerning history and religion. Here all perspectives are relativized. He is not denying truths of mathematics, physics, or biology. Claims for truth about history reflect the perspectives of the historian. Humanity cannot achieve justice, but only tolerable approximations. Theorists' concepts of justice reflect their own ideology, and tolerable orders in society reflect the forces that support them.

Social pressures and the relativity of our perspectives impel us toward seeking tolerance. Tolerance is for Niebuhr a social principle similar to equality and liberty. He explains these social virtues historically. All these virtues are to be sought without the expectation of total success. Christian love for the neighbor strives for justice, but in this book their relationship is paradoxical. Love seeks justice but is in tension with it, as the kingdom of God is relevant to all social approximations of the kingdom, which cannot be obtained. Throughout the discussion he tips toward the Reformation's pessimistic realism, but he refuses to go the whole way into Luther's social pessimism. Karl Barth too is overly pessimistic and overly biblical. The insights from humanistic philosophy have their partial validity and are not to be despised. He criticizes cynicism, but his skepticism approaches it. The Christian imperatives of love and the possibilities of human achievement keep him from cynicism. He is more of a Christian stoic committed to the social struggle for justice.

The concluding chapter is on the Christian symbols of the end. He distinguishes the individual's end and fulfillment from that of the civilization. The theme of the two volumes—that the good and the evil are mixed until the end of history—comes to symbolic expression here. The symbols are not used literally, but in a manner that illumines the meaning of history before the end. He uses Schweitzer's term, "interim," to describe the era between the revelation of meaning in Christ and the end/fulfillment of history.

He explains the meaning of the Parousia, the last judgment, and the resurrection. They all symbolize the reality of judgment and the grace of forgiveness. They are known through faith and they explain history better than the alternative philosophies he has reviewed. History is not redemptive. Wars and rumors of war will continue. Humanity is unable to achieve a government to provide for the welfare and security of all. Disavowing pride in principle will provide the best possibility of doing our duties for the common good without creating illusions leading to monstrous conclusions. Accepting the limits of our knowledge and power "can prompt people to accept their historical responsibilities."[4] Each civilization contributes to others even as it falls, and individuals contribute to their children and their works to their communities. There is both individuality and unity in history, and both have partial fulfillments. In faith, he accepted in his conclusion as in the beginning that ultimate security was found in the Pauline theology of recognizing there was no separation from a loving God. He repeated: "I am persuaded that neither death, nor life, nor angels, nor principalities, nor powers . . . shall be able to separate us from the love of God which is in Christ Jesus our Lord."[5]

These theological guidelines persuaded him that politics and international relations were a mixture of sinful and cooperative actions. Universal peace was not to be expected. Real gains for aiding the suffering, protecting the vulnerable, and reducing conflict could be made. The evil of men could become so bad that their evil had to be resisted, sometimes even by taking on the sinfulness of armed conflict as one's own duty. Love required that justice be pursued, but justice grew from the minds and actions of morally ambiguous humans. The best understandings of justice related them to their time and place and granted their humanely historical origins. The historical sinful inheritance of institutions and ideas made visionaries only partially helpful in politics. Their visions could blind them to the necessity of forceful action in politics as they trusted too much in the goodness or rationality of humans. Or their visions could lead in the opposite direction, to the need to attempt to create a new society and new humans by cruel measures to eliminate the recalcitrant. His theology inclined him to appreciate the value of prudence in all things political and to appreciate historical developments rather than rationalistic schemes. Given his history, he was forced

4. Niebuhr, *Nature and Destiny*, 2:321.
5. Romans 8:35–39.

to the defense of democracy against the utopian cruel visions of fascists and Communists. Democracy with checks and balances fit his vision of morally ambiguous humanity. Even when he used theological symbols less, he held to the virtues of prudence and historical explanations for human politics.

5.

Beginning the Kennedy Era, 1960

> Basically, love means that life has no meaning except in terms of responsibility; responsibility toward our family, toward our nation, toward our civilization and now, by the pressures of history, toward the universe of mankind which includes our enemies.

Niebuhr published a short piece of autobiographical reflection in his final month of tenure at Union.[1] He was reticent about autobiography. It was so hard to write objectively. He conceded to Scribner's the publication of June Bingham's *The Courage to Change*.[2] This first biography was written by a devoted friend and he feared too much adoration. Moreover, his wife Ursula had indicated her wish to attempt a biography later. His reflections on his self and thinking stayed at the impersonal, rational level. He stressed his difference from neo-orthodoxy and described himself as "a liberal at heart." He admitted some of his earlier polemics "against liberalism were indiscriminate."[3]

He refused to dampen his critique of pacifism, rejecting nuclear pacifism. The peace between Russia and the United States depended upon the strategy of the nuclear deterrent. He urged actions to reduce tensions between the superpowers, and he thought some gains in arms control were possible as both powers recognized that war would be a catastrophe. Miscalculation could still lead to war, and steps to reduce the danger of accidental war were needed.

While still deeply sorrowful about the inadequate role of the white

1. Reinhold Niebuhr, "The Quality of Our Lives," *The Christian Century* 77, no. 19 (May 11, 1960): 568–72.

2. June Bingham, *The Courage to Change* (New York: Charles Scribner's Sons, 1961).

3. Niebuhr, "Quality of Our Lives," 568.

church in overcoming racism, he now celebrated the vitality of the black churches in leading the revolt against white racism. He thought their revolution comparable to his favorite movement in Christian social ethics, the Puritan sects in the Cromwellian revolution in England in the seventeenth century. He concluded by criticizing the Christian support for apartheid and the nationalist party in South Africa.

He devoted one-fifth of his essay to distancing himself from Karl Barth while recognizing the creativity of the early critique of liberal culture in Barth's commentary on Romans. He could not recognize in himself any continuing influence of Barth's later scholasticism. He particularly rejected the Barthian overreliance on eschatology and the consequent tendency to neutralism on the important issues of the Cold War. Niebuhr continued to argue for the discriminate role for humanistic disciplines in the formulation of Christian social ethics. It seems obvious that Barth's neutralism was influenced by his Swiss politics, but Niebuhr stayed more at the level of theological vocabulary in his critique.

This 1960 reflection contains an interesting paragraph on linguistic analysis, as it recognizes religious statements as meaningful even if not scientifically verifiable. Arguments for the existence of God remain irrelevant, but religious discourses about the meanings of life are important. The significant verification for Christian life is in the quality of life it produces in its followers. In the confrontation with the problems of life and the nonchalance about death, truth can be found. The prophets, Jesus, and Paul all witness to realism about the human condition, and the response to life in terms of love and justice. He concluded that reflection with his Pauline text: "Whether we live or whether we die we are the Lord's."[4]

In personal relations, love should lead to mutual forbearance and toleration in which we seek to avoid harm and practice forgiveness.[5] For congregations it means nurturing communities of acceptance and comfort from the hurts of industrial civilization. In social life love leads to justice and developing social instruments for justice. In the Cold War, love means building bridges across the chasm separating us from our foe. We should not renounce responsibility to protect, he argued. However, the biblical commandment to forgive our enemies and pray for those who hurt us needs to be joined with human wisdom to find imaginative ways to move away from humanity's wrestling on the edge of a nuclear

4. Niebuhr, "Quality of Our Lives," 572.

5. Niebuhr's words about the interrelatedness of people and the need for forgiveness and acceptance indicate he never abandoned his earlier work on the psychology of the self. An example of this reflection was his foreword for his colleague's book on the self. See Earl Loomis Jr., *The Self in Pilgrimage* (New York: Harper & Brothers, 1960).

abyss. The church should not abandon its responsibility here and drift into irrelevance.

His agenda for the remaining decade of his life is his commitment to two problems for his analysis: the Cold War and race relations. The greater weight was on the nuclear dangers of the Cold War. He called the church to the work, but fearing the triviality of the church, he took upon himself the task of "establishing or helping to establish a frame of meaning in which the adjustments of coexistence can take place."[6]

INTERVIEW

Before Niebuhr left New York City for his 1960 summer in California, he was interviewed by Henry Brandon, US correspondent of the *Sunday Times* in London. Brandon intended to use the interview for his book, *As We Are*. It was published in *Harper's* magazine[7] the month following the publication of his interview of Arthur Miller and Marilyn Monroe. Brandon's questions reflected some knowledge of Niebuhr's writings at a general level, but also some intellectual confusion. For example, he regarded Niebuhr as theologically conservative and as one who thought the governing Marxists in Russia were idealists.

Brandon teased out of Niebuhr his crediting the vitality of religion in the United States to the sectarian and immigrant communities of the church. The strength of Judaism and the non-antagonism toward religion of American secularism also contributed to the religious underpinnings of American society. Niebuhr also explained he was not among the religious critics of the intellectual and political contributions of secularism. He shared his distaste for American revivalism and Billy Graham's naïveté.

As in other general essays, Niebuhr judged the quality of a religion by its capacity to ameliorate racial discrimination and to provide a frame of meaning for living with the Cold War. Central to living through the Cold War was the recognition of the common fate shared by the United States and the USSR. Both religious imagination and secular learning could contribute to this recognition and to the reduction of danger.

Niebuhr praised Eisenhower's world trip at the beginning of 1960. He was particularly enthused by the receptions Eisenhower received in his visit to India. He thought that in his last year as president, some of the

6. Niebuhr, "Quality of Our Lives," 572.

7. Reinhold Niebuhr, "A Christian View of the Future," Interview by Henry Brandon, *Harper's* 221, no. 1327, December 1960, 71–77.

rigidity and harshness of the policies of the late John Foster Dulles were being overcome.

But, by the middle of the year, he regarded Eisenhower as completely outplayed by Khrushchev in the embarrassing Paris Summit.[8] He exaggerated it as the worst diplomatic defeat for the United States in his time. A Russian missile, with capacity greater than the United States had calculated, had destroyed a U-2 spy plane. Eisenhower was caught flatfooted by his denials, and the ill-planned summit failed. Khrushchev seemed to be luring the neutrals toward Soviet influence.

The United States appeared to Niebuhr unable to balance the missile gap or to suggest policies to overcome the Cold War. The initiative was with the Soviets led by the adroit Khrushchev. At the UN, the Russian goals for the Congo seemed thwarted while Khrushchev attacked Dag Hammarskjold and proposed his fatuous *troika* governance for the international body.

Britain was preoccupied with withdrawing from Ghana and Nigeria. France sought a way out of Algeria after losing in Southeast Asia. The inability to negotiate a German solution and the renewed pressure on Berlin left a European Atlantic alliance less sure of itself than when Eisenhower had directed NATO.

THE 1960 ELECTION

Early in 1960 Niebuhr was supporting Governor Stevenson for another run for the presidency. He shifted to support his friend Hubert Humphrey. Gradually Arthur Schlesinger's persuasion and John F. Kennedy's primary successes turned Reinhold into reluctantly supporting the brash, bold senator.

He was in Santa Barbara in residence at the Fund for the Republic's Center for the Study of Democratic Institutions during the Democratic Convention in the summer. The time there encouraged him in his third emphasis of writing for this final decade: democratic political philosophy. Niebuhr contributed an essay to Professor H. Odegard's collection of essays on *Religion and Politics*.[9] Odegard, a former president of the American Political Science Association, was concerned to create an academic discussion of the issue of a Roman Catholic president of the United States. Odegard's conclusion was yes, the nation could have a

8. Reinhold Niebuhr, "Failure at the Summit," *Christianity and Crisis* 20, no. 9 (May 30, 1960): 73.

9. Reinhold Niebuhr, "Religion and Politics," in *Religion and Politics*, ed. Peter H. Odegard (New York: Oceana, 1960), 107–12.

Catholic president. Niebuhr contributed his 1954 essay from *Perspectives*, "Religion and Politics." He noted that he did not "like religious parties as they exist on the continent of Europe." He thought the Catholic tendency to identify the church and the kingdom of God was a mistake. He rejected overdependence on natural law theory, as for example, in the prohibition of birth control and divorce. But after these reservations, the essay detailed the pluralism of Roman Catholic parties in Europe and the positive contributions of Catholicism in protecting democracy and in many cases its alignment with socialist parties. Often Catholicism was more creative than Protestantism. Even in the United States, Protestantism's individualism tended to direct it toward more conservative Republican politics while Jews and Catholics aligned closer to Niebuhr's preferred politics. He appreciated the more spiritual and organizational power of Catholicism, which could act creatively in democratic society. The use of the essay in 1960 rebuked overly simple or bigoted positions on the election of a Catholic president. The ruthlessness and money of the young senator won him the day. Both Kennedy and Nixon were regarded as relatively unscrupulous. Niebuhr mused that he and his friends, looking for eloquence mixed with moral rigor and real compassion, seemed idealistically irrelevant. The deal with Lyndon Johnson surprised Niebuhr, but he thought he might be the southerner Kennedy needed to win. When Arthur Schlesinger phoned him to discuss his own nervousness about Johnson, Niebuhr assured him it would help in the South and reinforce the idea that the Democratic Party was a truly national party. He expected both Nixon and Kennedy to be stronger on the burgeoning push for African American civil rights than President Eisenhower. Schlesinger assured Niebuhr that Kennedy's sexual immorality had been suppressed and that he would be scandal free in the White House. Niebuhr gradually came around, and Niebuhr introduced him to the Liberal Party dinner.

The Niebuhrs moved out of Knox Hall into an apartment at 304 Riverside Drive. With the support of a grant from the Rockefeller Foundation, he became a Fellow of the Institute of War and Peace Studies of Columbia University. Union Seminary asked him to give his seminar on social ethics for seniors and graduate students one more time. As usual, about half of it consisted of Niebuhr's presentations and about half of student presentations.

One day as the crowded rotunda elevator ascended to the library, a gruff voice from the back of the elevator exclaimed: "This is the slowest elevator in the Western world!" It was Reinhold Niebuhr expressing his disgust at the elevator but revealing his own impatience about his condition. Earlier he was known for running up the steps to the library two steps at a stride.

The decade in New York City seemed to open to new flowers peeking through the concrete of the older order of the 1950s. But many of those flowers would fade and some would soon be regarded as weeds.

Protestors against apartheid were shot in Sharpeville, South Africa, killing more than fifty Africans. The resultant economic pressures would lead to international banks forming a consortium to support South Africa's apartheid economy. Within a few years, students in New York would respond against those banks with the movement toward divestment and boycott, which would become major tools of moral-social action. Independence was won for eleven African countries, but the movement for self-determination birthed civil wars in Algeria and the Congo.

The attempt to integrate a beach in Biloxi, Mississippi led to the shooting of eight blacks and two whites. Martin Luther King Jr. called for federal intervention in Mississippi. The movements in South Africa and the United States were moving together for some students and activists. Nationalist rhetoric by Malcolm X and rising discontent among young black leaders in the Student Nonviolent Coordinating Committee threatened the mixed idealistic rhetoric and action of King and pointed toward breaks in the movement not obvious to white supporters of the Southern Leadership Conference. Liberals and radicals were cooperating in reforming race relations. But oppression, strong resistance to reform, and the brutality of white power threatened to undo reform strategy.

In international affairs Nikita Khrushchev seemed to be setting the stage. He startled the United Nations with dramatically rude behavior in New York City. The United States launched nuclear-powered and -armed submarines and pushed ahead in developing its space program. The old general, Dwight Eisenhower, three days before Kennedy's inauguration warned of the scientific, industrial, military complex. He pleaded for world peace without expecting it. Here Eisenhower feared the combination of weapons and technology development in a computer age that he had encouraged while in office. The boldness of the young president pointed toward a continuation of increasing the combination. France's nuclear tests in the Sahara confirmed it as the fourth member of the nuclear club, and Charles de Gaulle's rhetoric matched the soaring nationalism of Kennedy.

Castro spoke in Harlem on 125th Street to a large enthusiastic crowd. The emerging issues of Cuba and invasion were passed on by a negligent president to an inexperienced Kennedy, leaving the crucial decisions to the CIA. Castro's speech at the United Nations and his nationalization of US resources in response to the boycott moved him closer to Russia. Cuba would provide a major forum of action for the young president until his death.

In 1960 the leaders of the decade were all on stage: Kennedy, Nixon, Khrushchev, Johnson, and King. Two would die by assassination, two were forced to resign because of opposition, and one retired due to hidden ill health and criticism. It is assumed that there was an excess of idealism in the early rhetoric and spirit in the decade. However, the wars against Communism in Vietnam and Cuba would fail. The war against drugs never would succeed, and the war against poverty had its funds diverted to Vietnam. These failings and murders produced moralistic rage and dropping out among a dispirited youth, which produced weaknesses in the public sphere, in government, and in the churches. In one interpretation of the 1960s it was Reinhold Niebuhr's realism that was overthrown first by idealism and then by cynicism. However, while many withdrew from Christian theology and action, its understanding of ambiguity, tragedy, and the irony of history provided better guides than mystical experience, drugs, dropping out, or moralistic crusades.

Niebuhr hailed the election of the bright, vigorous young senator. He suppressed his criticism and hoped that Kennedy's toughness and political sense would lead him to accomplishments reminiscent of Franklin D. Roosevelt. He noted the awful responsibilities of any president in confronting and extricating the nation from the Cold War. He concluded the essay with a wish for a new national humility and sense of duty.[10] The substance of the Center conversations and the frequent political visitors from the convention provided the stimulus for his next book and influenced his teaching and other writings.[11] His reflections on the Democratic convention indicated that his early support for Adlai Stevenson placed him, in his own expression, among the Old Guard.

THE KENNEDY YEARS

In the first months of the president's tenure, Niebuhr called for review of several foreign policy issues, from the overextension of worldwide military bases to questions regarding Laos and Cuba. His respect for neutral-

10. Reinhold Niebuhr, "The Election and the Next President," *Christianity and Crisis* 20, no. 20 (Nov. 28, 1960): 170.

11. Reinhold Niebuhr, "Stray Thoughts on the Political Scene," *Christianity and Crisis* 20, no. 14 (Aug. 8, 1960): 124.

ism led him to be cautious about involvement in Laos. He regretted the breaking of diplomatic relations with Cuba, but he regarded the threat of US invasion of Cuba as absurd.[12] The inability of the new president to handle these two issues of Cuba and Indochina would destroy the possibilities of the next two administrations. These cautions were ignored by the assertive Kennedy approach to the Cold War. Reinhold Niebuhr and Paul Tillich spent the month of January at Arnold Wolfers's Washington Center for Policy Research. Tillich attended the inauguration while Niebuhr for health reasons could only watch it on television. A month later he pleaded for an end to unsightly demonstration of religious pluralism at the ceremony. Four prayers were too much, and the ceremony should be revised to include only a reasonably short invocation and a benediction.[13]

The special issue of *Christianity and Crisis* on Africa was written mostly by supporters of Niebuhr. Robert C. Good had written a dissertation on Niebuhr's politics and coedited *Reinhold Niebuhr on Politics*. He had joined the Kennedy administration as the President's Coordinator of the Task Force on Africa. His sharp criticism of previous American policies combined with a plea for realism regarding Africa so that disillusionment with Africa could be resisted. George Hauser discussed the European-oriented African policy of the United States seen in recent UN votes supportive of colonialism. Kenneth W. Thompson, a Niebuhrian political scientist, and Arthur J. Moore contributed their warnings concerning US policies toward Africa. As a whole, Africa as seen in Niebuhr's journal was in crisis as it assumed independence and new roles for the twenty-five African states in the United Nations. Niebuhr's lectures on Africa in his Harvard course of 1961–62 reflected the meager prospects for democracy there and the reality of the Cold War in Africa.

Niebuhr's ignorance about the Central Intelligence Agency's plan in January to have Cuban exiles invade Cuba was not surprising. President Kennedy was not briefed on the planning underway until after his election. Allen Dulles and Richard Bissell had briefed him on Cuba during the election season without mentioning invasion planning. President Eisenhower, learning of the failure to develop a Cuban government in exile, was probably innocent of CIA plans to assassinate Castro or to invade the island. The invasion plans were certainly not worthy of Eisenhower, who had planned D-Day.

By the time Kennedy assumed office he had inherited an invasion plan

12. Reinhold Niebuhr, "Laos and Cuba: Problems for Review," *Christianity and Crisis* 20, no. 24 (Jan. 23, 1961).

13. Reinhold Niebuhr, "Pluralism at the Inaugural," *Christianity and Crisis* 21, no. 2 (Feb. 20, 1961): 15.

with exiles trained in Guatemala.[14] At that point, it was his to amend, modify, or continue. During the election campaign, he had asserted the need to back Cuban exile organizations and the decision was laid before him. Originally the planning called for a US airstrike and the insertion of the force near mountains where they could adopt guerrilla tactics. The second choice, of the Bay of Pigs, was a tactical mistake. The president's canceling of the air strike doomed the mission, which the Joint Chiefs of Staff had regarded as having "a fair chance of success."

Several in the CIA believed the US armed forces would back up the invasion if necessary. President Kennedy had said that under no circumstances would the United States invade Cuba. Neither the CIA nor the president understood each other. There was a fatal miscommunication. The famous spy, Allen Dulles, was in the middle. He would later recall he had estimated the chance of success to President Eisenhower as no more that 20 percent and that he promised Kennedy no more than "a fighting chance."[15] Of course, CIA apologies are not to be trusted. The timidity of the failed attempt encouraged aggressive forces in the Soviet Union to take a future risk in Cuba.

On April 17, 1961, the invasion, not having been stopped, went ahead. On April 19, the invasion was defeated and over 1100 Cuban exiles were taken prisoners. Options to use US airpower or the two battalions of marines cruising offshore were not taken. Assumptions of Richard Bissell and Allen Dulles that Cuban exile failure would be covered by the United States were mistaken. The Bay of Pigs would remain a prime example of the CIA operating without adequate understanding or supervision by elected administration officials. Niebuhr's critique of the CIA deepened during the 1960s.

Allen Dulles was fired and the transition for him was delayed until November 1961, when John McCone replaced him. Dulles had hoped to stay on an additional two years and to move into the new CIA headquarters in Langley that he had planned and supervised in construction.[16] Various commentators and reporters concluded, to no avail, that the intelligence functions needed to be separated from military actions. The CIA was still gathering intelligence and carrying out its own war with secret drone strikes and interrogation prisons throughout the world after 9/11.

Niebuhr's critique of President Kennedy's failed invasion of Cuba made use of the denunciation of others closer to the sources, including

14. Peter Grose, *Gentleman Spy: The Life of Allen Dulles* (Boston: Houghton Mifflin, 1994), 316.

15. Grose, *Gentleman Spy*, 159.

16. Grose, *Gentleman Spy*, 534.

Joseph Alsop, Cyrus Sulzberger, and James Reston. Kennedy's aphorism, "Victory has a hundred fathers, but defeat is an orphan," neglected the many conceptual mistakes of the administration. He came down hard on the Central Intelligence Agency.[17] He spared Allen Dulles, whereas his critique of John Foster Dulles had been regular and unrelenting. Niebuhr seemed willing for the CIA to take the bulk of the responsibility for the blunder and for misunderstanding the Cuban situation and Latin America.

Allen Dulles had nominated Niebuhr to the Council on Foreign Relations, and the connections at the Council provided him with much of the inside information that fueled his foreign policy writings. The brother who was the spy necessarily wrote less than the lawyer who became secretary of state under Eisenhower. Allen Dulles was a Presbyterian like his brother John Foster, but he did not make a public fuss about it as had the secretary of state. John Foster, as the son of an Auburn theologian and a board member of Union Seminary, had been in one sense Niebuhr's boss. John Foster was also a close friend of the president of the seminary, Henry van Dusen, and Reinhold told me President van Dusen's ideas on foreign policy never progressed beyond J. F. Dulles. Van Dusen told me once that John Foster had jokingly told him that the problems of the world resided in the fact that van Dusen should have been secretary of state and he, John Foster, should have been president of Union Theological Seminary. Niebuhr had a long and engaged relationship with John Foster Dulles. They had worked together in international relations at the Federal Council of Churches, the World Council of Churches, and the founding conference of UNESCO. Niebuhr became very critical of John Foster's stewardship of the State Department. Dulles complained to van Dusen that he could not understand why Niebuhr was so critical of his work, and that he had never criticized Niebuhr. For Niebuhr, Dulles's work, and writing, was far too moralistic, legalistic, and overly committed to international organization. To Niebuhr, Dulles represented the policies of Woodrow Wilson as well as the illusions of Wilson.

He criticized the president for his bold statement about the United States following its own security and national interests. Latin America always assumed that was the North American way; it would have been better to note mutual interests at such a time of defeat.

A month after his critique of the failed Cuban invasion, he approved of the citizen's group that met Castro's request of trading tractors for the

17. "President Kennedy's Cuban Venture," *Christianity and Crisis* 21, no. 8 (May 15, 1961): 70.

captured invasion force. He regarded it as impossible for the US government to make the exchange. He thought Castro had lost face by making the demand for a trade with the government. Moreover, Niebuhr wished that President Kennedy's request to Walter Reuther to expedite the process had been kept secret.

He dismissed the political critics of the deal such as Richard Nixon and Everett Dirksen, but he found the moral critics more disturbing. They apparently rejected both deals with Communists and blackmail payments. Niebuhr thought the lives of the Cuban prisoners were more important. He suggested that moral norms are compromised in history as part of the whole web of contextual relations. Norms were not always realizable and moral prudence in cases like the one involving 1,100 prisoners launched by the United States was necessary. "It is the complexity of this web that makes moral prudence one of the virtues of political morality and frequently the supreme virtue."[18] The web of complexity would deepen as Russia moved to support Cuba, and the United States engaged in assassination plots against Castro. The utilization of the Mafia "mob" in the plots to kill Castro and the deepening Russian involvement pointed toward the death of the president. His own major success in avoiding war while thwarting Russian missile emplacements humbled Khrushchev, and the Cuban quagmire encouraged hatred among Cuban exiles and in the troubled mind of Lee Harvey Oswald. The distrust of the Warren Commission's report contributed to the loss of confidence in the government during the 1960s.

The second special issue of *Christianity and Crisis* on "Race in America"[19] was edited by Roger Shinn on the protest movements and concluded in a review of Eric C. Lincoln's *The Black Muslims in America.* The contents of the issue were mostly on voting rights, residential desegregation, and the desegregation of Christian colleges. Niebuhr followed in the next issue with an editorial titled "The Montgomery Savagery."[20] He called for rigorous enforcement of the law against racist violence and concluded: "The whip of law cannot change the heart. But thank God it can restrain the heartless until they change their mind and heart."[21]

A month later the journal published an account of the freedom riders across the South by Professor John D. Maguire. For the professor, it was an overriding of his usual preference for more moderate action. That

18. Reinhold Niebuhr, "Tractors for Freedom," *Christianity and Crisis* 21, no. 11 (June 26, 1961): 109–10.

19. Roger Shinn, ed., "Race in America," *Christianity and Crisis* 21, no. 9 (May 29, 1961).

20. Reinhold Niebuhr, *Christianity and Crisis* 21, no. 10 (June 12, 1961).

21. Reinhold Niebuhr, *Christianity and Crisis* 21, no. 10 (June 12, 1961): 103.

same month, Niebuhr published his own essay on the freedom rides in his local newspaper, *The Berkshire Eagle*, titled "The Death Throes of a Way of Life."[22]

The fruit of Niebuhr's summer in Santa Barbara began to be published in 1961, and it concluded in 1969. The discussants of the summer responded in August to a paper by Robert M. Hutchins, "Two Faces of Federalism,"[23] which summarized findings of the Center's work. Government could be limited by (1) restrictions on the states' sphere or (2) restrictions as to the means and ends allowing for governmental functions. Niebuhr, joined by others, disagreed particularly with John Courtney Murray's reliance on natural law defined as reason. Niebuhr kept interjecting the contingencies of history and the historical relativism of principles into the discussion. William O. Douglas generally aligned with Niebuhr. The discussion focused on the possibilities of unity and pluralism in democracy, and themes of Niebuhr's future writing emerged. Niebuhr's previous paper for the Fund for the Republic on June 1, 1960, in Washington, DC, "A Study of American Character," formed the first chapter of his next book, *A Nation So Conceived*.[24]

He developed his arguments from the Center in his midsummer publication of "The Unintended Virtues of an Open Society."[25] Communism's evil rests in its dogmatic religious character. The virtues of an open non-Communist society were their openness to criticism and revision according to the dynamics of the people's wisdom and choices. History itself as well as human nature was a mixture of destiny and freedom. Freed from the oppression of traditional society, open society had to protect itself from pretensions of utopian absolutism wherever it appeared. These open societies—particularly of Western Europe and North America—were blessed by tolerance, freedom to overcome error, the lack of unity in society, and conflicting purposes among democratic states. They required wise statecraft and they were located in a very dangerous situation. His closing prescription was:

> Our modern task is to escape the hell of mutual annihilation while exorcising the false heaven of utopian credo. Fortunately, the two tasks are not as incompatible as they seem.[26]

22. *The Berkshire Eagle* 70, no. 34 (June 12, 1961), 16.

23. Robert M. Hutchins, *Two Faces of Freedom* (Santa Barbara: Center for the Study of Democratic Institutions, 1961).

24. Reinhold Niebuhr, "A Study of American Character" (Fund for the Republic). Printed in Congressional Record 87th Congress, August 7.

25. *Christianity and Crisis* 21, no. 13 (July 24, 1961): 132–38.

26. Niebuhr, *Christianity and Crisis* 21, no. 13 (July 24, 1961): 138.

That hope was dimmed by Russia's new weapons testing in October, which he referred to in the closing of his essay:

> This modern history has moved into the eschatological dimension in which all our judgments are made under the shadow of the final judgment. May the Lord have mercy on our souls.[27]

In his prime, Niebuhr had turned down offers from Harvard to join its Divinity School faculty and to accept a position as University Professor there. He had opted to remain at Union with its congenial faculty and church orientation. He had regularly preached at the University Chapel to large crowds. His coming to Harvard in his retirement led him to teach the one course on democracy to the university and to provide a course for the Divinity School. His inaugural address to the Divinity School was published as "The Present Encounter between Christian Faith and Western Civilization."[28] The relationship of the faith to the civilization was that of the faith as foundational, but in a paradoxical relationship to it in civilization's modern situation. It had both given and taken from Western civilization, and still its genius could provide resources to the situation.

He understood Christianity as a synthesis of Greek and Hebrew religions as foundational to Western civilization; in particular it had contributed a sense that history was meaningful and not just a corruption of divinity. Second, the dignity of individual life was affirmed, and in human freedom both the grandeur and misery of the human were found. Finally, he emphasized the Hebrew attitude toward nature as contributing toward the capacity of humans to develop and use nature and its Hellenic spirit as contributing to an understanding of nature that could explore its laws. He understood modern science as combining induction, mathematics, and empiricism to allow the mastery of nature. Only later in the decade would he see the dangers of modern science in destroying its natural base. He painted the picture with broad strokes, analyzing both the drive and the fanaticisms of that history. Historical developments also spun off messianism, utopianism, and apocalyptic understandings of history. The impossibilities of messianism as in the dream of an innocent ruler were overcome, he thought, in the interpretation of the Messiah as the suffering Christ. He emphasized the dangers of utopianism and apocalypticism, cutting the nerve of historical action or alternatively of supporting fanaticism. He hurried through Augustine and the

27. Reinhold Niebuhr, "The Resumption of Nuclear Testing," *Christianity and Crisis* 21, no. 16 (October 2, 1961): 161–62.

28. *Harvard Divinity Bulletin* 26, no. 1 (October 1961): 1–11.

church's role in civilization. His passion was to point out how utopianism and messianism within the materialism of Communism made it so dangerous, "perhaps the most grievous of evils."

The emphasis on the dignity of the individual was explained in terms of the Christian existentialist thread from Augustine to Kierkegaard. His dialectic of sin and grace was referenced, and the hope of preserving the dignity of the human in a technological society and community was grasped. He expected and hoped that the Christian understanding of the self would be enriched by the modern sciences and projected in the civilization.

Technology is the major gift of the West that the new nations covet. Ways to transfer that technology to the poorer nations are needed in a humane and just manner. The technology accentuated the dynamism of the West and gave it power in its imperialism over other peoples. The growth of freedom expanded both the good and evil in history. Christian symbols can enrich the discussion of these developments, but he feared both the Catholic tendency toward absolutism and Barth's eschatological irrelevance. Christian contributions to the alleviation of the misery of the modern age threatened by nuclear weapons could be found in the pursuit of the Christian understanding of love expressed in terms of justice. Justice requires both rational understanding of the requirements of modern society, but also new balances of power. The moral ambiguity of the modern situation of great imbalances of wealth, technology, and learning needed to be grasped realistically. Covetousness and cultural vulgarization threatened modern civilization as well, and there were useful resources in Christianity that taught people to pray for their daily bread, but also to realize we cannot live by bread alone.

He concluded with three imperatives. Eternal verities about the dimensions of human life needed to be lifted up and protected. The faith had to be freed from irrelevant and literalist versions from its past that prevented modern humans from believing it. The moral imperatives of the faith had to be adjusted and applied to the new realities of the technical society.

The address laid out a heavy vocation for the assembled divinity students. Some of its themes would be radically challenged before the decade was out. The perspective of Walt Whitman Rostow in *Five Stages of Economic Growth* presupposed by the talk would be challenged by liberation theology. New eschatologies of radical political hope would criticize Niebuhr's realism. New identity theologies of the third-world poor, women's liberation, and black liberation theology would attack his universalism. Ecological theologies would challenge the easy acceptance of the scientific manipulation of nature. During his life, though, the issues of democracy on the world scene, the Cold War, the challenge of Communism, and the threat of nuclear war would remain. His basic theology would guide the National Council of Churches, the Christian Council for Social Action, the World Council of Churches, and many of the seminaries during his lifetime. The faith barely suggested in this complicated lecture, when expressed in politics, would inform several progressives in American government. Through the Americans for Democratic Action (ADA), it would inform the liberal side of American politics.

From Harvard in 1961–62 he made modest contributions to the *Christianity and Crisis* debate over nuclear deterrence. John Bennett initiated it, discussing an essay from the book he was publishing on nuclear weapons. Kenneth Thompson, Paul Tillich, Paul Ramsey, Tom Driver, Hans J. Morgenthau, and Niebuhr all joined in the discussion. Niebuhr's most insightful comment was that NATO had already decided without national debates to use nuclear weapons to thwart a Russian invasion. It was not clear that the others had digested that reality. While deploring arguments justifying armed defense, he accepted the president's policy of providing public shelters from nuclear weapons explosions. Both Bennett and Niebuhr accepted nuclear deterrence, rejected first use of the weapons, and justified their use only in case of a response to a nuclear attack toward the end of preventing further attacks. Niebuhr particularly stressed the responsibility for Russia and the United States to accept the fact of the deterrent and to try to reduce tensions in the competition under the jointly managed nuclear umbrella.

COLLOQUIUM AT THE CATHEDRAL

Many colloquia have been held in New York City on Reinhold Niebuhr's thought, but the deepest one was held in 1961. A few days before Halloween, on October 21, 1961, the colloquium held at the Cathedral Church of St. John the Divine involved his intellectual friends. Paul Tillich, John Bennett, and Hans Morgenthau applauded his thought and raised questions from theology, social ethics, and political philosophy. Others joined in the intellectual feast, and it was recorded for publication.[29]

29. Harold L. Landon, ed., *Reinhold Niebuhr: A Prophetic Voice in Our Time* (Greenwich, NY: Seabury, 1962). An earlier form of the argument over sin and ontology is found in *The Theology of Paul Tillich: A Revised and Updated Classic*, ed. Charles W. Kegley (New York: Pilgrim, 1952).

The mammoth stone edifice with one tower left incomplete dominated its corner of Morningside Heights on Amsterdam Avenue. Between Central Park and Columbia University, its solid presence symbolizes the presence of the Episcopal Church's guidance of the republic. The historical tour of the cathedral connects with the history of Christian faith from its Hebrew origins to its central figure, visions of the end of the Roman Empire, through English church history to present conflicts. The walk through its pillars, altars, and art needs the spoken word of interpretation to reveal its meaning. Most of those present at the colloquium remembered that Reinhold Niebuhr often worshipped, sang, and prayed there. Half a century later, I would be interviewed there for the making of the film *An American Conscience: The Reinhold Niebuhr Story*.

Tillich described Niebuhr changing the theological scene in the 1930s. Even the questions students brought to Tillich's public and academic lectures around the country reflected Niebuhr's influence. He was *en kairoi*; his words met the present in transcendent terms. Tillich reflected upon a phone call from Niebuhr that offered him a life after he had been dismissed from his academic position in Germany. He warmly remembered their walks on Riverside Drive and their different attitudes toward man in nature.

Tillich agreed with Niebuhr basically about the doctrine of humanity. He believed that the philosophy of the human was decisive for Niebuhr and consistent with the rest of Tillich's system. Their differences were minor and derivative from their differing Christian sources: one more biblical and one more philosophical. Niebuhr feared Tillich's ontology and drive to universals would obscure the particular human responsibility for human evil. Niebuhr wanted to affirm the separation of the two biblical stories of the goodness of creation and the human responsibility for sin. He feared Tillich collapsed separation of the essence from existence into sin. Niebuhr, defending responsibility, wanted to keep the two stories separate. Niebuhr resisted moving onto Tillich's grounds of metaphysics. Tillich insisted that Niebuhr could not avoid ontology without making mistakes. Niebuhr as the ethicist refused the responsibility of the metaphysician. Tillich as a systematic thinker wanted to criticize Niebuhr's use of symbols as unsystematic. Niebuhr had more of a sense of basic human innocence, and also that by giving oneself to a cause one could lose the self somewhat and be closer to innocence than Tillich could concede. Tillich lived with personal sin more than Niebuhr, and his ethic encouraging self-fulfillment seemed dangerous to Niebuhr. Tillich's sense of sin, drawn from his experience and his ontology, was more determinative than Niebuhr's.

But both were Augustinian, Lutheran, and socialist in their intellectual development. Tillich's German idealism never understood Niebuhr's pragmatism, and they developed in their respective differences. Tillich delighted in pointing out the unorganized ontological assumptions in Niebuhr's theology. But their mutual friend Wilhelm Pauck pointed out there was no need for Niebuhr to follow Tillich's ontology. Both Niebuhr and Tillich remained with Martin Luther—in that the "New Being" meant justified but still a sinner. Tillich would not move into John Mackay's request urging him to assert that the "New Being" or the "new person in Christ" was ontologically a different person. Tillich affirmed the Lutheran realism he shared with Niebuhr. Tillich said that he thought they were closer now than earlier because of conversations with Niebuhr at Harvard. According to Tillich, Niebuhr said he was no longer throwing the concept of "original sin" in "the teeth of modern culture."

Tillich had retired from Union Seminary at the required age of sixty-eight in 1955. He and Niebuhr saw less of each other, as Tillich moved on to Harvard and later to the University of Chicago. Elisabeth Sifton's judgment that they remained friends seems correct to me. Others may have exaggerated the tension between Reinhold and both Tillich and Reinhold's brother, Helmut Richard. Their correspondence in both cases reflects their partnerships and deep respect for each other even when their methods were different. Particularly in ethics Reinhold emphasized responsibility and duty while Tillich stressed personal fulfillment. However, Reinhold graciously accepted the dedication by Paul of his book on ethics, *Morality and Beyond*, in 1963. Before New Year's in 1963, he wrote:

> I thank Paul for his generous dedication of his book *Morality and Beyond* to me. You are quite right we have been close friends for many years and we have had a creative dialogue about ethics and ontology without, incidentally, convincing each other.[30]

John Bennett presented Niebuhr's social ethic as having one absolute: love. Without seeing how love required justice, Christian ethics would be utopian or sentimental. Love through justice was always committed to struggling to improve the lot of the oppressed. Niebuhr struggled against both the moral relativists and the moral absolutists, settling for neither natural law nor radical contextualism. With love as the only absolute, he strove to show the relevance of a principled ethic developed

30. *Letter of Reinhold Niebuhr to Paul and Hannah Tillich* (December 27, 1963), Reinhold Niebuhr Papers, Library of Congress.

from the human wisdom of Western Christianity. Bennett, rather than pronouncing a eulogy, asked for more development in Niebuhr on foundations for hope, more ethics for the welfare-capitalist economy, and strategies for overcoming the terror of nuclear holocaust. Hans Morgenthau praised Niebuhr's recent book, *The Structure of Nations and Empires*. He regarded Niebuhr as the most creative political philosopher of the time. He philosophized about political situations and emergencies. He did not develop a total philosophy but thought rigorously about politics. Both Niebuhr and Morgenthau were pragmatic, but Morgenthau's German positivism probably did not understand how Niebuhr's epistemology was drawn from science, empiricism, and pragmatism. As a regular teacher of Aristotle, Morgenthau was drawn to Niebuhr's empiricism and realism, but he may not have understood, as much as he tried, the total theology and transformative thrust of Niebuhr's politics. Niebuhr still possessed some social gospel drive to reform society that Morgenthau understood less well than Schlesinger. Inasmuch as the colloquium reached back to the Old Testament, Jesus, Plato, and Augustine, it filled the cathedral with the voices that gave rise to the imposing structure itself.

Niebuhr's poor health and commitments at Harvard made it impossible for him to attend. His written responses to their comments and criticisms were humble and appreciative without surrendering any ground to Tillich or Morgenthau. He summed up his position against Eduard Heimann's criticism: "I am a pragmatist who tries to be guided in pragmatic judgments by the general principles of justice as they have developed in Western culture."[31]

Meanwhile at Harvard, Niebuhr was developing a new course on the struggle and prospects for democracy in its worldwide clash with Communism. Hundreds of students enrolled in the course. It assumed the directions of both Kennedy and Khrushchev—that the conflict was to be enacted in the Global South. He explored the uniquely Western historical origins of democracy, and the difficulty of applying democracy in the non-Western world. He would teach the course the following year at Princeton. It was political philosophy in grand design within the world crisis of the Cold War.

DIMENSIONS OF THE 1960S

The articulation of a Christian social philosophy or change in race relations and politics was only one strand of the 1960s. There were devel-

31. Landon, *Reinhold Niebuhr*, 123.

opments in sexuality, drugs, music, student rebellion, and lifestyles. This Christian philosophy, developed differently by Martin Luther King Jr. and Reinhold Niebuhr, was countercultural as the movements above were countercultural, but it was more serious in its claim to mold the whole society from Christian insights.

Martin Luther King Jr. was the dominant moral voice of the 1960s. His belief in God and the power of love revolted against the status quo of Jim Crow. Uniting theological liberalism from the social gospel and the rhythms of the black church, he unleashed a new vision of just-peace into the 60s. He was the essential voice of rebellion expressed through reform in the terminology of American history and Christian liberation. His hope in black-church terminology had more radical social energy than Niebuhr's "irony" and "ambiguity." Niebuhr knew that, and he learned to say it, pronouncing King as the greatest Christian social theologian. King believed to his death in a Christian vision of hope that Niebuhr regarded as a necessary illusion for change. King found the power to overcome the sense of inferiority that had been pounded into the slaves and their descendants. He found it in the black church and its message of God's power through love. This revolt discredited the laws and practices of Jim Crow and shook the ethos of establishment and quietism of the 1950s. After the war, America had settled in with Eisenhower. But in that quiet, forces were brewing that would insist all Americans had a place on the bus. Court decisions encouraged hope while King studied Niebuhr on social change and the possibilities of revolt through Gandhi. He studied Paul Tillich and Henry Nelson Wieman on the theological-philosophical concepts of God and hurriedly finished his dissertation to complete the study for the doctor of philosophy degree at Boston University. But his incomplete studies melded into the southern black Baptist experience of his life to produce a synthesis to rise to leadership in the midst of a bus crisis.

Kennedy too, brought his Catholic Boston sense of justice and courage to the sixties. He relied more on King's movement than the aid he could be persuaded to give to it. He wrote on courage with the help of a ghostwriter, and he brought it to the sixties. He had demonstrated virtue in World War II. Conscious of his own mortality, he continued to act boldly. The decade began with hopeful Christian social awakening fueled by courage, threatening to undo the complacency of the 1950s. The revolts they unleashed would ricochet beyond their expectations. The movements and the music changed as it moved to the white culture.

Vocal groups like Peter, Paul, and Mary translated the hope. Pete Seeger and Joan Baez popularized it with new groups.[32]

The four students who subjected themselves to abuse in North Carolina in February 1960 at the lunch counter had no idea that in the same year Union Seminary students would support them demonstrating at Woolworths on 125th in Harlem. Revolt looked like it was succeeding, and students began revolting against rules that thwarted them and sometimes against real injustice systems.

The snow piled up in the winter of 1960–61. New York City became quiet for a couple of days. The traffic stopped briefly. How beautiful it was. Bob Dylan hitchhiked from Hibbing, Minnesota; he was far from quiet. His harmonica and guitar recorded by Columbia Records enlivened student life. They loved the songs against the never-ending war. "Blowin' in the Wind" and "The Times They Are a-Changin'" spoke to their hearts. "Highway 61 Revisited" enlivened student hitchhiking. I heard him at the Washington Monument in 1963 with Martin Luther King Jr. and finally at the Cosmopolitan in Las Vegas the day after he won the Nobel Prize. This kid from Minnesota brought the folksong tradition and his own version of rock and roll into many hearts for the major struggles for peace and racial justice. Tony Norman noted that Dylan's music is haunted by the blues.[33] It is a very American sound. Later he was missed from the movements, but he had his own spirit to follow. Even Hibbing, Minnesota's great open-pit iron mine had a place in the American mythology around industrialization.

David R. Williams rightly interprets the Free Speech Movement and disruption at Berkeley in 1963–64 as a continuation of the southern civil rights movement.[34] The issues were relatively simple and the students relatively innocent. The early Student Nonviolent Coordinating Committee and the Students for Democratic Society were also innocent utopians at the beginning. University overreaction spurred them into more profound rebellion. Accompanying the social movements for reform was the abandonment of older sexual mores.

32. David R. Williams, *Searching for God in the Sixties* (Newark: University of Delaware, 2011), 59.

33. Tony Norman, "Bob Dylan's Never Ending Masterpiece," *Pittsburgh Post-Gazette*, Oct. 13, 2016, 2.

34. Williams, *Searching for God*, 30.

6.

International Politics, 1962

> We believe the task of defending the rich inheritance of our civilization to be an imperative one, however much we might desire that our social system were more worthy of defense.

In the early 1960s Niebuhr planned to write a book on democracy and Communism. It would have been a development of his Union Seminary course, Christianity and Communism, which he had taught since 1949 with John Bennett. Most of the course was on the practice of Communism, as the students at the seminary studied Christianity in their other courses. The second year of the course was additionally shared with Professor Searle M. Bates, an academic missionary who had taught Chinese history in China. The course description from the Union Seminary catalogue:

> *Christian Ethics 394*: A course on the nature of Communism and on the Christian approach to Communism. There will be a study on the classical Marxist theory and on the contemporary theory and practice of Communist parties. Emphasis will be placed on the problems created by Communism for the Christian church, for its world mission, and for the younger branches overseas.[1]

Niebuhr had given four or five lectures in the course during the term, and he was the leader of the course. He taught that Karl Marx equated empiricism with the history of materialism from the time of his dissertation to the writing of *Das Kapital*. He used his materialism to attempt to overthrow Hegel for the sake of the liberation of humanity from

1. *Union Seminary Catalogue* (1953), 82.

capitalism. Marx had rejected his baptismal tradition of Christianity. His secularism and materialism had much in common with Christianity, but it was tied to a particular party and praxis.

A following lecture dealt with the determination and human freedom question in revolution. He particularly focused on Engels, Trotsky, and Lenin and their hopes for a Marxist utopia. Stalin's perspective on Marxist philosophy was analyzed. Throughout his career, Niebuhr reviewed many books on Communism, Russia, and other countries.

He compared Communist and Christian ethics. Marxist ethics were not essentially opposed to Christianity on many subjects of interest to Niebuhr like the use of force in society or revolution, or class struggle, or the end justifying the means of change in society, but they were all used for Communist strategy. The Marxist ideal of "from each according to ability and to each according to need" had its New Testament roots, but it was not achieved in either Christian or Marxist civilizations.

He also lectured on Marxist interpretations of history, as he had written about it several times. His comments on Communist parties in Europe drew upon his constant reading in European politics and his many visits to Europe beginning in 1923. He also drew upon his own experiences with Communists in New York City in united front organizations.

Niebuhr, of course, was a heavy critic of Communism in the years he taught the course. The FBI File No. 121-033418 noted that he taught a popular course at Union titled "Christianity and Communism." There is no known record of FBI agents sitting in on the course, though they were around Union perusing the library card catalogue and interviewing people who knew Niebuhr.

He regarded the Marxist logic of history as a fantasy. That which Marxism took as science, Niebuhr interpreted as religion. Errors in Marxist philosophy, in his view, condemned Communism to inadequacy in checking tyranny and to moral pretensions. He exposited six errors in Communism: (1) Its trust in building a utopia on earth; (2) The dualism of good and evil people; (3) The deriving of evil from a human institution; (4) Overestimation of the power of ownership rather than managerial power; (5) Underestimation of the power of the state; and (6) Overestimation of the determinate role of economic production.

John Bennett was less critical than Niebuhr of Communism. Both knew of the plurality within Communism. Bennett regarded Niebuhr's critique as exaggerated. Bennett's book, derived from the course "Christianity and Communism Today," was more hopeful about Communism's constructive role in the poor world leading to revolution.

Niebuhr saw the same phenomenon as confrontation. He saw himself as an ideological critic of Marxism. He welcomed the philosophical struggle while hoping to avoid, where possible, the military struggle. Bennett's reservations about the severity of Niebuhr's criticism of Communism encouraged others to develop the theme. Russian critique of the terrors of Communism after the Soviet Union dissolved reinforced the truth of Niebuhr's critique, as did the secrets of Soviet archives as they were opened and analyzed. Niebuhr's own writing recognizes John C. Bennett and Roger Shinn as his best friends. They were not always in absolute agreement, though it is hard to separate Shinn's judgments from his mentor and senior colleague. Typically during times of crisis during the 1960s Bennett, Shinn, and Niebuhr would discuss the issue over the phone or in person if the opportunity presented itself. Sometimes in the late 1960s, I would be included in these discussions over the phone or in the advisory meetings for *Christianity and Crisis*.

The student response to the seminar was quite positive in the survey of his students taken in 1990. Professor Beverly W. Harrison, a critic of Reinhold Niebuhr on the subject, expressed criticism and ambivalence regarding the course she took in 1955–56.

> Christianity and Communism was truly awful pedagogically, with three unrelated lecturers. But A. F. Kerensky took the course, so that was interesting. To hear Kerensky's accounts of his and Lenin's conversations the night before the Bolsheviks formed a government was worth the price of admission. His and Niebuhr's conversations were fascinating and provided the best sessions of an otherwise dismal seminar.[2]

The Reverend Mr. Richard Poethig, an industrial and urban affairs expert, reported from the first time the course was given in 1949.

> My first experience of Niebuhr as teacher came in a 1949-50 seminar on "Christianity and Communism" with a focus on China. The Communists had just taken over the mainland and Chiang Kai-shek had fled to Taiwan. John Bennett and Niebuhr drew upon the experience of missionaries who were present at Union. The seminar holds vivid memories. It was as relevant as the latest news coming off the press-wire. It was an experience in shared knowledge. Niebuhr and Bennett respected what others had to say about the situation.[3]

Niebuhr's hopes to write a book on democracy and Communism were never fulfilled fully, though his 1969 book on democracy absorbed

2. Response to Nov. 15, 1990 Survey in author's possession.
3. Response to Nov. 15, 1990 Survey in author's possession.

aspects of the earlier project. The general perspectives of the course and the project were laid out in other occasional writings and in his 1959 *The Structure of Nations and Empires*.

The standing of Niebuhr in the area of philosophy of politics and international politics was particularly high in the 1960s. Friends of his and those influenced by him entered government in the 1960s. Arthur Schlesinger Jr., who regarded Niebuhr as the most important political thinker in the nation, called Niebuhr's daughter, Elisabeth, to the president's attention, and she was appointed to a position in the State Department. Dissertations on his thought were numerous, as were the published essays and books. Some of his earlier books will stay in print longer than these of the 1960s. However, his stature in the field is caught by his publication in *The Annals* of the Academy of Political Science in 1962, "American Hegemony and the Prospects for Peace."[4] It lays out the philosophy undergirding his essays on a variety of foreign policy issues.

The major reality was a sort of peace between two hegemonic nations dependent on nuclear terror. Each was hegemonic in their respective alliances. Both were imperialistic in the sense of great power imposition on weaker nations. Each tended to deny its own policy of imperialism and had anti-imperialist ideologies.

The United States could tolerate the loss of Laos in 1962, but it had to remain firm in holding on to its European allies. Vietnam was thought of as a client state like South Korea or perhaps Saudi Arabia. The United States would for the foreseeable future often ally with one-party states or dictators, hoping to maintain a possible openness toward long-term evolution of democratic developments.

The emerging power of China was difficult to evaluate for the prospects of ongoing peace. Niebuhr saw the competition of two Communist powers in a triangular relationship with the North Atlantic Alliance.

He welcomed the use of foreign aid and diplomacy to help allies overcome social pathologies that would weaken their resistance to Communism. He celebrated the Alliance for Progress and the preserving of the unity of the Congo, including Katanga.

Democracy and its non-Communist allies had plenty of problems holding together and creating social health. Probably the Communist tyranny had greater problems enforcing its authoritarian structures, with developments in education and technology challenging the hierarchy.

The burden of defense of the West and its allies was a worthwhile

4. *The Annals* 342 (July 1962): 154–60. Republished in Ronald H. Stone, ed., *Politics and Faith* (Macon, GA: Mercer University Press, 2012), 213–22.

task. Peace could not be guaranteed. Even a nuclear war and destruction was a possible outcome. But prudence, patience, and the development of societal and military strength could show a way through recurring crises. Niebuhr's whole theology and his sense of the ironical complexities of history prevented him from articulating bold visions for the future. But, he hoped for noncatastrophic outcomes from policies of humble strength. For him there were analogies between individual existence and national existence.

His own body was battered and subject to pain and infirmities, but he exercised humility and strength. As bad international news could depress the country, which would struggle to overcome it, so bouts of pain and weakness could encourage depression and he would need companionship and encouragement to overcome them. He revealed more pain and tendency toward depression to Bishop William Scarlett in his correspondence than he revealed to his friends at Union or to his students. Both of them were much weaker than when they founded the Delta Farm and worked together in the South, and their correspondence echoed that decline in a way that reinforced both of them in their musings about illnesses and death. The strokes that Justice Felix Frankfurter suffered in 1962 led Reinhold to reflect in his correspondence with the judge as he retired. Niebuhr thought both of them may have saved their lives by being forced to slow down their hectic pace. Niebuhr regarded Frankfurter as the most vital human being he knew, and thought the necessity of measuring his efforts could be good for his health. Meanwhile, Niebuhr that same year fell and suffered a concussion, which he thought was aggravating his paralysis. The two had corresponded on issues of legal and political philosophy since the 1940s, and they enjoyed a unique friendship grounded in their both having summer cottages in Heath, Massachusetts. Frankfurter was a reader of *Christianity and Crisis* as well as occupying a pew in Heath whenever Niebuhr preached in the ecumenical chapel in the village. Niebuhr would chide Frankfurter on his extreme secularism in some court cases, and Frankfurter countered by serving as a part-time critic of Niebuhr's journal—though his criticisms were more often of some of Niebuhr's writers than they were of the master himself. Once the judge needed expert advice on religious matters in a case before the court, he wrote the firm "Niebuhr & Niebuhr" to get the joint opinions of Ursula and Reinhold.

Despite what the Vietnam debacle became, it made very little appearance in his extensive writing on international affairs in 1962. In 1955, Niebuhr applauded President Eisenhower's decision to refuse stronger intervention to save the French in Indochina. He had not been an advocate for deeper involvement in China than financial support as the Communist revolution succeeded. The balance he achieved was in the refusal to intervene with military force in Asia if there was inadequate social strength to sustain a regime. Both the French regime in Indochina and the Kuomintang in China lacked the support of the population needed to maintain sovereignty. The defense of Western Europe was a different situation. He anticipated more Communist gains in the Global South. He was not against supporting regimes threatened by Communism, but he trusted more in indirect support than military intervention by US forces. He had written in 1955:

> No doubt military action must frequently be the ultima ratio in a struggle with a foe. We saved the whole situation by military action in Korea. But the contemporary situation in Vietnam should certainly instruct us on the limits of military power in the long cold war.[5]

He appreciated Eisenhower's caution over military intervention in Vietnam against Nixon's arguments for the need of a stronger US military intervention. He refrained from criticizing President Kennedy's continuing policies of support for the US-backed government in Vietnam in 1962.

He is best understood as a cautious interventionist recommending indirect support for non-Communist governments. He appreciated containing the rebellious Katanga province in the Congo through the United Nations' interventions. He refused to support European and American mining interests that hoped to wrest a pro–mining business province away from the nation in the name of anti-Communism. He was enthusiastic about the Alliance for Progress intervention to strengthen non-Communist forces in Latin America. His occasional writings on international politics corresponded closely to his liberal, anti-Communist editorials in *The New Leader*, which had moved from its earlier socialist origins to liberal anti-Communism. His friend and advisor to President Kennedy, Arthur Schlesinger Jr., advocated middle-class revolution for Latin America, and Niebuhr's support for Christian Democratic ideas was similar. Reflecting on the first year of the Kennedy administration, Niebuhr granted it a pass.

On the race issue, he appreciated the greater rigor of the New Frontier. Black appointments in government were up, and the Justice Department had initiated lawsuits or action in transportation, voting,

5. Reinhold Niebuhr, "The Limits of Military Power," *The New Leader* 38, no. 22 (May 30, 1955): 16–17. Reprinted in *The World Crisis and American Responsibility*, ed. Ernest W. Lefever (New York: Association Press, 1958), 115.

and the elimination of poll taxes and literacy tests. The administration had not supported new suffrage laws or closure in the Senate. Eight months later[6] he regretted the intransigence of Governor Barnett to James Meredith's education. He admired the Kennedys' overpowering of him and the enforcement of the law. Racial prejudice he regarded as universal, and justice required the power of the state. He moved quickly to foreign policy, neglecting to focus on Arthur Schlesinger's contribution to the State of the Union address on domestic issues. The Cuban misadventure caused the president no harm in the popularity polls, and the Alliance for Progress could improve US and Latin American relations, in his opinion.

The severe Berlin crisis seemed to be managed while avoiding moving any closer to nuclear war. The president's emphasis on striving to avoid atomic war, perhaps for decades, while resisting Communism, echoed Niebuhr's own hopes. While Kennedy was not an expert reader of Niebuhr, many in the inner circles of the New Frontier had been influenced by him, including at least one speechwriter. His friends Arthur Schlesinger Jr. and Adlai Stevenson, at the UN, were probably the closest to Niebuhr and they were normally on the liberal peacemaker side in the administration's arguments over foreign policy initiatives.

Haunting the administration were the renewal of nuclear tests by Khrushchev's Soviet Union. The president was harassed by advisors on both sides of the question of further testing, the possibility of a neutron bomb, and the consequences of using tactical nuclear weapons. While advisors assured the president of the necessity of keeping ahead of the Russians by resuming tests, the benefits of resuming tests were not so obvious to the president. Schlesinger and Stevenson were among those resisting the resumption of testing.

Niebuhr wrote a four-page review of the book edited by John Bennett on nuclear weapons.[7] He began with David R. Inglis's estimates of the consequences of nuclear war. Inglis, a physicist at Argonne National Laboratory, detailed the differences between a World War II "blockbuster"—a Hiroshima-size bomb—and an H-bomb. From the description he moved to the discussions of disarmament, finding some hope in regional schemes of inspection. Finally, the author's advocating of accommodation with Russia and small trust-building steps met Niebuhr's own sense of hope and realism. However, war through miscalculation could still lead to the catastrophe the authors hoped to avoid.

6. "The Intractability of Race Prejudice," *Christianity and Crisis* 22, no. 18 (Oct. 29, 1962): 181.

7. Reinhold Niebuhr, "Nuclear Dilemma," *Union Seminary Quarterly Review* 17, no. 3 (Mar. 1962): 239–42.

The two Union Seminary realist essays by Shinn and Bennett in the volume both resolved to keep the deterrent and to appreciate peace under terror.

The Khrushchev gambit to fortify Cuba with SAM missiles, IL-28 bombers, short- and intermediate-range nuclear missiles still defies analysis. It challenged US dominance in its own neighborhood, took a great risk for a weak ally, and would theoretically have changed the balance of power.

Could Khrushchev and his advisors have underestimated the resolve of the Kennedy administration? Was the United States perceived as too liberal to respond? The Roosevelt administration had waited until attacked at Pearl Harbor. Would the United States absorb a strategic defeat if the Russian installation succeeded? Had the Bay of Pigs confusion portrayed a weak president? If the Kennedys were still playing with the Mafia vis-à-vis Cuba, and entertaining failed plots to assassinate Castro, was a Russian gamble worth the risk?

The failure of US intelligence permitted the Russians to install a surface-to-air missile defense system, begin preparing, in some cases succeeding in readying the nuclear missile sites, and the intrusion of Russian air forces into Cuba before discovery by the U-2s. Once they were discovered and confirmed, the Kennedy administration moved quickly with diplomacy and mobilization to remove the missiles. The means of removal were debated, and eventually the naval quarantine of Cuba was decided upon by a narrow margin of the president's team. A direct attack on the island was reserved as an option if the blockade should fail.

Though the Soviet Union attempted stalling a decision, hoping to complete the project and to establish the facts on the ground, the US threat of invasion moved the Kremlin to withdraw. Faced by a reinforced US fleet, the Russian transports turned around and the work on the nuclear missile sites was ended.

The Kennedy government agreed early that the missiles had to be eliminated, as they threatened the United States in a new and immediate way. The debates raged between invasion, air strikes the Sunday after discovery, United Nations resolution, and naval blockade. At the time it was not known that the freighters were accompanied by nuclear-armed submarines. According to Robert Kennedy, a concept of a ladder of escalation was arrived at along with communication with Khrushchev. If all else failed, air strikes and an invasion would be launched. The degree of readiness of missiles already in place to fire was unknown. So, nuclear war could not be ruled out. Khrushchev had been pushing on Berlin and blustering since the failed Geneva Conference with President Eisenhower. The weakness of the New Frontier in the Bay of Pigs attempt encouraged the militants around Khrushchev to take a risk. However, he underestimated US resolve under Kennedy. He moved a major piece too far on the chessboard of competitive geopolitics. Castro had seconded the risk. Agreements were made, including Russian withdrawal of missile forces, eventual withdrawal of medium-range missiles in Turkey, and a nonaggression promise from the United States to Cuba. Niebuhr's first printed comment on the crisis regarded the outcome as Khrushchev's capitulation.[8] Perhaps, but the US president had given him enough secretly that he could save face among those who would support him in the Kremlin. In my early teaching of international relations midway in the decade, I used Robert Kennedy's moral courage and the ladder of escalation as appropriate responses.

The major issues of 1962 for Niebuhr were race relations and the nuclear issues around Cuba and Berlin. The Cold War issues were more dominant than race. When at the end of the year he wrote a long piece on the church, it focused on the same two issues. He was willing to judge the church by its moral exertion. He could not find much in church life that was relevant to the great moral issues of nuclear war and race. He judged the modern church as trivial.[9] Protestant churches were particularly weak. The churches developed more sophisticated social action projects following Niebuhr's exertions. Many of the leaders of the social action bureaucracies of the churches were Niebuhr's followers. Almost all of the leaders of the Council for Christian Social Action of his church, the United Church of Christ, were either Niebuhr's former students or his followers. The thoughtful, aggressive Commission of the Churches on International Affairs was also led by his students or allies. The studies of the World Council of Churches on social issues were staffed by Paul Abrecht. Abrecht and Shinn were among the last visitors from Union Seminary to visit Reinhold in 1971 as he rested on his deathbed. Niebuhr spoke at all of the assemblies of the World Council of Churches until ill health led him to just send his essay to the last one during his lifetime at Evanston, Illinois. He not only spoke but led the work in international affairs at the meetings in Amsterdam and Oxford. Later in the century, this important work of the churches in attempting to lead the consciences of Christians on important social issues weakened. Budgets of mainline, social-action workers were reduced and staff decreased.

8. Reinhold Niebuhr, "Cuba: Avoiding the Holocaust," *Christianity and Crisis* 22, no. 20 (Nov. 26, 1962): 204. The study by Arthur Schlesinger Jr., *A Thousand Days* (New York: Greenwich House, 1965), 784–841, presents an insider's view of the crisis.

9. Reinhold Niebuhr, "The Problem of the Modern Church Triviality," *Christianity and Crisis* 22, no. 21 (Dec. 10, 1962): 223–28.

The drift of the World Council of Churches toward liberation theology inclined many of its statements to sound utopian or socialist to American Christians at the same time that Roman Catholicism was opposing its liberation theologians. Parachurch movements similar to those Niebuhr founded now have a relevance that Niebuhr had hoped for while the mainline efforts seem more trivial. The rise of the Christian right is, of course, a post-Niebuhr phenomenon that he had not anticipated.

7.

The Mounting Racial Crisis and Democracy, 1963

> In the United States, we are conscious, as perhaps we were not a few years ago, how difficult it is for democracy to deal with race, especially when it is reinforced by economic handicaps.

The ethos of Union Theological Seminary of 1960 was one of alliance with the civil rights movement led by Martin Luther King Jr. Professors and students had been arrested for the cause. However, it was still a minority that picketed the Woolworth Dime Store on 125th Street in support of demonstrators at lunch counters in the South. Only a few joined the Social Action Committee's attempt to unionize the Union Theological Seminary staff. There were no African Americans on the faculty yet. Several students joined King's March on Washington, DC. There were only a few African American students, so the senior class made a gift sufficient to bring a black student to Union. He later became an outstanding Methodist bishop. The Social Action Committee organized a busload of Methodist students and an equal number of Methodists from Harlem to travel to Pittsburgh to demonstrate and lobby the Methodist Church to eliminate its race-based jurisdiction and to integrate the church. The same year the committee also organized pickets at Idlewild Airport protesting Mrs. Nhu's visit to the United States, and opposition to the war began among the students.

Probably no students were aware of Niebuhr's long history of progressive writing and action on race relations. The record stretched from chairing the Mayor's Commission on Race Relations in Detroit in 1925, to chairing the boards of the Delta Cooperative Farm in Mississippi and the Highlander School in Kentucky, to advocating economic boycotts by African Americans, influencing Martin Luther King Jr. and other black intellectuals, and to writing every year on the progressive side of the racial crisis. But all, I think, at Union knew that racial prejudice was sinful, and that the power structures of the country and the churches needed to be changed.

Niebuhr's end-of-year essay in *The Christian Century* focused on Protestantism, as it had in 1962. The issue had shifted from the Cold War nuclear threat to the church's failure in race relations. The individualism of Protestantism as analyzed by Max Weber left it unfit to deal with social problems and particularly with racism. Protestantism had previously failed to relieve the suffering caused by industrialism. Only the organizations of big labor and big government had been able to overcome the meanness of big business. Heroic Protestants and the social gospel movement had taken stands, but industrial oppression had been overcome by labor, not by the church. Niebuhr affirmed Adolf Berle's judgment in *The American Economic Republic* that through social forces a tolerable economic justice had been obtained. But a tolerable justice in economic affairs of white America was irrelevant to the facts of the failure in racial justice.

He spurned Gunnar Myrdal's characterization of American failure as a "Dilemma": "It was a scandal."[1] His paragraphs about the failure of Thomas Jefferson, the Constitution, the Hayes election, the retreat from Reconstruction and the Emancipation Proclamation, and the deprivation of 10 percent of the American population indicted the nation and the church. The catastrophe was more shocking because the moral issues were so clear.

The evangelical tradition within Protestantism had tolerated the worst racism in the nation in the South. It put up with segregated schools until tardily the Supreme Court acted, and then the combinations of individualism and racism conspired to create a new racist school system for whites and blacks. The "deliberate speed" of the court was overwhelmed by previous sentiments of the heart.

Niebuhr praised the renewal of the black church in joining the civil rights struggle. Martin Luther King Jr.'s efforts had propelled him to the role of outstanding churchman and leading citizen. The Protestant church could not be renewed without joining the social struggle for righteousness in race relations. So far, the church had failed in this

1. Reinhold Niebuhr, "The Crisis in American Protestantism," *The Christian Century* 80, no. 49 (Dec. 4, 1963): 1499.

most significant issue in the nation's life.[2] In the middle of the summer Niebuhr had been able to hope for the enactment of President Kennedy's legislative reforms. He had expected the resistance of white supremacists to increase as they lost the legal battle and faced the increasing impatience of awakened and organized African Americans. The demands on Niebuhr for contributions to periodicals, journals, and books often led to his rewriting his thoughts in several places. He wrote new pieces, but they often used the same arguments, examples, and historical references. His lecture at Barnard College, in a course his wife had initiated, analyzes American religion briefly and then continues with his usual polemics about the dangers of Protestant individualism and the need for the Protestant churches to focus on the nuclear holocaust and the tragedy of white racism. The lecture, published in Harold Stahmer's book, continues the same balance. His critique of "the most segregated hour in the nation" is harsh.[3] His essay is the most explicit and critical essay on race of any of the lecture-essays in the book delivered at Barnard College, nine blocks from the central street of Harlem.

BIRMINGHAM

The hatred of the racists exploded on September 15, 1963, killing Denise McNair, Addie May Collins, Carole Robertson, and Cynthia Wesley, Sunday school children at the 16th Street Baptist Church in Birmingham, Alabama. A week later the Protestant Council of the City of New York presented James Baldwin and Reinhold Niebuhr in dialogue on the radio on the meaning of the outrage. The dialogue was moderated by Thomas Kilgore, a former student of Niebuhr who was now minister of the Friendship Baptist Church and director of the New York City Southern Leadership Conference. James Cone, the founder of black theology, and I have discussed this conversation more than once. We later both wrote on the subject independently.[4] I, maybe foolishly, offered to write with Jim on Niebuhr, but he needed to have his own say. We would have agreed on much, but our perspectives are different.

2. Reinhold Niebuhr, "The Mounting Racial Crisis," *Christianity and Crisis* 12, no. 12 (July 8, 1963): 122.

3. Reinhold Niebuhr, "The Religious Situation in America," in *Religion and Contemporary Society*, ed. Harold Stahmer (New York: Macmillan, 1963), 150.

4. Reinhold Niebuhr, "The Meaning of the Tragedy in Birmingham," unpublished typescript. Reinhold Niebuhr Papers in the Library of Congress, Washington, DC. Ronald H. Stone, *Politics and Faith: Reinhold Niebuhr and Paul Tillich at Union Seminary in New York* (Macon, GA: Mercer University Press, 2012), 431–33. James H. Cone, *The Cross and the Lynching Tree* (Maryknoll, NY: Orbis, 2011), 53–57.

Baldwin and Niebuhr agreed on the moral failure of the white churches in race. The Birmingham image of the destroyed Christ without a face was raised by Kilgore. Baldwin indicated the white church's failure in love and the history of distortion for centuries of the image of Christ. Niebuhr thought it was a failure of justice. He did not anticipate the races loving each other, but love should drive them toward achieving justice.

Niebuhr knew through reading *The Fire Next Time* that this great writer had been a preacher. James Baldwin as a youth had gone through a shaking religious experience and followed it into preaching. Contrary to Niebuhr, Baldwin hated his preacher father, who perceived the young Baldwin as a rival. Niebuhr had stayed with the Christ of his youthful conviction whereas Baldwin had rejected Christ. Faced with the destroyed image of the white Christ in Birmingham's black church, they both deplored the failure of the church to overcome racism, but with different accents.

Baldwin had dined with Elijah Muhammad and affirmed with him that the white man was a Devil to blacks. The two previously published essays of *The Fire Next Time* expressed the despair of blacks as strongly as any writer of 1962. The portrait of most white men actively grinding the human dignity out of the black child may have been exaggerated. But their system certainly drove the black population to despair, as Baldwin insisted.

However, in the 1960s Baldwin was read more than Niebuhr. Baldwin had won fame and fortune with his books on black despair. He had overcome the horror of Harlem he described. Their fates were interlocked. Black Muslim hopes for a region of America under black power was an illusion. For him the white man was lost in his oppression of the black. The only hope Baldwin saw was for the relatively enlightened whites to join the relatively conscious blacks "to end the racial nightmare, and achieve our country, and change the history of the world." Either this minority would change the consciousness of the country and save it, or we would face the biblical prophecy: "God gave Noah the rainbow sign, No more water the fire next time."[5]

Niebuhr was less apocalyptic. He hoped for change through melioristic change using boycotts, demonstrations, the courts, politics, and education. However, in the dialogue over Birmingham James Baldwin expressed the political strategies for change more forcefully. Baldwin, using his personal knowledge of suffering under racial oppression, was the more powerful of the two in the conversation even without the

5. James Baldwin, *The Fire Next Time* (New York: Vintage, 1962), 105–6.

apocalyptic. It would take the aging, crippled Niebuhr a few more months to arrive at the level of Baldwin's strategic outrage. By then Malcolm X would have been assassinated by Elijah Muhammad, Baldwin would be in self-imposed exile, and the fires in the cities would be burning.

Niebuhr commented on the renewal of the black church by its leadership in the civil rights movement. He repeated his praise of Martin Luther King as one of the great Americans of the present. Baldwin responded:

> What I think is that there is a very great paradox in this country now. What you say about the Negro church for example, is, I think, entirely true. Martin has used the Negro church really as a kind of tool, not only to liberate Negroes but to liberate the entire country. They are the only people in this country at the moment who believe either in Christianity or the country, and are the most despised minority in it. It is ironical, I am trying to say, that the people who were slaves here, the most beaten and despised people here, and for so long should be at this moment, and I mean this, absolutely the only hope in this country. It doesn't have any other.

Niebuhr took the conversation to the level of revolution, calling the African American to be the only true proletarian in the country. "He is the revolutionist; he has got to be the revolutionist." Still, he wanted to say that as he had read most of what James Baldwin had written he did not see him throwing the white person out completely.

Baldwin responded that he was saying the white Protestant majority in the country, the white Christians, were irresponsible. They are immoral, and they don't know what is going on in their own kitchens. "I don't mean to say the white people are villains or devils or anything like that. They are irresponsible." Niebuhr did not hear exactly, and he asked: "They are irresponsible you say?" Baldwin replied: "Yes, they are morally irresponsible, criminally responsible. But this is their country too. What I want to say is that I don't suppose everyone in Birmingham, who lives in Birmingham, are monstrous people. But there may be silent people, you know, and that is a crime-in-itself. That's what I mean."

Baldwin moved the conversation to Niebuhr's ground of politics and economics. Niebuhr's comments on revolution seemed beside the point. The issues for Baldwin needed to move to Washington, DC to address integration of the neighborhoods, expecting the schools to follow. Employment among the minorities had to be resolved. He did not want political opponents to like him. Racists had seized the political momentum from the vacuum and it had to be won back.

Niebuhr was asked about the church. He responded, citing the failure of Protestant individualism and praising the black church in its struggle for justice. Sentimental or individual love was not very relevant to the structure. Love was to be the motive, but the tools of social forces toward justice were the way forward.

The moderator asked Baldwin about his hopes for a boycott of Christmas shopping. He urged all listeners to boycott Christmas and to boycott the large corporations that were engaging in business in Birmingham. Niebuhr responded in terms of James Reston's morning editorial in the *New York Times* urging the national corporations to open up channels of communication, and he started a reference to the president's investigative commission. Baldwin responded to the president's appointees as an insult. They sparred verbally a little until Niebuhr seconded Baldwin's reference to boycotting Christmas, saying it might save Christmas and its horrible canned music in the department stores. Baldwin threw in "with a record of Ray Charles."

The moderator asked about a sign he had seen in a picket line at the United Nations: "Arm the Negro." Baldwin responded in terms of the history of American violence and marked the concern in America about an armed African American. Why would America praise King's nonviolence, but not help in the struggle? Niebuhr admitted the legal system was violent to black people, but still urged, for pragmatic reasons, the strategy of nonviolent resistance for a minority's social strategy for change.

In conclusion, Dr. Kilgore thanked the speakers and announced rallies at Foley Square and the Salem Methodist Church in Harlem to continue the discussion.

James Cone confesses that he has learned much from Niebuhr. He has criticized Niebuhr sharply for not bringing the same moral passion to the defense of blacks as he brought to the Jews.[6] Niebuhr dialogued more with Jewish intellectuals than he did with black intellectuals. He appreciates Niebuhr's critique of the failures of the white churches and the strengths of the black churches.

Cone and I agree that Niebuhr was more deeply involved in writing about the Cold War in those later years than on race. I think race relations during the 1960s were his second issue. Cone admits Niebuhr may be better on race in America than other white theologians, but he failed to bring the passion that James Baldwin exhibited to the issue. I would add that he could not bring James Cone's passion to the issue, as he had never walked through the insults and oppression directed at blacks by

6. Cone, *The Cross and the Lynching Tree*, 178.

his own white tribe. Cone is a very passionate theologian, and Niebuhr in his old age was no match for the passion of either James Baldwin or James Cone. The power of the white, moderate liberal reformer to achieve change over against the most radical black theologian or radical is another issue.

Central to Cone's critique of Niebuhr is that Niebuhr did not use the metaphor or the analogy of the cross and the lynching tree. To Cone it is an obvious analogous symbol. Niebuhr praised imagination in religious language, but still failed to make the connection as far as we know. He could have made it in the case of Dietrich Bonhoeffer and Martin Luther King Jr.; as far as I know, he did not. He regarded them as martyrs and that may be as much identity as either of them would have claimed. In 2016, I sent Cone the one reference I had discovered of Niebuhr arguing for an anti-lynching law in the 1930s. Niebuhr had become a progressive moderate or liberal with some radical impulses. Cone is a radical, a liberation theologian who personally experienced insults to his human dignity. Their positions and interpretations are different. He credits Niebuhr's 1968 essay on race, which I published, as sounding almost like Malcolm X in some sentences. That is radical enough for me. In 1972 I was accused by the black theological ethicist, Preston Williams, as sounding like James Cone, and that's sufficiently radical for me.

I fault James Cone's interpretation on two points. He criticized Niebuhr for not being present at a major council on race in Chicago on January 14–17. He praised Abraham Heschel for walking with Martin Luther King Jr. and "Niebuhr did not."[7] Heschel and all of us who walked with Niebuhr knew better. He could hardly walk. He could lecture at Barnard a few blocks from his home for a short time in 1963 by leaning on a lectern. He could not travel as far as Chicago in 1963, and I assume managers of the council knew that. In 1964, he could not travel to Washington, DC even to receive the nation's highest civilian award from the president. Even given that James Cone is a more passionate speaker than the elderly Niebuhr, I do not expect him to exhibit the passion or production on behalf of white laborers or Jews that Niebuhr exhibited on their behalf.

Niebuhr's comment to James Baldwin that he had read most of Baldwin's works seems accurate to me. But I don't have good data on how many black authors he read over the years. Interestingly, the best data James Cone and I have on the subject comes from the course Dietrich Bonhoeffer took with him, "Ethical Viewpoints in Modern Literature." If I read Cone correctly, he credits Bonhoeffer with reading black

7. Cone, *The Cross and the Lynching Tree*, 178.

authors in Niebuhr's course. He mentions particularly Countee Cullen, Langston Hughes, and Alain Locke as being read in Niebuhr's course; he credits Bonhoeffer for being existentially involved, but Niebuhr is regarded as distant from the issue.[8] I accept Cone's point that Niebuhr did not quote black authors in his published works. But the crediting of the student, and not the teacher, for reading assigned books indicated a deeper argument. Niebuhr, from southern Illinois, deepened his perspective on the race issue, but by the time his last decade ended, he had gone as far as liberals went. Cone is a liberation theologian, and he bears all the glory and criticism that such a position deserves. Niebuhr just refused to believe that overtly indigenous theologies exhibiting passion and moralism would carry the day for reformation and social change.

Niebuhr lectured on race on December 16, 1963, in the seminar on social ethics he was teaching in the ground-floor seminar room across from the bookstore. It was a lecture on race and group relations. The first third was on anti-Semitism and the following two-thirds on white racism. Several of us students had participated in antiracist actions in various cities. The tutor John Raines had been a freedom rider integrating transportation in the South. I and one other student had been in the March on Washington earlier that year. Niebuhr presented a historical lecture indicating how the country had oppressed the black minority from its earliest days. He explained that the black revolt in 1963 was stemming from the rising of hopes of the oppressed due to Supreme Court decisions and the civil rights movement led by King. He deplored the failures of Jeffersonian democracy and evangelicalism. He repeated his conclusions of the superiority of Roman Catholic institutionalism versus Protestant individualism and congregationalism. He appreciated the criticisms of James Baldwin and Adam Clayton Powell on the corruptions of the black church, but he thought it was renewing itself through the civil rights movement. The free society according to Jefferson demanded education and universal suffrage, and of course both were denied to black people. He praised Martin Luther King Jr. as the leading Protestant, but he still faulted him for having liberal illusions about white people responding to moral arguments. I do not remember, nor do my notes show, that he advocated any different policies than the civil rights movement was promoting. A student paper in the seminar[9] was on housing integration.

John Raines had asked me to lead off the student presentations. My paper was on the political philosophy of Hans Morgenthau. Niebuhr's

8. Cone, *The Cross and the Lynching Tree*, 42.

9. Lecture notes from December 16, 1963, in author's possession.

response to the paper and his calling me to come over to his apartment later to discuss some of the points I had raised between Morgenthau and himself strengthened my academic relationship with him. I do not remember any of us who were actively engaged in action, demonstrations, and working on race relations as regarding Niebuhr's presentation discouraging our actions or differing from the strategies we were developing as activists ourselves.

A NATION SO CONCEIVED

Following his summer at the Center for Democratic Institutions in 1961 in Santa Barbara, the Fund for the Republic commissioned a book by Niebuhr to follow up on his address at the Fund in June 1961 on the American character. The following years of retirement were busy, and he was not in good health. According to Richard Fox,[10] Hutchins was so dissatisfied with Niebuhr's progress that the Fund arranged for a young Harvard professor, Alan Heimert, to assist Reinhold in the project. The book, coauthored by Niebuhr and Heimert, was published in 1963.[11]

Alan Heimert was newly appointed to the departments of English and American History in 1961. The previous year he had been at the Institute for Advanced Studies at Princeton. Niebuhr provided most of the philosophy of history and the themes of the book. Heimert's obvious contributions are in the details of American history and in the production of the manuscript. Niebuhr authored chapters 1 and 4: "American Character" and "The American Sense of Mission."[12]

The authors' purpose was to portray the American character resulting from its early English-transplanted messianic vision tested and traumatized by forces of history into its present imperial responsibilities. The character moved from its romance of an agricultural nation blessed by "nature and nature's God" into expansion by immigration into an industrial power. Its power led it painstakingly away from its anti-imperialism into the responsibilities of world power in the Spanish-American War. Presently (1963) it ironically exercised the responsibilities of nuclear power as one of two hegemonic powers on the world scene still grappling with the vision of its earlier innocence and its present morally ambiguous role.

10. Richard Fox, *Reinhold Niebuhr: A Biography* (New York: Pantheon, 1985), 278.

11. Reinhold Niebuhr and Alan Heimert, *A Nation So Conceived: Reflections on the History of America from Its Early Vision to Its Present Power* (New York: Charles Scribner's Sons, 1963).

12. Here as elsewhere in scholarship on Reinhold Niebuhr the determination of authorship is best guided by knowledge of previous known writing, by sources used, and the grasp of Niebuhr's repeating phraseology, insights, concepts, and generalizations.

The book improves on some of Niebuhr's earlier works of historical writing in mentioning the national sins of slavery in six pages. Still, the conflicts of African Americans and their contributions to the American character are much deeper than Heimert and Niebuhr reveal in this volume. The more grievous failure is the naïveté of the presentation in two pages of reflections on Native Americans. Partially this judgment is due to my personal experience in sections of the country other than those familiar to Niebuhr. We were both Midwestern: he from Illinois and I from Iowa (both states named after Native American tribes). The Black Hawk wars in Illinois and eastern Iowa were concluded before the Civil War, and Niebuhr was born in 1892. The issues among and with the Native Americans were still alive for me in western Iowa in my college years. My acquaintance with southwestern Native Americans dates back to my high school years. The wars with the Apaches were settled in the 1890s. My grandfather still talked about meeting Sioux at the homestead cabin. The neglect of the Indian Wars is a serious omission. The sentences describing Anglo-Saxons assuming "the virgin character of the Northern Hemisphere and 'disregarding' the indigenous Indian population" will not suffice. Nor is the description of national expansion into "the empty spaces of the western territories" adequate.

Genealogical records of Puritan life in Massachusetts in the 1600s are full of terrible warfare between the colonists and the natives. The Americans may not have been very aware of how their germs decimated the landscape before their actual taking of the land, but they were quite conscious of the almost genocidal violence against the natives. From New England to California the land of each state was taken by germs, native starvation as the animals were killed, and by warfare and massacres.

Similarly, the picture of expansion over a "virgin continent" forgets that the continent was occupied by empires—the Spanish, French, Russian, Mexican—and by smaller colonies of Swedes and Dutch. The empires had to be conquered or persuaded to sell or cede their land. The young nation could also sometimes claim to have purchased land from supposed leaders of Native Americans. But the history of forced removals, massacres, and broken treaties reveals the character of violence and terror of the new colonists over the Native Americans. There, of course, was resistance to the displacement, some assimilation strategies, and some violent reactions. But whether the Native Americans assimilated or fought, they lost the continent.

The overconcentration of the volume on the perspectives of New England and Virginia also neglects the Spanish contributions to North American civilization. The Southwest and California were conquered and converted not by Anglo-Saxons, but by Spanish conquistadores and their allied Catholic missionaries. The region from Texas to California had its own character and its own policies vis-à-vis the Native Americans, which are still felt in those regions, religions, and races. The return of Mexicans and Hispanics to those regions in large numbers is a large part of the American character today even if it was less apparent in 1963. Niebuhr and Heimert may have been aware of these different historical trajectories, but they failed to write about their significance. The American character was developed not only in slavery but in slaughter, and that character is inherently violent. The vision of democracy and capitalism is more dangerous than Niebuhr and Heimert explained because it has been armed and relatively merciless from the beginning. The decline of the religious elements in the vision may leave it even more vicious for some of its pro-war or nuclear-terror proponents than before. Of course, religion like business was often imperialist. But both religion and business sometimes restrain violent impulses.

The book consists of three chapters and an introduction from Niebuhr's original paper for the Fund for the Republic on "The American Character." The three themes are standard Niebuhr, often repeating other essays he had written in the 1960s. The first is that the Anglo-Saxons have been forced by immigration into accepting religious and ethnic toleration for a pluralistic and open society. The references to the Kennedy inauguration echoed the religious tolerance in the use of four prayers, as he had previously written in *Christianity and Crisis.* Second, he repeats his story of the movement from agrarian society to great industrial power, emphasizing the religion and secular reforming movements that produced a relatively just settlement between labor and capital. Finally, the third theme is the messianic and secular hopes that were mixed together in "Manifest Destiny." The United States overcame isolationism and but was now particularly vulnerable in a peace between two superpowers in a balance of power guaranteed by nuclear terror.

An alternative vision stresses the Native American wars of the seventeenth to nineteenth centuries and the conquest of the continent represented in the town and state names representing Native American words and the number of towns still named "Fort." The open society of chapter 2 was never achieved for the majority. The lives of industrial workers were more mean and squalid than the book represents, and the tolerable justice required the alliance of government and big labor, an alliance that suffered defeats soon after the book was published. Issues regarding the openness of society remain debated for persons of alternative gender identities, and only in the twentieth century were women granted the vote; the struggle for women's rights remains unfinished. If, in a book reflecting on American history, we neglect the violent suppression of Philippine patriots, opponents in the Caribbean, annexation of the republics of Texas and California, our role in wars in China and interventions in Russia, we will not prepare readers to understand the other wars in Asia that the Kennedy administration and its successors were already entering. Of course, Niebuhr knew all of this and wrote about it elsewhere, but this book is misleading. Niebuhr has been criticized for avoiding detailed discussion of slavery and black oppression in his historical books. I agree with the critique as represented by the few pages in the introductory chapter of this book and its later neglect. But criticism for what one does not undertake in one genre of work is weaker than argument over that which one has written. Niebuhr published so much more on race in 1963 that its near absence in this book is not as major a fault as the neglect of the American Native. He consistently neglected analysis of the ongoing conquest of the indigenous nations, as do most American historians. Part of the American character, including the seventeenth-century ancestors, is murder and near genocide of the original inhabitants.

INTERNATIONAL RELATIONS

Niebuhr wrote enthusiastically about the test ban agreement.[13] He saw in it less relaxation of tension than many, but he saw potential for a Russian-American partnership at the expense of the Chinese. He was uncertain as to what the "next steps" might be. Moreover, commenting on the dark world situation, he quoted Cardinal Newman's hymn: "I do not ask to see the distant scene; one step enough for me."[14]

On Vietnam, Niebuhr assumed that in our contest with Communism the United States would support nondemocratic nations against Communism. He regarded the Central Intelligence Agency as supporting many dictators against the threat of Communism. Democracy was an ideal and not the reality of many US allies. He thought the US would do well to confine the CIA to intelligence gathering and interpretation. Its military exercises were often not helpful, and sometimes their extreme anti-Communism backfired against the United States. He regarded the CIA as innocent of overthrowing Diem, though it had supported the Special Forces of his brother. He recognized that United States author-

13. Reinhold Niebuhr, "The Test Ban Agreement," *Christianity and Crisis* 23, no. 15 (September 16, 1963).

14. Niebuhr, "The Test Ban Agreement."

ities knew of the plans to overthrow Diem and that the United States had signaled its displeasure with him to the coup plotters. His earliest recorded direct attack on US Vietnam policy was in November 1963. *The National Guardian* reported that he and eleven other clergymen had formed a "Ministers' Vietnam committee to protest the persecution of Buddhists in Vietnam and US involvement in the Vietnam War."[15]

Niebuhr wrote immediately on the death of the president.[16] He noted the grief beyond the nation around the world. Kennedy's youth and promise had been cut down too soon. He praised his accomplishments: confrontation of the Russians in Cuba, the test-ban agreement, progress in race relations, and powerful leadership of the non-Communist world. Niebuhr used the "American dilemma" symbol that he had rejected only a few months earlier. He praised the president's nonvacillation in race relations, when he knew better. His praise of Kennedy's intelligence, political shrewdness, and courage touched on qualities that the world, in its grief, responded to powerfully. His grief was real, and his tribute was fitting for an obituary.

His "A Tentative Assessment" credited John F. Kennedy first with style. His cool detachment and appreciative support for intelligence and the arts marked his three short years. Second, he recognized Kennedy's ability in confronting the Soviets without realizing the full price paid for Khrushchev's retreat. He gave him credit domestically for the tax cut and active engagement of the administration in the civil rights struggle. He recognized the eulogy quality of saying nothing negative about the dead.[17]

Doubts about the assassination continued to spark controversy during Niebuhr's life. Lee Harvey Oswald's affection for Russia and Cuba and Jack Ruby's Mafia associations connected the president's death with his foreign policy. The facts don't suggest a deranged loner as strongly as they point toward deeper connections in the Russian-Cuban imbroglio. The Kennedys used the Mafia in assassination attempts on Castro. Allen Dulles's leadership in the investigation of the killing of the president points toward deeper and shadowy connections through the CIA. The Warren Commission quieted most of the public, but I believe there were deeper international policy issues at stake, and the actors' associations with Russia, Cuba, and the Mafia suggest conspiracies reminiscent of traditional international politics. Too much remains hidden, and I don't know what Niebuhr knew or suspected. The president's bedding of a

15. Federal Bureau of Investigation report on Reinhold Niebuhr in File 121-33418, p. 60.

16. Reinhold Niebuhr, "John Fitzgerald Kennedy, 1917–1963," *Christianity and Crisis* 23, no. 21 (Dec. 9, 1963): 221.

17. *The New Leader* 47, no. 25 (Dec. 9, 1963): 7, 8.

Mafia mistress also sparked issues around Mafia involvement with assassinations on both sides of the Florida straits.

SOCIAL ETHICS

Niebuhr's major essay on method in social ethics placed the discussion in the history of the church and in the recent ecumenical developments. The first half of the essay presents his survey of the historical development of the social teachings of the Christian churches. The second half details ecumenical council teachings from 1925 to 1963. The liberal Christian ethic of the 1925 Stockholm Conference developed toward realism in the 1937 Oxford Conference. German theologians were prohibited from attending Oxford by the Nazis. Barth and Niebuhr shared dominance of that pre-war consultation. John Foster Dulles and Josef Hromádka of Czechoslovakia clashed. The development toward the Amsterdam Conference of 1948 was in Niebuhr's perspective toward pragmatism and empiricism. By the World Council meeting in 1954, Niebuhr could only send his address due to crises in his health. By this time the responsible society theme was suggesting the conjoining of welfare with the productive capacity of capitalism. Human rights and technical aid for economic development were affirmed. Race relations moved to center stage at the conference. In his interpretation, his reliance on the social sciences or at least social philosophy and pragmatism paralleled the World Council of Churches. So he characterized the work as empirical studies "under the Love commandment," guided by changing social principles. He regarded as helpful the "middle-axiom" principled approach of Archbishop Temple, represented at Union by John Bennett. The essay approved of principles if they were not held too tightly, as Roman Catholicism natural law tended to become rigid. He concluded with the threat of nuclear weapons and the "revolution of race and nations" as the world context.[18]

18. Reinhold Niebuhr, "The Development of a Social Ethic in the Ecumenical Movement," in *The Sufficiency of God: Essays on the Ecumenical Hope*, ed. Robert C. Mackie and Charles C. West (Philadelphia: Westminster, 1963), 111–28. Reprinted in Ronald H. Stone, ed., *Faith and Politics: A Commentary on Religious, Social, and Political Thought in a Technological Age* (New York: George Braziller, 1968), 165–81.

BARNARD LECTURES ON DEMOCRACY, 1963

Niebuhr was appointed the Virginia C. Gildersleeve Professor for Barnard College in 1963. He participated in one course in the religion studies department for Ursula, who chaired the department. The course that caught my imagination was on democracy, its past in the United States and Europe, and its future in the countries of the Global South. There were 110 girls in the course and thirty boys, myself sitting in the back as an unregistered student. The lectures presented on political philosophy evolved from his Harvard and Princeton lectures of the previous two years. In Cambridge and Princeton hundreds of students and several professors filled the auditoriums. Neither most of the professors nor the students understood fully what he was undertaking. Peter Laslett followed the general consensus when in 1957 he announced: "For the moment, anyway, political philosophy is dead."[19] Laslett collected the best essays suggesting that a resurrection of the undertaking might be beginning. But, as a whole, the study had fallen on hard times under Marxist and sociological analysis. Linguistic analysis had driven other nails into the coffin.

Niebuhr had defined his vocation as teaching political philosophy in a Protestant seminary. Political philosophy, classically, was an extension of ethics, and ethics also had undergone a period of eclipse under the language philosophers. Niebuhr's retirement lectures for his three years of post-Union teaching were political philosophy in the grand scale with use of historical material. Given the threat of the end of civilization in a nuclear war launched by the superpowers, he set out to analyze the ruling ideology of the United States with reference to the Soviet Union.

The context was the Cold War between the Bay of Pigs and the Cuban missile crisis. The New Frontier administration was subjecting the policy of deterrence through the threat of massive assured destruction to evaluation. Kennedy wanted other options than nuclear war to deter Khrushchev.

Niebuhr accepted "containment" of the fanaticisms of the Communists. He expected the contest to be waged in the new nations freed by European decolonization. Hardly any of them had achieved stable governments; fewer had achieved democracy. He intended to contribute to the context in the ideological debate. In World War II he had contributed a realistic defense of democracy in *The Children of Light and the Children of Darkness*. Now facing nuclear destruction partially fueled by

19. Peter Laslett, "Introduction," in *Philosophy, Politics and Society* (Oxford: Blackwell, 1963), vii.

philosophical struggle between Russian Marxism and Western democracy, he set out to analyze "democracy" historically.

He was doing neither political science nor theology. His work was philosophy fueled by a lot of historical data and interpretation. The funding of the study by the Rockefeller Foundation and its move from Scribner's (Niebuhr's usual publisher) to Prager (where his daughter Elisabeth worked as an editor) indicated its political use. It was philosophy with a purpose in the midst of the Kennedy administration and the world nuclear crisis.

The lectures in a revised format were published in 1969 by Niebuhr's assistant at Harvard, Paul Sigmund, as *The Democratic Experience: Past and Prospects.*[20] The significance of Sigmund's contribution should not be minimized. The introduction is clear that Niebuhr's concepts and outline were utilized. Sigmund had by 1969 already published on ideology, politics, and development in the Global South. The book also incorporates many studies past 1963 that Sigmund utilized. However, Niebuhr's distinctive phraseology and style appear in both parts of the book, while he wrote the first part of the book on the origins of democracy. Niebuhr's 1963 lectures also used empirical data and literature from the developing nations. So, though Niebuhr's work clearly predominates in the first part, the second part also follows his outline and has some of his content.

Niebuhr wrote essays on democracy without defining it. Even in the 1969 volume containing the lectures with an additional essay on democracy by Paul Sigmund, there is not a precise definition. He means by the term a governed system that limits the power of government while allowing individuals and groups to pursue their own agendas. It requires the capacity of the people to replace those who govern them, protection of human liberties, and toleration of various agendas within the system. The achievement of a tolerable degree of justice requires social mobility and some balancing of powers. Both constitutional monarchies and republics are regarded as democracies.

Rather than define the concept, he accepts the commonsense meaning of democracy to Americans while explaining how it arose in Europe from contingent historical struggles. His most famous aphorism implies that his understanding contains strains of both idealism and realism: "Man's capacity for justice makes democracy possible, but man's inclination to injustice makes democracy necessary."[21] Democracy in the modern expression was preceded by the national states and empires. Its

20. Reinhold Niebuhr and Paul Sigmund, *The Democratic Experience: Past and Prospects* (New York: Prager, 1969).

21. Reinhold Niebuhr, *The Children of Light and the Children of Darkness* (New York: Charles Scribner's Sons, 1944).

presuppositions normally included the dignity of the individual; some dominant language, a sense of community, a diminution of tribalism, the achievement of a degree of toleration, and often a dominant religion projecting a sense of human dignity. Extreme competition among religions, languages, and classes could thwart democratic developments. However, Belgium, Switzerland, Canada, and Lebanon suggested the rivalries could be overcome. Democracies emerged when traditional societies were overthrown by rising middle classes. High points in the rise of governments regarded as democracies were the Cromwellian, Glorious, French, and American revolutions. Disunity in Germany and Italy prevented their early evolution toward democracy, and then democracy was thwarted. Germany, Italy, Japan, and South Korea all struggled toward democracy after the war, with American tutelage. The Scandinavian countries along with the Netherlands and the United Kingdom maintained their monarchist symbolism while moving into parliamentary democracy. The lectures told his version of these struggles and then moved into the legislative battles, as suffrage alone did not permit participation by unorganized workers or minorities in power. The struggles for unionization and organization were a necessary part of achieving democracy. In the United States it required a Civil War and the later black revolt to achieve democracy. The achievement of unionization and women's suffrage moved the European nations and the Commonwealth of Nations toward fuller democracy.

In Niebuhr's thought, democracy was a contingent historical development realized in the American Revolution. Exported to the British colonies, it flourished in India except for caste, but was thwarted in South Africa by apartheid. In 1963 it existed in principle in the newly formed nations in Africa, but in reality the African nations lacked linguistic, ethnic, and religious harmonies and were largely illiterate. Without educated middle classes or economic viability they soon fell into one-party states, dictatorships, or military-run governments.

Niebuhr was deeply pessimistic about democracy emerging in the traditional Islamic states of the Near East. Turkey's secular revolution was promising, and while Lebanon had democratic features its future was doubtful. Niebuhr did not conceive of Islamic revival pushing democracy. The attempts at modernization under traditional Islam seemed remote. He was optimistic about Israeli democracy if it was supported by the United States. He was aware of the dangers to Israel's democracy as power shifted toward non-European immigration and in the absorption of the original Muslim and Christian Arabs.

In Asia the Communist countries could not be expected to evolve into democracies. Their exaltation of the community and state power over individual freedom thwarted some tendencies toward democracy. Japan's religion lacked some trajectories toward democracy, but US imposition and power could sustain tendencies toward democracy there. Paul Tillich was more pessimistic about democracy in Japan than Niebuhr because of the religious tendency there toward negation of the individual self. The trends of Pakistan and Indonesia were not supportive of democracy, but they sometimes preserved parliamentary structures and might evolve toward more open societies.

Niebuhr and his later colleague Sigmund were more positive regarding the chances for democracy in Latin America than in Africa, the Middle East, or Asia, but they remained pessimistic. In 1963, Niebuhr saw most of Latin America alternating between military governments, civilian dictators, and movements toward paramilitary government. The class structure of Spanish feudalism was overlaid with parliamentary forms following the republican revolutions. Niebuhr's formula was of Latin American feudalism supporting democratic forms and occasional reform movements continuing unless interrupted.

He regarded Uruguay, Costa Rica, and Mexico as the most democratic, with Venezuela and Colombia showing trajectories toward democracy but threatened by guerrilla warfare. Niebuhr remained enthusiastic in 1963 about the Alliance for Progress pushing for land reform, education, aid, and social progress, but the capacity of its limited funds moving the oligarchs, rulers, generals, and church of Latin America toward fundamental change were small. Niebuhr saw some democratic tendencies in Mexico's PRI, and he was encouraged by Christian Democrats in Chile. Niebuhr could not anticipate the unborn liberation theology in 1963. The book published in 1969 was pessimistic about liberation theology challenging the dominant feudal church in Latin America. Sigmund foresaw that the Marxist elements in the movement would encourage ruling oligarchs to shout "Communism" and the United States would overreact with its military control. Neither of the large countries of Brazil or Argentina showed much progress of lasting democratic reform. Niebuhr's friends had some influence in the Latin America policy of the Kennedy administration. But, the realities of the Cold War and the social-ideological bent of most of Latin America provided few grounds for democratic tendencies there. The growing middle class of urban Latin America was an encouraging factor, but centuries of dependence of the Indian, mestizo, and black populations reinforced the white oligarchic domination of the population.

Niebuhr dismissed utopian dreams of American democracy along with libertarian claims for it that emphasized only "freedom." He preferred to note it as a phenomenon of European, Commonwealth, and American experience. Approached realistically, it was a way to limit government power that previously had been tyrannical, and to add to it welfare, organizational, and human rights expression that allowed individuals a chance to flourish.

As part of his grand strategy, the lectures encouraged a rational defense of democracies where they existed and where "open societies" with future democratic possibilities could evolve. He did not encourage the export of democracy to societies where its foundations were lacking. In the Cold War world, the decrease of Communist fanaticism could be hoped for over time. Communist analysis failed in understanding the poor-developing world of largely agricultural economies. The United States could defend bastions of "open societies" where the substance was present. These calculations needed to be made in terms of national interest and power, and not in terms of utopian or libertarian campaigns for democracy. Similarly, analysis of the possibilities of human-economic development needed to be on a case-by-case basis and not on ideological grounds.

In 1963, I dissented from the lectures in three areas. From my year of work with children from Harlem and in my Harlem camp experience, I thought the situation of black youth's oppression needed more attention than the lectures revealed. Furthermore, my association with graduate students from wealth and other contacts with the wealthy in New York City persuaded me the economic inequalities had not been resolved in a tolerably just way. Finally, my analysis of the Vietnam War persuaded me that democracy's restraint on its unjust war-making tendencies was less secure than Niebuhr represented. These failures of democracy would present me many opportunities for further discussion with the professor. By the time the lectures were published in 1969, the authors noted that democracies had not succeeded very well in race, social justice, or peacemaking. They repeated Churchill's aphorism that democracy was the worst form of government except for all the others that had been tried.[22]

Johnson kept the Niebuhrians of Kennedy's cabinet, but he added his own reformers as he sought to continue the New Deal of Franklin D. Roosevelt. His mother's Christian activism led Johnson to see no discontinuity between his father's progressivism and Christian social action. As biographer Randall B. Woods put it:

22. Niebuhr and Sigmund, *The Democratic Experience*, vi.

> LBJ decided to retain Kennedy's cabinet, but he had his own brain trust, a group that he had assembled over the years, a collection of men whose pragmatic liberalism was tinged with the theological realism of Reinhold Niebuhr.[23]

According to Woods, Johnson was himself a Niebuhrian, as were his closest advisors.[24]

Johnson like Niebuhr presupposed the content of the social gospel, but his practical politics and the words of his advisors pushed him into sober progressivism. His 89th Congress would push through progressive legislation even more far-reaching than Roosevelt's. Medicare, Medicaid, voting rights, aid to education, National Endowment for the Humanities and the Arts, antipoverty legislation, highway beautification, research monies for heart disease and cancer, the Department of Housing and Urban Development, and the National Institute of Health were all achieved. But by 1965 Republican and Chamber of Commerce opposition was growing. The conservatives of the Democratic south were digging in their heels against his liberalism. Some of the programs were bigger in funding and conception than they were in deep knowledge of their difficulty. Social engineering for the sake of reform was loosed on the American public, but gradually the war soaked up the funding and the promises were bigger than the reality. It was agreeable that Niebuhr would receive the Freedom Medal from Johnson in 1964. But, by the end of 1965 Niebuhr was becoming a severe critic of the administration, which thought war and social engineering could make a successful country out of a distant nation resisting its Communist revolutionary origins. Schlesinger left the administration before Niebuhr's polemics castigated the regime, but by 1965 the realist liberal spokesmen had moved away from their earlier hopes for the Johnson presidency. Niebuhr's hopes were higher than Schlesinger's, I believe. Schlesinger had been too identified with Kennedy to share Niebuhr's hopes for the administration. The sordid realities of both American classism and racism resisted reform, and the costs of the war made it impossible.

23. Randall B. Woods, *Prisoners of Hope: Lyndon B. Johnson, the Great Society and the Limits of Liberalism* (New York: Basic Books, 2016), 19.

24. Woods, *Prisoners of Hope*, 19.

8.

President Johnson, 1964

> The [*Mississippi Black Paper*] documents disclose a society in which the instruments of justice are tools of injustice.

President Johnson perceived the resentment of inheriting the victory of the martyred John F. Kennedy. His own health since a 1955 heart attack was less than robust. Lady Bird encouraged him to win the presidency in his own right. He hesitated; sometimes he denied to her that he would run. Still agonizing over the decision, he chose just before the convention that he would campaign while intending not to repeat in 1968.[1] His victory over the sentimental-nativism of Senator Goldwater was total except for the votes of five Southern states. His choice of Niebuhr's friend and fellow Americans for Democratic Action, Hubert H. Humphrey, could not have been more pleasing to Niebuhr.

Though Niebuhr's health continued to deteriorate, he managed with help from colleagues to complete his seminar at Union. The Dean of Instruction, Roger Shinn, wanted the seminar to succeed, and so it did with several other lecturers. The contributions of Jose M. Bonino, Henry Clark, and M. M. Thomas were particularly well received.

Before the outcome of the election was decided, Niebuhr counted on Johnson winning and he wrote on "Johnson and the Myths of Democracy." His journal commented: "[Niebuhr's] one continuing activity is his writing which he does under great handicap."[2] This seemed exaggerated criticism from his heirs at *Christianity and Crisis* to those of us in his thrilling seminar. Myth in the Johnson essay meant: "Myths have the

1. See Betty Boyd, *Lady Bird and Lyndon* (New York: Simon & Schuster, 2015), 235–48.
2. Reinhold Niebuhr, editorial note, *Christianity and Crisis* 24, no. 21 (Dec. 14, 1964): 248.

function of sanctifying historically contingent value with absolute worth and of simplifying the complex realities of political life."[3] He regarded democracy's myth to be that of freedom, even though it defended tyrannies and police states. While Republicans added the myth of "free enterprise" in the Rockefeller and Goldwater campaigns, most recognized that the United States, as subject to social forces, achieved a mixed economy with collective bargaining. The power of unions with the threat of strike was central to Niebuhr's strategy of achieving social gains and more freedom with collective bargaining. Without unions powerful enough to win gains from capitalists, Niebuhr's hopes for tolerable justice were utopian. He wrote sorrowfully the same year on "The End of an Era." Union power was decreased both by automation and by the interests of the government preventing utility strikes that would disrupt the political economy. The role of the unions in his social strategy is revealed in a sentence: "[Collective bargaining] has become one of the most cherished democratic rights, second only to the right of suffrage."[4] He saw their power weakening and Johnson using myths of collective bargaining to cover his enforced settlements on the railroads and their unions. President Johnson's industrial policies and settlements were the work of a "manipulator of political myths."

Later he would see Johnson as a Machiavellian, but not in 1964. The defense of freedom in Vietnam was a myth, but relevant. Niebuhr was baffled. He spurned the president's assertion that, "If any nation wants to fight for its freedom we will help them."[5] The reality was imperial competition, of which the peasants of Vietnam had little knowledge. "Undoubtedly we must continue our support of South Vietnam indefinitely, though there is no indication that more technical support will hasten victory in a vicious guerilla war."[6] Some students in his seminar had gone further, rejecting Johnson's myths as untrue and demonstrating against the support of Diem and the successor client regimes. The events of August 1964 set the stage for the remainder of Niebuhr's life. Ambiguous reports of small Vietnamese craft attacking US destroyers in the Gulf of Tonkin produced overwhelming support in Congress for a resolution authorizing President Johnson to use all necessary means to defend the US forces operating in Vietnam. That became the basis for expanding the civil war into an American war, eventually leading to

3. Ronald H. Stone, ed., *Faith and Politics: A Commentary on Religious, Social, and Political Thought in a Technological Age* (New York: George Braziller, 1968), 245.

4. Reinhold Niebuhr, "The End of an Era," *Christianity and Crisis* 24, no. 9 (May 25, 1964): 97.

5. Niebuhr, "The End of an Era," 250.

6. Niebuhr, "The End of an Era," 251.

a million and a half American service personnel in Vietnam until they were finally reduced to a fifth of a million in Niebuhr's last year, 1971.

In September 1964, President Johnson awarded Niebuhr the highest civilian award, the Medal of Freedom. His health prevented him from attending the ceremony. His children Christopher and Elisabeth made the trip and accepted on behalf of their father. In this early point in the Johnson presidency, the Kennedy team, including many Niebuhr admirers, were still in the administration. McGeorge Bundy, Hubert Humphrey, Adlai Stevenson, and Arthur Schlesinger Jr. were all devotees, and any of them could have recommended the award as fitting and smart politics. The domestic agenda of the president corresponded closely to Niebuhr's as seen in ADA policies. Niebuhr's break with Johnson would come the next year over foreign policy regarding Vietnam. It is well to remember that it was disagreement with socialist-pacifist foreign policy issues that had driven Niebuhr to break with the Fellowship of Reconciliation and the Socialist party in the 1930s.

Khrushchev's fall from power increased President Johnson's freedom of movement. Khrushchev's risk-taking had cost him support, and the traditionalist-centralist Russians replaced him. His agricultural policies could not produce enough food. But, Hans J. Morgenthau regarded his fall as due to his destruction of the infallible Marxist science by his attack on the record of Stalin in 1956. The polycentrism unleashed in 1956 and then repressed in Poland and Hungary exposed the weaknesses in Russian leadership of Marxist-Orthodox science. China challenged the new liberalism of the Soviet leadership directly. The transitional period in which Leonid I. Brezhnev emerged as leader was far less dangerous than the brinkmanship of Khrushchev. If the 1962–63 struggle had been dominated by the Khrushchev-Kennedy struggle and then a nuclear rapprochement in the partial test-ban treaty, both major players were now gone.[7]

Goldwater's announced positions failed to take into account the web of relationships governing and limiting action in domestic economic affairs or in an interrelated world of nations and organizations. *Christianity and Crisis* endorsed President Johnson in an issue after it had rejected Goldwater's campaign in the previous issue. This first-time editorial presidential endorsement was protested by Goldwater's letters to Bennett and Shinn. For a period, the tax exemption of the journal was withdrawn due to its partisan endorsements. Later that judgment was overturned, and the journal agreed not to publish endorsement editorials

7. Hans J. Morgenthau, "The Myth of Soviet Politics," *The New Leader* 47, no. 22 (Oct. 26, 1964): 3–6.

and to confine political endorsements to essays.[8] Ironically the day after the election, I preached in Union's James Chapel. John Bennett, the editor of the journal, reminded me that my sermon celebrating Johnson's victory would not be appropriate for a Christian church. I responded that I understood that, but this was the Union Seminary Chapel.

Niebuhr's choice of the title, "Goldwater vs. History," made clear to readers the direction of the essay. His other three essays on Goldwater in 1964 were just as critical. He argued that Western culture was resolving the tensions of order and justice by "commonsense adjustments and consolidations of power."[9] The recent Ford Motor Company agreement with the United Auto Workers was evidence of the adjustments. Senator Goldwater seemed to challenge the historical evolution of society by his alliance with Southern racists and tobacco farmers. The denunciations of the Supreme Court and federal officials harkened back to a less sophisticated age.[10] The claims of Goldwater for simplicity ignored the cosmopolitan and social balance of a diverse society. The malice of the Goldwater campaign tended to sow distrust against the functions of government. Niebuhr wanted to affirm the social gains toward justice in the economy and the pursuit of "more racial justice" against those "yahoos" who failed to understand how justice in America had advanced.[11]

RACE RELATIONS

Niebuhr reviewed *The Quest for the Dream*, which covered some of the same history as *A Nation So Conceived*.[12] John Roche's book focused on overcoming the ethnic repression that characterized American history. He criticized the failure of the melting pot to achieve the dreams of the country's founding documents in freedom and justice. Then it moved swiftly through the transition from agricultural society to industrial world power. Niebuhr criticized it for an inadequate treatment of the transition from agriculture to industry. He thought the civil rights issues had overshadowed the more important transition to industry. Yet, he praised it as a history of civil rights. The yes-and-no evaluation of the book was a very typical approach for Niebuhr. He found in the volume

8. Mark Hulsether, *Building a Protestant Left* (Knoxville: University of Tennessee Press, 1999), 77.

9. Reinhold Niebuhr, "Goldwater vs. History," *The New Leader* 47, no. 2 (October): 16–17.

10. Niebuhr, "Goldwater vs. History," 16.

11. Niebuhr, "Goldwater vs. History," 17.

12. Reinhold Niebuhr, "Progress toward Society," *The New Leader* 47, no. 1 (Jan. 6, 1964). John Roche, the president of Americans for Democratic Action, was like Niebuhr a regular contributor to the journal, addressing issues of liberal political thinking and morality.

both truth and error. But it also indicates the incompleteness of his work the previous year, which was relatively strong on transition to industry but very weak on the civil rights struggle. For Niebuhr, the brutality of ethnic privilege in the United States refuted Roche's overly optimistic projections of the innocence of the American population.

A theme of Niebuhr's next book, *Tribalism*, appeared in his 1964 essay "Man the Unregenerate Tribalist." After Martin Luther King Jr.'s "Letter from the Birmingham Jail" was published in *Christianity and Crisis* and the release of *Why We Cannot Wait*, the resistance of whites toughened. Despite legislation, basic rights were still denied, school segregation persisted, and integration was opposed. Economic oppression grounded in inadequate education, increasing technology, and discrimination pressed down on African Americans. Resentment continued to grow among the young, but their lack of power meant progress would be slower than the idealists hoped. African Americans were almost without power, lacking votes or powerful unions.[13] Consumer boycott was a relevant tool, but it was a frail instrument against white tribal prejudices.

Niebuhr respected Senator J. William Fulbright on foreign policy, especially his criticism of the US obsession with outrageous military budgets. As Chairman of the Foreign Relations Committee he provided wisdom and foresight. However, on race relations he had not been able to lead. He remained a prisoner of his Southern politics. Niebuhr recommended pity rather than castigation of him for his compromises.[14]

Niebuhr admitted that he was slow to recognize the despair of the unemployed African American in the North.[15] Though in the North black people had rights still denied in the South, the Civil Rights Act could not deliver jobs or a way out of poverty. Integration of schools and housing moved very slowly, with widespread white resistance. He reflected on the impossibility of enforcing prohibition law against local custom. Of course, change would come, but it would probably be slow. Tactics of resistance would change as the movement toward justice gained ground.

Niebuhr predicted not only a long, hot, troubled summer, but decades of struggle to achieve justice. The validation of human rights had a long struggle against white racism. The impulses of tribalism were usually less vicious than those of the Nazis, "yet even so they are cruel."[16]

13. Reinhold Niebuhr, *Christianity and Crisis* 24, no. 12 (July 6, 1964): 33–35.

14. Reinhold Niebuhr, "Prisoner of the South," *The New Leader* 47, no. 9 (Apr. 27, 1964): 17–27.

15. Reinhold Niebuhr, "The Struggle for Justice," *The New Leader* 47, no. 14 (July 6, 1964): 10.

16. Niebuhr, "The Struggle for Justice," 11.

Developments in 1964 encouraged idealism. Martin Luther King Jr. received the Nobel Peace Prize. President Johnson signed the Civil Rights Act, the most sweeping civil rights legislation the country had seen. Elsewhere though, James E. Chaney, Michael Schwerner, and Andrew Goodman were turned over for murder to the Klan. Rochester, New York, exploded in riots and Governor Nelson Rockefeller repressed it with a thousand National Guardsmen.

Several factors influenced Niebuhr's realism about overcoming racism. He knew of his own evolution on the subject. He understood the triviality of the church on the issue. His appreciation of organic social change rather than idealistic social contract theory led him to expect slow improvement. He regarded it as unusual for many to sacrifice privileges of the self for justice. Law could be overcome by self-interest and resistance. Still, his own evolution continued and by the end of the decade he would be advocating more tools of social change for justice.

However, among his students other strategies were developing. Graduate students were meeting to conspire. They were asking, How do we get ahead of social conflicts? In particular, How do we avoid US intervention supporting apartheid if there is a race war in South Africa? A room at the Interchurch Center across from Union served as a meeting place where the decision was made to act proactively on the apartheid of South Africa. Rather than waiting for race warfare to break out, strategies were developed to influence US policy toward South Africa. One strategy was to encourage US banks to end their support of emergency loans for the nation. This took years to develop, but it became the divestment, boycott strategy of social corporate responsibility. The second strategy was direct action. Students led a sit-in of the South African embassy to the United Nations. The sit-in responded to the threatened execution of Nelson Mandela after he was found guilty. It was part of a larger demonstration on the ground. The coalition of Union Seminary students, Student Nonviolent Coordinating Committee, and members of Local 1199 were eventually arrested after the New York Police Department consulted with Adlai Stevenson, the US ambassador to the United Nations. They spent the night in the Tombs, but a couple of months later, charges were dropped when South Africa refused to appear in court to press charges. Twenty-five years later Nelson Mandela was released to become president of the renewed nation.

KARL MARX

Niebuhr's introduction to Karl Marx and Friedrich Engels's *On Religion* is a six-page critique of Karl Marx. Written in 1963 and published in 1964, it was reprinted in the 1982 Scholars Press of the American Academy of Religion. That was followed by a more appreciative introduction of Marx by John Raines in the Temple University Press edition. The volume does not disclose who chose or why the enclosed selections were published. There are many more of Marx and Engels's writings on religion that were translated by 1982. Niebuhr's introduction is Cold War philosophy; the first selection by Marx is an attack on the religious tradition of the Western world. Niebuhr had used the early humanistic writings of Marx in his 1932 edition of *Moral Man and Immoral Society* as a critique of capitalism. Here against both Marxists and post-Marx humanists, he recognizes that humanism was subject to the revolution. Niebuhr does not quote Engels at Marx's graveside: "that above all else he was a revolutionary," but that is the spirit of the essay.

Niebuhr had no quarrel with the empiricism of Marx. He is no more an idealist than Marx. But, he writes that Marx collapsed empiricism into materialism to critique religion and therefore the foundations of the Western world. Niebuhr began his short essay quoting Marx: "In Germany the criticism of religion is the premise of all criticism."[17]

Niebuhr saw a lack of empiricism in Marx's charge that capitalism produced human alienation. Wasn't it as probable that the patriarchs of nineteenth-century industrialism alienated the proletariat? Niebuhr objected here to the humanism of the early Marx more than to *Das Kapital.*

In the "Introduction" Niebuhr repeated his analysis of Communism as an apocalyptic-violent religious movement akin to early Islam. Its distinctive features were religious rather than scientific. Marx gave up his position as a learned philosopher to project a revolution, and some of the weakness of the Lenin-Marxist philosophy is due to Marx's own rush to revolution in apocalyptic religious terms.

HUMAN NATURE

Niebuhr's preface to the 1964 edition of *The Nature and Destiny of Man*[18] threw a bomb into the studies of Niebuhr's work. In many quarters the

17. Reinhold Niebuhr, "Introduction," in Karl Marx and Friedrich Engels, *On Religion* (Chico, CA: Scholars, 1982), vii.

18. Reinhold Niebuhr, preface, *Nature and Destiny*, 1964 ed., xxv–xxvi.

explosion has not yet been felt. Here he surrendered the symbols of fall, original sin, the eschatology of final struggle between Christ and the anti-Christ, and the messianism of the kingdom of God. He still quoted his original assertion that the universality of sin seemed to be empirically established. The move is similar to the argument of *Man's Nature and His Communities* (analyzed in the following chapter) and confirms the direction of Tillich's report on their conversation in *Reinhold Niebuhr: A Prophetic Voice in Our Time*. While refusing further development of these symbols, he retained his central positions on the meaningfulness of human history and the reality of human nature as selfhood in transcendence. The heavy biblical vocabulary of his early work is absent in his books of the 1960s. He had not taught "Theological Ethics" since 1957, and his work now fit, as he said, in the vocabulary of political philosophy while still based on the conclusions he had developed theologically regarding humanity and history. H. Richard Niebuhr's comment that Reinhold's work was like an iceberg with much of it hidden beneath the surface is particularly true for this final decade. Human evil still originated in human freedom and not in ignorance or passions of the body. Rejecting idealism, materialism, or dualism, he thought the self is best understood in poetic terms.

Paul Tillich and Reinhold Niebuhr had their last meeting at the wedding of Marion Hausner and Wilhelm Pauck at Riverside Church on November 21, 1964. Marion Hausner was researching a biography of Paul Tillich that she and her husband would eventually publish together. Wilhelm was particularly close to Tillich, and Marion had worked at *Christianity and Crisis* and knew Reinhold well. Reinhold served as best man for the service and Tillich presided as clergyman for the ceremony in the chapel. Marion has recorded a remark of a Union faculty member as saying: "That wasn't a wedding; it was a Protestant summit meeting." Paul Tillich died the next year, and so his plans to return to New York City, the New School, and Union Theological Seminary remained unfulfilled.

9.

Man's Nature and His Communities, 1965

> I am not now so sure that the historic symbols will contribute much to the understanding of modern man of his tragic and ironic history, with its refutation of the Messianic and utopian hopes of the Renaissance and Enlightenment.

As Niebuhr's theological emphasis moved away from orthodox Christian symbolism in the 1960 revisions of his thought, his recognition of the necessity of federal coercion in matters of racial justice deepened. The burning of American cities and associated violence revealed to him the depth of black anger. His functionalist-organic-social philosophy and caution gave way to a more moral critique and welcoming of federal force in 1965 than he had revealed earlier in the beginning of the decade. The interpretation of Niebuhr on the ethics of race relations takes account of his 1925 chairing of the Mayor's Commission on Race Relations in Detroit and the regular writing and organizing on race throughout his career. The 1965 "Foreword" to the *Mississippi Black Paper*[1] is different. Rather than appealing to white moderates to correct the injustice, he is feeling the pain of the people's testimony gathered in the collected documents and calling for federal action.

"FOREWORD" EXCERPTS

This collection of notarized affidavits and statements gathered by the Council of Federated Organizations—an association concerned, among its other goals, with helping Mississippi Negroes register to vote—gives eloquent

1. Reinhold Niebuhr, "Introduction," *Mississippi Black Paper* (New York: Random House, 1965). Unnumbered.

testimony to the horrendous conditions of justice in a state that lacks both the democratic disciplines and an independent judicial system. Yet this state is part of a nation which prides itself on having attained these two forms of political justice.

The documents disclose a society in which the instruments of justice are tools of *in*justice. On the evidence of these affidavits, it seems that there are no limits to inhumanity, cruelty and sheer caprice in a closed society once social and communal restraints are no longer in force. . . .

The murder of the three freedom workers, after their arrest and detainment on a charge of speeding, is more understandable in light of the picture of legalized injustice these affidavits present. The affidavits also help to explain why the alleged murderer of the Negro civil rights leader, Medgar Evers, is still unpunished after several jury trials. The jury trial, in theory the final guarantee of justice, is in fact the criminal's final source of immunity in a corrupt society.

These documents will serve two purposes. On the moral level they reveal to the reader an important fact about human nature: that social discipline is the chief source of our much praised political humanity, so that in a community in which that discipline has been corrupted—in Nazi Germany, South Africa and some of the most benighted Southern states—cruelty and inhumanity flourish. But these documents also serve a more pragmatic purpose: they offer proof, if that is still needed, of the absolute necessity of the Civil Rights bill for the sake of this country's political health. . . .

Not all of the states of the Southern Confederacy have sunk to the standard of inhumanity described in these documents. . . . Admittedly the national community has its own problems of racial prejudice and injustice, but the majesty of the law in the United States as a whole is preserved in no small part by the recognition by state and local communities that the federal government is the final source of law and order.

There are no quick or simple ways to eliminate the monstrous injustice revealed in these pages, but perhaps these affidavits will suggest to their readers that justice in Mississippi is corrupted to such a degree that without aid from the outside it is doomed.

His foreword to *The Mississippi Black Paper* was followed by a lead editorial: "Civil Rights Climax in Alabama."[2] The editor of *Christianity and Crisis*, Wayne Cowan, had been in the march from Selma to Montgomery.[3] Niebuhr's piece stressed the national gains for the civil rights movement and his hope that the violence and martyrdoms would give the Civil Rights Act momentum to pass. He also celebrated the alliance of the unity of organized religion in supporting the struggle. He, for a

2. Wayne H. Cowan, "Selma at First Hand," *Christianity and Crisis* 25, no. 5 (Apr. 5, 1965): 17–18.

3. Reinhold Niebuhr, "Civil Rights Climax in Alabama," *Christianity and Crisis* 25, no. 5 (Apr. 5, 1965): 1.

change, remained silent on the irrelevance of the church to support the movement.

PRESIDENT JOHNSON AND VIETNAM

Shortly before President Johnson ordered marines into combat in Vietnam and began air attacks on North Vietnam in retaliation for guerrilla raids in South Vietnam, Niebuhr editorialized on the war.[4] He regarded Vietnam as an insoluble problem. He feared losing all of Southeast Asia to Communist pressure, but Vietnam was not solid ground on which to stand. The American enemy, Ho Chi Minh, was a national hero, the "Father of His Country," and the substance of South Vietnam's government was very weak. The protestation that the United States was defending democracy in Vietnam was false, as the conditions for democracy were not there. Our imperial policies of containment were too hard for American leadership to explain, but their substitution of "defending liberty" was not candid. The critical journalists were more convincing, but as Niebuhr's title stated, he had no solution.

He contributed in the same vein in February as the war was increasingly Americanized. He criticized the administration for claiming to "protect their freedom." "The problem," he wrote, "itself remained insoluble." By the next month he began to hope that a general conference might find a tolerable compromise. He surmised that this hope could be increased if the China-Russia competition could be exploited. Ho Chi Minh was pro-Russian and he feared China. This reaching for possible compromises was more typical of Niebuhr than his statement the previous month of an insoluble problem.[5]

His criticism of the intervention in the Dominican Republic was less hesitant. The administration's action was hasty and ill informed. Its anti-Communism led it to neglect the Organization of American States and to invade on the basis of misinformation from the CIA and the assistant secretary of state, Thomas Mann. The United States paid a price in alienating Latin American leadership and pushing some students in the United States into more radical opposition to US policy.[6] Military force

4. Reinhold Niebuhr, "Vietnam an Insoluble Problem," *Christianity and Crisis* 25, no. 1–2 (Feb. 8, 1965): 1–2.

5. Reinhold Niebuhr, "Prospects of the Johnson Era," *Christianity and Crisis* 25, no. 2 (Feb. 22, 1965): 1–2. "From Bad to Worse in Vietnam," *The New Leader* 48, no. 5 (Mar. 1, 1965): 6–7.

6. Reinhold Niebuhr, "Caribbean Blunder," *Christianity and Crisis* 25, no. 9 (May 31, 1965): 113–14.

without legitimacy might prevail, but its push was weaker than power that combined legitimacy and force.

The following month, he joined the editorial board of *Christianity and Crisis* in calling for direct negotiations among the hostiles, including the National Liberation Front. The board refused the Munich analogy and regarded Communism as different from the Nazis' primary military threat. The bombing above the seventeenth parallel could pull in China or provoke a more general war. The journal joined the general questioning of the presuppositions of the administration and declared it could never sanction the bombing of population centers in the North. It did not call for US withdrawal but recommended negotiations and the ending of the bombing in the North. The same issue in another article noted the ferment on the campuses as student groups evolved from civil rights toward anti-war causes.[7] The professors' own campus contexts were becoming more explosive. Students for a Democratic Society organized and 15,000 protested the war at the White House.

Despite pain, deteriorating health, and necessarily shortened work effort, Niebuhr produced philosophical-historical reflections on the contemporary struggles. The themes were not new, but few could combine philosophical reflection and relevance as well as he. With John Bennett shouldering major editorial oversight, Wayne Cowan acted as editor; Niebuhr surrendered control of his journal and published his major international political essays in *The New Leader*.

"The Fateful Triangle"[8] raised to consciousness the complications of the relationship of China, Russia, and the United States. Those who had overthrown Khrushchev and banished Stalin were losing influence in the Communist world to China. China and Russia still appeared as ideological allies while competing for power. The United States, while engaged in the world struggle for power, was ideologically opposed to both. The Kennedy-Khrushchev partial test-ban treaty seemed threatening to China. Niebuhr saw China as more aggressive than Russia and as more of a threat in Asia and Africa than the USSR. He expected the balancing of power among the three would determine the prospects for avoiding major war for a long time. He, of course, had no idea that Kissinger and Nixon working on the same triangle would attempt to leverage China into more competition with Russia. Nor did he have an idea of the USSR imploding. Both of the Communist powers were more susceptible to

7. Reinhold Niebuhr, "U.S. Policy in Vietnam: A Statement," *Christianity and Crisis* 25, no. 10 (June 4, 1965): 125–26. Among the board only Robert W. Lynn and Kenneth Thompson did not sign.

8. Roger L. Shinn, "Ferment on the Campuses," *Christianity and Crisis* 25, no. 101 (June 4, 1965): 126–27.

change under economic duress than he realized. He thought the fiction of Chiang Kai-shek ruling China should be abandoned, but he did not perceive the United States helping China rejoin the economic world of nations.

His comparison of Presidents Roosevelt and Johnson[9] found them both successful in beguiling the country into social reforms. Roosevelt's leadership of a reluctant, isolationist, somewhat pacifist nation toward world responsibility to resist Germany, Italy, and Japan succeeded because of Japan's ill-conceived attack upon US forces. Johnson's domestic policies were appropriate. His anti-Communism led him to rely too easily upon military force in both the Dominican Republic and Vietnam. Allies were pulling away from US leadership. He hoped for the best in a quick removal of US forces from the Dominican Republic as opposed to Woodrow Wilson's long-term occupancy of the island. Vietnam remained insoluble. Military force without moral support or legitimacy was a recipe for failure.

The month of publication,[10] US troops were authorized into active battle, moving beyond their "advisory role" and the protection of US bases. Before autumn 14,000 marines were fighting in the Dominican Republic, 125,000 soldiers were in Vietnam, and 20,000 National Guard were deployed to repress the riots in Watts, Los Angeles. Johnson's accomplishments in the Voting Rights Act, the establishment of the Housing and Urban Affairs Department, and Medicare under Social Security were obscured by the violence.

MAN'S NATURE AND HIS COMMUNITIES

Niebuhr's last book contained fifty pages of political philosophy in a 110-page manuscript. This preponderance of political philosophy points to his self-definition.

> They dealt with the social and political philosophy because that has been the author's chief vocation as a teacher of social ethics in the context of a Protestant theological education at Union Theological Seminary in New York.[11]

This book, published six years after *The Structure of Nations and Empires*, indicates not only the revision of "previously held opinions," but it

9. *The New Leader* 48, no. 1 (Jan. 4, 1965): 18–20.

10. Reinhold Niebuhr, "Roosevelt and Johnson: A Contrast in Foreign Policy," *The New Leader* 48, no. 15 (July 19, 1965): 5–8.

11. Reinhold Niebuhr, *Man's Nature and His Communities* (New York: Charles Scribner's Sons, 1965), 15.

reveals the lighter side of Niebuhr's theology. It confirms the radicalness of his departure from the symbolism of *The Nature and Destiny of Man* and the greater incorporation of secular resources in his thought. In the 1963 preface he suggested the fall, original sin, heaven on earth, and kingdom of universal peace were not as symbolically useful as he had believed in 1939 when the lectures were delivered at the beginning of World War II.[12] In both of these revisions he doubted the adequacy of the symbols, but he did not retract the substance of his argument. So the Preface of 1963 and the Introduction of 1965 are less biblical and less theological than his earlier published work of the 1940s. Very learned interpreters of Niebuhr, namely Charles Brown, Paul Merkley, and Richard Fox, do not emphasize their difference, and they may disagree with me on the importance of Niebuhr's later work. Certainly they do not emphasize the work of the 1960s.

Other changes Niebuhr noted included a greater appreciation of Roman Catholic and Jewish strength in supporting an ethic of justice. He recognized earlier work as uniquely Protestant, and now he welcomed thinking in religiously pluralistic ways. At the time he was publishing, John C. Bennett was opening the seminary to Catholic presence on the faculty, and its shared work with Jewish Theological Seminary was increased. Ursula's writing particularly stressed his late-life friendship with Rabbi Abraham Heschel of that faculty. He still regretted earlier uneasiness in the Vatican concerning democracy and he rejected the inflexibility of metaphysically based natural law teaching. He mentioned judging religions by their contributions to society in "wholly pragmatic sources of my appreciation."

He refers to the suggestion of a young friend, John Raines, who during a seminar proposed an alternative title of "The Not So Moral Man in His Less Moral Communities." Ursula has reported she provided the original title of *Moral Man and Immoral Society*. Niebuhr held to the point that collective egoism was stronger and less amenable to repentance or change than individual egoism. While still holding to the *London Times Literary Supplement* view that original sin was the most verifiable of any point of Christian doctrine, he opted to abandon the symbol for this book.[13]

Knowing that realism could become a support for bastions of conservatism of "unjust privilege," he assured readers that he intended it to support progressive justice and democracy without illusions. While

12. Niebuhr, *The Nature and Destiny of Man*, vol. 1, *Human Nature* (New York: Charles Scribner's Sons, 1941), xv–xvi.

13. Niebuhr, *Man's Nature and His Communities*, 24.

repeating the mistaken interpretation that Martin Luther and John Calvin consistently denied resistance to unjust authorities, he recognized early foundations for resistance and liberty in John Milton, John Locke, and Cromwellian revolutionaries.

In the introductory paragraphs he reflects on Ursula's teaching in a religiously pluralistic setting at Barnard College. He confesses intellectual debts to his wife. He mentions their discussions together and her greater ability in biblical studies, psychology, and literature's relationship to social dynamics. His humility and love are obvious in his confession that it was hard to separate his thought from hers. He recognizes that "joint authorship is not acknowledged except in this confession."[14] I would add early church history to the areas in which Ursula's learning surpassed Reinhold's.

Niebuhr was generous in attributes: he could give more than due credit to editors and collaborators. I personally benefited from this generosity. So it is hard to know how much to make literally of her contribution. I would regard an argument of joint authorship as too bold. They jointly authored a few short pieces and both names appeared therein as authors. Adding the wife's name to an autobiographical essay would be peculiar and, in this case, overdone. It is better to accept the literal attribution to joint authorship where they placed both names. A prominent example is their joint comment on the Vietnam War in 1966.[15]

Reinhold explained to me Ursula's sensitivity about June Bingham's biography of him due in part to her own intention to sometime write a biography. While he was alive they planned for a while to produce a volume of their conversations.[16] These tentative transcripts are in her papers in the Library of Congress. After his death she edited two outstanding volumes. The first, *Justice and Mercy*, is a collection of his prayers and sermons. I gathered the recordings from John Bennett's closet and secured Doris Liles for the original typing of the sermons from the tapes. The second is a collection of their letters from times they were apart, and additional selected letters from distinguished friends. The collection, *Remembering Reinhold Niebuhr*,[17] contains his letters and delightful memoirs by Ursula. It is necessary reading for understanding the person of

14. Niebuhr, *Man's Nature and His Communities*, 29.

15. Reinhold and Ursula Niebuhr, "The Peace Offensive," *Christianity and Crisis* 25, no. 24 (Jan. 24, 1966): 301–2.

16. Letter: Ursula Niebuhr to Ronald Stone, n.d. In author's possession, and in Niebuhr Papers, Library of Congress.

17. Ursula M. Niebuhr, *Remembering Reinhold Niebuhr* (San Francisco: HarperSanFrancisco, 1991).

Reinhold. On my writing, she was full of praise for the first volume and bought copies to present to friends. She was less appreciative of *Professor Reinhold Niebuhr*, and critical of my paper from the Tantur Ecumenical Institute on his Zionism. She was also unhappy with my talk at Union on his use of books. In fact, she produced a list of books they read and owned. It is deposited in the Library of Congress. She was comforted and moved by my "In Memoriam" writing on him and critical of my homily at his memorial service at Riverside Church.

I was very fond of her. I admired her and treasure memories of her giving me his books as they closed their Riverside Drive apartment. Visits to their home in Stockbridge included not only conversations with Reinhold, but lunches at their home, tours of Stockbridge with her as the knowledgeable guide, sherry in the late afternoon, and lunch with her at the Red Lion Inn in Stockbridge. Participation with the two of them and on occasion with Christopher were intellectual whirlwinds. I'm sorry neither a biography by her nor their conversations were ever published. Keeping up with requests to republish his writings and for comments tired her. In one letter to me she suggested I relieve the strain on her by acting as literary executor. But, she immediately noted I was probably too busy.

POLITICAL PHILOSOPHY

The fifty-three-page heart of this book is on realist and idealist political theories. The tale of the history of political ideas is derived partially from his early reading in German of Ernst Troeltsch, *The Social Teaching of the Christian Churches*. Versions of this narrative appeared in many of his writings from 1927 to 1965. Idealism had prevailed in *Does Civilization Need Religion?* (1927), and realism was dominant in *Moral Man and Immoral Society* (1932) and in *Structure of Nations and Empires* (1959). In 1965 most of the realist, historical reflection on politics seems to have been overdone.

> The realists are inclined to obscure the residual moral and social senses even in the most self-regarding men and nations.[18]

Both religious and secular idealists overestimate the capacity of religion and rationality to overcome the natural self-regarding impulses of the human in society.

Through the labyrinth of written political philosophy, he traces the

18. Niebuhr, *Man's Nature and His Communities*, 31.

mistaken impulses of idealists and realists until he concludes with a dialogue portrayal of the thought of his friend Hans J. Morgenthau. Niebuhr in a letter mistakenly attributed this chapter to my influence because of my seminar paper on Morgenthau and our follow-up conversations. We received a letter from him while we were in Oxford in 1965, giving me credit for inspiring the chapter on political theory and concluding with issues from my paper on Morgenthau.[19] This generous attribution neglects his previous writing on Morgenthau and their relationship, and reflects more on the generosity of the professor than on the student or on the accuracy of his memory. There is no doubt, however, that the depth of our intellectual relationship sprang from this early work on Morgenthau. He works out a balanced critique and appreciation of Morgenthau's thought on interest and power. The analysis of Morgenthau gently critiquing his opposition of the search for power and love, and proposing his own solution to the ideal-real contrast in politics, should be required reading for all who would study politics. Whereas Morgenthau sees ideal claims justifying power impulses as hypocrisy, in Niebuhr's view, the hypocrisy reflects the residual values of the beneficent-cooperative spirit of humans. It is real. The power impulses are real, but the understanding of the interest pursued is shaped by values and human ideals.

As the human sexual impulse is more than the animal drive that Aristotle saw, so the power political impulse is framed, defined, and to an extent shaped by the ideal. Nationally the pursuit of interested parties is shaped by the balancing of powers, power of the government, and values, as James Madison understood better than other prominent founding fathers.

It is where Morgenthau follows Paul Tillich on love and power that he slips. Tillich correlates the two and relates them to justice. Morgenthau opposes power to love and thereby, often, is overly realistic. Niebuhr understands brutal realism as the corruption of love. The values of a culture are real. The pursuit of self-interest is normal in people and nations, and they use power to obtain it. However, the ideals qualify the definition of self-interest and the means of power that both nations and persons will use. Niebuhr concludes with a position of moderate realism. He moves somewhat beyond Morgenthau's realism, and in this book his appreciation of James Madison's institutional realism is affirmed more strongly than elsewhere. I had put in my seminar paper that whereas in some of his writings Morgenthau regarded pursuit of national self-

19. Letter: Reinhold Niebuhr to Ronald Stone (Dec. 15, 1965). Letter in author's possession and in Niebuhr Papers, Library of Congress.

interest in terms of power as normative, Niebuhr saw it as only normal and reserved more of a place for real values and ideals. Niebuhr's chapter here was quick to point out that human ideals were often beyond the grasp of people. Political thought at its best proceeded from social realities and sought reforms rather than starting from ideals and spurning social reality. For example: total nuclear disarmament was not possible, but the Kennedy-Khrushchev test-ban treaty was an important reform.

Obviously, fifty-three pages are not sufficient for a subtle history of Western political theory. It omits too much, especially French political philosophers: Montesquieu, Rousseau, Condorcet, and the French Revolution. Roman, Greek, and early church political thought are hastily run over. Niebuhr had reviewed Eugen Rosenstock-Huessy's *Out of Revolution: Autobiography of Western Man* thirty years earlier, and knowing Wilhelm Pauck, he could have presented a more positive interpretation of Martin Luther. If Ursula had advised him more on the essay, there would have been more of a role for English theorists, many of whom he had discussed previously. There is much to criticize in the essay, but in his usual way of criticizing previous theory he clears the way for an appreciation of James Madison and constitutional republican government founded in Christian realism. His dialogue with Morgenthau subtly presents his own revised version of moderate realism, which characterized this later period of his thought.

Tribalism was dividing emerging nation-states in the decolonization process. Niebuhr chose in the third chapter to discuss the race problem in the United States under the rubric of tribalism. He accepted Stoic, Christian, and scientific analysis that humanity is one race. However, tribalism—the division of humanity into groups—inspired the worst inhumanity between peoples.[20] Factors of language, religion, culture, class, or race can all serve as distinguishing marks identifying the other. Unifying languages like Latin or English have helped maintain unity among those of different origins. The war in Cyprus exhibited many of the different factors. Oppression made use of the differences in South Africa, Nazi Germany, and Mississippi. Class in India was reinforced by religious belief to divide the country into castes. Latin America exhibited the feudal system built up on language, race, and political power.

All of the discussion of tribalism was to set a discussion of the American inability to overcome the vestiges of slavery. The African American was seen by Niebuhr as a national proletariat denied participation in the promised universalism of the nation. Only political pressure could change the oppression in the South through the achievement of universal

20. Niebuhr, *Man's Nature and His Communities*, 84.

suffrage. The denial of economic power to black people foreshadowed a lengthy struggle to overcome white oppression.

History showed that rationality demanding universalism often could not overcome parochial loyalties to one's own tribe, which inflicted brutalities when possible on other groups. Ancient Stoics saw the universalism but underestimated the power of tribalism among humans.[21] Christians set up universalism within the church, but in refusing to include Jews who remained loyal to their origins, set up the brutalities of anti-Semitism. Even the conversion of African slaves to Christianity denied them common humanity for economic reasons.

Nation-states with their own languages and religions in Europe seemed to have overthrown imperial tendencies toward universalism in Catholic Europe in the Middle Ages. But in modern times the recognition of universal human rights and movements toward European unity seemed again to move toward human universality. Democratic modern governments with concern and programs for human welfare reinforced these tendencies. But the United States still resists in practicing human rights for its black population. Both moral consideration and issues of the national interest required the full emancipation and fulfillment of the black minority.

For Niebuhr, the power of the national government to enforce human rights was the major instrument of their liberation in housing, education, voting, and economic opportunity as in the War on Poverty. For him, world opinion also had its role to play in helping America achieve universal human rights. Still, there would be no quick victory. He thought the program for achieving black potential had a good beginning and he was glad to see the white churches were following black churches in joining the issue. However:

> The problem will probably concern the nation for at least a century as the tolerable solution of the problem of economic justice required the resources of democracy throughout the 19th century.[22]

Though he may have casually written "a century," half a century after he wrote it the damage being done to black lives would take a very progressive half-century to overcome. Others, even Robin Lovin in his 1996 introduction and other writings, regarded Niebuhr as too conservative about the urgency in overcoming racial prejudice.[23] Half a century

21. Niebuhr, *Man's Nature and His Communities*, 94.

22. Niebuhr, *Man's Nature and His Communities*, 105.

23. Robin Lovin, introduction to *The Nature and Destiny of Man* (Louisville: Westminster John Knox, 1996), xxvi. My extended discussion of Niebuhr on race is in *Politics and Faith*

later Niebuhr's realism seems more accurate—that more could have been accomplished after King's assassination.

Does the short concluding chapter offer a new interpretation of the self, and can we detect another hand in the writing? This chapter on the self is particularly illuminated by his brother's comment that Reinhold's thought is like a great iceberg with most of it hidden under the surface. In this case there are two major works under the surface. There is, also, his wrestling with his own self-understanding in pain and near the end of his career and life. The chapter is sharpened by one of his favorite texts of Jesus: "He who finds his life will lose it, and he who would lose his life for my sake will find it."[24]

For him it means self-seeking is self-defeating, while self-giving or losing oneself in a cause (in this text the cause is that of Jesus) will result in self-realization. The penultimate paragraph of this concluding essay is devoted to the explication of the self-giving self. The remainder of the chapter interprets grace in its common form and its "saving form."

The footnotes defining grace and crediting Erik Erikson are contributed by Ursula. Reinhold's earlier work does not use Erikson, though he had many conversations with him in Stockbridge. Ursula used Erikson in her teaching at Barnard College and they knew him personally in Stockbridge. Terry Cooper's book on Niebuhr's psychology refers to Erikson only incidentally and does not use this chapter, but does discuss extensively Niebuhr's use of Freud, Carl Jung, Karen Horney, and Erich Fromm.[25]

The discussion of various church confessions about grace and its irrelevance or harmful relevance to many issues of social justice seem vintage Reinhold, though some of the sentences reflect Ursula's editing. The paragraphs on Lincoln and Churchill reflect his earlier writing. The criticisms of evangelical individualism and perfectionism reflect early standard works of his.

The general critique of the churches is found elsewhere in his writing, as is the thesis that undue self-concern is a mistake and fulfillment and happiness are added incidentally to the life given to a great cause. Love remains the law of moral life. An additional, between-the-lines theme is the criticism of an ethic of pursuing self-fulfillment, which is one possible reading of Paul Tillich's moral philosophy. Niebuhr argues that

(Macon, GA: Mercer University Press, 2012), 428–38. Also on p. 215 of the same book, I criticize his omission of discussion of the genocide of Native Americans. This, in my opinion, is an even more important omission in this chapter on American tribalism.

24. Reinhold Niebuhr, *The Nature and Destiny of Man* and *The Self and Dramas of History*.

25. Terry D. Cooper, *Reinhold Niebuhr and Psychology* (Macon, GA: Mercer University Press, 2009).

we should love God and go to work with discriminate, informed judgments. In my reading, editorial contributions are present, but the essay is a summary and often a rewrite of that which he had written and spoken repeatedly.

Both Ursula and Reinhold encouraged me to pursue study of political philosophy in Oxford. One evening we left the dinner party of the college president's daughter to catch the film *Reinie* on BBC Television. The film, *Reinie: The Life and Times of Reinhold Niebuhr*, was inadequate and mistaken in a few places. His ministry in Detroit was slighted by the substitution of the song "Tin Lizzy" and footage of the Depression and World War I. The omission of his early work in the Mayor's Commission on Race Relations in Detroit and later work and writing on race is misleading. We would not learn from the film of his role as the Secretary for the Evangelical Synod's War Welfare Commission. Similarly, the film is mistaken about Niebuhr's early appointment at Union. The film is accurate on the theology and ethics of which it speaks, but it spoke very little about the content of his thought. The clips of Roger Shinn speaking of his thought correct the deficiency somewhat. It is a British film, but it concentrates overly on Britain. It was natural for the film to speak of "his suffering at the hands of the McCarthyists," but Niebuhr would not have spoken that way: they were simply opponents that he criticized and fought against. J. Edgar Hoover was more of a persecutor. They referred to his writing *Man's Nature and His Communities*, but the film did not seem to have a clue about the project. The final pictures of Ursula and Reinhold walking slowly toward the door of their Stockbridge home were moving. A few days after viewing it I wrote him about how glad I was to see it, and I included a few points critiquing the film. He responded as the year ended.[26]

26. Letter (Dec.15, 1965).

404 Riverside Drive
New York, NY 10023
December 15, 1965

Mr. Ronald Stone
37 Museum Road
Oxford, England

Dear Ronald:

It's so nice to have a letter from you and a report on the BBC program on my thought. You agree with the great historian E. L. Woodward that the program was, on the whole, amateurish. But I am grateful both to you and Dr. Preston and Dr. Boyle for the contributions.

Would you give Ursula's and my greetings to Joan? We are so happy that you are enjoying Oxford and that you are ensconced on Museum Road.

You must not be surprised at Dr. Van Dusen's signature on the Viet Nam declaration. As Dr. Bennett says, he follows the Dulles line long after Dulles is dead.

You congratulate me on my new book. I should have sent you a copy. To tell you the truth, the first chapter on "Idealist and Realist Political Theories" which ends with Morgenthau's and my realism was inspired by your questions in my seminar.

We both send our heartiest greetings to both of you.

Sincerely yours,
Reinhold Niebuhr

Ursula added a note as she frequently did:

All best wishes. I do hope you visit some of my special spots: Old Marston, Ely Lantern, Berkshire Downs . . . as well as Oxford—Merton Street-the Meadows, Do you over look St. John's College Gardens? A Happy New Year—Ursula

Before the year ended, he wrote his last letter to Felix Frankfurter celebrating their friendship. He mentioned that he had experienced a second stroke. His lameness led him to sympathize with Felix even more. He would interpret Frankfurter's doctrine of judicial restraint in his *Harvard Law Review* essay and in his final *In Memoriam* the following year.[27]

27. Daniel F. Rice, *Reinhold Niebuhr and His Circle of Influence* (Cambridge: Cambridge University Press, 2013), 245.

10.

Christianity and Crisis, 1966

> In terms of religious leadership and religious tradition my life was formed by the left-wing of the Protestant liberal movement, made up of people who extricated the Christian enterprise from the relations with a moribund Calvinism and social Darwinism, and proclaimed that the Christian doctrine of love had to be implemented by the doctrine of justice.

The decline in the productivity of Reinhold Niebuhr is most obvious in 1966. He had contrary to many interpretations kept his production of books, essays, and editorials very high after his strokes in 1952 and in the following years. Most of his writings in 1966 were editorials on the Vietnam War as his opposition deepened. Additionally, he produced a wise essay on religious symbolism and the death of God debates.

NIEBUHR AS A JOURNALIST

He has not interpreted himself as a journalist. His interpreters have neglected to examine this vocation. Some insightful essayists have seen him as a preacher; even Ursula so regarded him. Others including myself have focused on him as a professor. His roles as political philosopher and interpreter of international relations have been generally emphasized. By his own admission he never spent a full year on a book other than his late sabbatical for *The Structure of Nations and Empires*. The task that occupied his entire adult life was that of a journalistic essayist and editor of publications. He started in high school, and followed the example of his older brother, a journalist and producer of movies, into the world of journalism. He never quit writing until immediately before his death, and notes on Martin Luther were found in his typewriter. Most studies of him indicate he came to New York as a professor at Union Seminary. Some make it associate professor. But most neglect that he also came as an editor of *The World Tomorrow*, for which he received half his salary. Editorships followed at *Radical Religion*, *Christianity and Society*, and culminating in *Christianity and Crisis*. Contributing editorships elsewhere completed the picture. The writing continued even after his 1952 stroke restricted his preaching, lecturing, and organizing to sites close to his home in New York City except for the post-retirement classes in succeeding years at Harvard and Princeton.

The one serious study of *Christianity and Crisis* is by Mark Hulsether, who unfortunately encountered Niebuhr first through his right-of-center devotees.[1] The author is more compatible with the left side of the debates in the journal than with Niebuhr himself. Hulsether divides Niebuhr and Bennett more sharply than I would, and records Bennett as something of a hero. Beverly Harrison did something similar by dividing Roger Shinn, whom she admired, from Niebuhr.[2] Neither of the authors would have divided themselves so sharply, nor did either leave evidence in their writing of such sharp distinctions. In both cases the differences lie more sharply in the chronological contexts of their writing than in their own perspectives.

CHANGE IN *CHRISTIANITY AND CRISIS*

The last issue of the journal bearing the name Reinhold Niebuhr as coeditor was February 4, 1966. There he summarized the history of *Christianity and Crisis* from 1941 to 1966. The crisis at its founding was the threat of Nazism. The threat of Communism was different but real. The central current threat was the danger of nuclear war. The social life of humanity continued in crisis. As he retired from leadership of the magazine, he wrote: "As long as this journal combines moral imperatives with moderate moral discrimination, it will have a creative future in both Church and Nation."[3] The most important domestic crisis was in the belated efforts to find justice for the large black minority.

In this last editorial as a member of the board he named Henry Sloane

1. Mark Hulsether, *Building a Protestant Left: Christianity and Crisis Magazine, 1941–1993* (Knoxville: University of Tennessee Press, 1999).

2. Beverly Harrison, "The Quest for Justice," in *The Public Vocation of Christian Ethics*, ed. Beverly Harrison, Robert L. Stivers, and Ronald H. Stone (New York: Pilgrim Press, 1986), 289–310.

3. Reinhold Niebuhr, "A Christian Journal Confronts Mankind's Continuing Crisis," *Christianity and Crisis* 26, no. 2 (Feb. 21, 1966): 11–13.

Coffin as the real founder of the journal. He regarded himself as only one of the journal's founders who assumed responsibility as editor because Coffin was too busy. He praised both John Bennett and Wayne Cowan for their success as chair and managing editor. The essay was his farewell. Many other editorials would follow from his typewriter, but he was no longer in control. His editorials would not always be accepted and sometimes, Ursula said, the office neglected to acknowledge their receipt. He did not mention Vietnam in the editorial; Bennett discussed the journal and Vietnam in the essay following Niebuhr's. Bennett hoped we were still Christian Realists in the changed position of using American military power. Issues 3–9 make no listing of Niebuhr's role in the journal's leadership. He roared back in issue 10 with the lead article and the important essay criticizing the "Death of God Theologians." He was now listed as "Special Contributing Editor" with nine others as "Contributing Editors." Cowan penned an announcement to the readers knowing that some readers would be pleased. Niebuhr told me that it was a pretentious title forced on him. Obviously, Niebuhr was not capable in 1966 of really leading the journal, but his displacement was not easy.

The first issue without Niebuhr's name spelled out the editorial board's criticism of the Vietnam War. The entire board except for Kenneth Thompson and F. Ernest Johnson, the two most known for international affairs expertise, signed the document. Thompson's essay in the previous issue had criticized overreliance on idealistic statements and consigned the Vietnam War to negotiations. Niebuhr's absence from the statement raised questions among readers as to how far he might have disagreed. The editors quoted Niebuhr[4] from a recent letter: "I would have signed if I had not meanwhile dismissed myself from the co-chairmanship."

COWRITING ON VIETNAM

Ursula and Reinhold began the new year of 1966 criticizing Hubert Humphrey, Lyndon B. Johnson, Dean Rusk, and Robert McNamara on their conduct of the war in Vietnam in a joint, leading editorial for *Christianity and Crisis*. They feared Johnson might lose his political consensus and support for progressive programs in domestic and racial issues. They also raised the possibility of his losing to a Republican in terms of Ike promising to end the Korean War. This joint editorial was at a

4. Reinhold Niebuhr, *Christianity and Crisis* 26, no. 5 (Apr. 4, 1966): 65.

time that their reading of the Harris poll showed national support for the administration standing at 73 percent.[5]

Despite President Johnson's attempt at Princeton to escape Senator Fulbright's charge of "the arrogance of power," Niebuhr seconded the charge. Self-righteous nations become arrogant, using their own dogmas to justify themselves. So Johnson used Wilson's ideals of self-determination to protect the nascent nation of South Vietnam. Self-righteousness prompted both superpowers to refuse a full partnership to avoid a nuclear catastrophe. Johnson cautioned universities against prejudice in foreign affairs. But it was first the university, without power, that was free to criticize folly in foreign policy when politicians would not.[6]

By October, Niebuhr noted the tide was turning against the United States continuing the war. Now the president was polling at his lowest, with only 50 percent supporting him. The pope and the secretary general of the UN were both opposing the war's continuance. Even the Republicans were remembering Eisenhower's promise to end the war in Korea. Ambassador Goldberg's speech to the UN showed some movement in the administration toward negotiations.[7] The following essays by John Bennett and George Kennan supported Niebuhr's hopes for a negotiated settlement. US casualties in the war exceeded those of the South Vietnam army by the middle of the year. President Johnson and Premier Ky promised they would win the war, effectively shutting out meaningful negotiations. That same year President Johnson made a short visit to US troops at Cam Ranh Bay, placing the prestige of his office squarely behind the war. The commitments of US presidents would continue until finally President Ford was thwarted by Congress. US prestige declined as it committed itself to the weaker side of the civil war. Supporting weak, unpopular governments that cannot secure the support of the population or government is a foolhardy policy. The vice president, who had opposed bombing North Vietnam in 1965, visited Vietnam in 1966 and after military briefings, returned to the United States to support the US war efforts.

The confusions of the 1960s were recorded in the colloquium[8] sponsored by *Christianity and Crisis* at the end of May. The conversations

5. Ursula and Reinhold Niebuhr, "The Peace Offensive," *Christianity and Crisis* 25, no. 24 (Jan. 24, 1966): 301–2.

6. Reinhold Niebuhr, "The President on 'The Arrogance of Power,'" *Christianity and Crisis* 26, no. 8 (June 13, 1966): 125–26.

7. Reinhold Niebuhr, "Vietnam: The Tide Begins to Turn," *Christianity and Crisis* 26, no. 17 (Oct. 17, 1966): 221–22.

8. "Call to Colloquium," *Christianity and Crisis* 26, no. 9 (May 30, 1966): 107–33.

among non-Niebuhrian cultural-political voices throughout the day echoed themes of "continuing never-ending revolution" and apocalyptic social thought. The spokespeople who might have spoken for the tradition of the journal, John Bennett and Roger Shinn, had their role in the evening of tribute to Reinhold Niebuhr featuring Professor Hans J. Morgenthau and Vice President Humphrey. They both spoke movingly about Niebuhr while disagreeing about the Vietnam War. Morgenthau's policy recommendations were similar to Niebuhr's critique. Humphrey's position would a year and a half later cost him his chance at being elected president. The apocalyptic-sociological tone of the colloquium soared beyond Niebuhr's politically oriented pragmatic policies. The journal would follow this direction after Niebuhr's resignation. It drifted into radical criticism of Niebuhr's trajectory after John Bennett departed Union Seminary and Roger Shinn became a less-frequent contributor. Meanwhile Niebuhr continued making his occasional contributions until his last essay in 1970.

CHURCH

Patrick Granfield, OSB, the managing editor of *Ecclesiastical Review*, teased out of Niebuhr his late views on the church.[9] Noting his thirteen years in the parish in Detroit, he asked about its influence. Niebuhr responded that the auto workers in his church taught him that Protestant individualism and preaching self-sacrifice were irrelevant to the power realities of modern industrialism. While in the parish he learned from Bishop Charles Williams the reality of social Christianity. The prophets talked about justice as did social Christianity, and he related the learning to the auto-industry personnel in his church.

He learned gradually to appropriate the social ethics of Catholicism and the Catholic assumption of social substance to human living. Eventually he abandoned his Protestant polemical criticism of Catholicism. That was part of his overcoming a polemical spirit in general. He welcomed Catholic-Protestant dialogue while not expecting unity. Catholic devotion to the pope and Protestantism's love for freedom prevent movements toward unity. Catholics chose order and Protestants liberty.

He expressed great appreciation for Catholicism's greater achievement in supporting justice for laborers and racial minorities than Protestantism. Protestant individualism as in the case of Billy Graham was

9. Patrick Granfield, "An Interview with Reinhold Niebuhr," *Commonweal* 80, no. 11 (Dec. 6, 1966): 315–21.

a great hindrance to the adequate development of social justice in the Protestant churches.

Near the end of the interview, Granfield raised Paul Tillich's criticism of his epistemology, his low view of the church, and the death of God theology. He accepted Tillich's critique unnecessarily but objected to his NeoPlatonic epistemology and perspective. He felt Tillich's view of the evil of temporal existence was heretical. He thought there was a need for more appreciation of the Hebrew realistic perspective.

On criticism of his perspective on the church, he thought the criticism may be valid even though it came particularly from his Anglican friends. The United Church of Christ, of which Niebuhr along with his brother was a founding member, is in fact quite low church. The posthumous, polemical criticism of Niebuhr's churchmanship by Stanley Hauerwas seems surprisingly unaware of Hauerwas's own move from Methodist to Episcopal, both of which are bishop-dominated. Varieties of polity hardly seem to me an adequate basis for criticism of one who while appreciating the Episcopal Church remained a low-church pastor. He was influenced by "the historical realities of the church as I know it—both Protestant and Catholic." There have been a lot of scandals in the church of which his secular friends remind him. "Religion needs an institutional church. I think a universal church is better than national churches."[10] The interview could have gone into his lifelong work for the ecumenical church and its social ethics, but this might not have been natural ground for a Roman Catholic editor. More fundamental is the divide between churches that regard themselves as somehow the institution of Christ, and Niebuhr's view, which was that the church was the institution in which to hear the gospel of grace preached.

He criticized the death of God theologians for failing to contribute anything positive.[11] They destroyed various symbolic constructions that have aided human meanings, and they did not put anything in their place.[12] Where are their new symbols?

DEATH OF GOD

Niebuhr criticized the younger death of God theologians for failing to provide a sense of meaning to replace the symbols they dismissed. He regarded the concept of God as a myth. He suggested they dismissed myth as illusory and failed to replace the meaning of the myth. This crit-

10. Granfield, "An Interview," 320.
11. Granfield, "An Interview," 321.
12. Granfield, "An Interview," 321.

icism may not be fair, for they too found tangents of meaning in Jesus or in humanism or reason.

However, the essential meaning for Niebuhr of the concept or symbol of God was that human life and history had meaning. He admitted the meaning may be obscure, but the symbol of God as the beginning of humanity and fulfillment of the human was important to the moral life of humanity. Earlier he had hoped for a metaphysic adequate to protect human dignity and reality. But, after conversations with Paul Tillich, he settled for religious symbols that expressed that meaning.

He did not totally reject metaphysics. Several times he testified to the adequacy of Alfred North Whitehead's metaphysics. He thought that God as "the principle of concretion" expressed the value structure that permitted particular realities to emerge from the groundless realm of possibilities. He even regarded the emergence of the human from the animal as one of those decisions imposed by "the principle of concretion."

The creation myths of religion are not to be taken literally, but they preserve the realm of mystery that hovers over scientific cause-and-effect explanations. Niebuhr uses myth to indicate humanity is of nature but transcends nature in limited freedom. For him: "Religious faith is permanently valid despite the discredit it suffers."[13]

The symbols are not scientifically exacting. The methods of science are not particularly helpful in interpreting the religious experience. The symbols point to nearly universal human experiences of ultimacy and of meaning beyond death. The statement, so common, that "I cannot believe he is dead,"[14] points toward humanity's search for eternity. Scientists who worship instinctively see the difference between religious language and scientific language. The one need not intrude upon the other. Their experience witnesses to a partnership in life between rational science and the mythical language of religion.

He asserted that (1) Previous atheists had substituted other interpretations of meaning for the gods they dismissed; (2) Even Bultmann distinguished between primitive and living myths; (3) Tillich's system based in Neoplatonism too easily abandoned biblical symbols; (4) Neither Bultmann's existentialism nor Tillich's Neoplatonism adequately protected the meaning of human freedom in historical social life. Niebuhr risked using the symbols to illumine historical experience to escape meaninglessness or the bareness of a purely empirical view of life. Niebuhr,

13. Reinhold Niebuhr, *Faith and Politics: A Commentary on Religious, Social, and Political Thought in a Technological Age*, ed. Ronald H. Stone (New York: George Braziller, 1968), 6.

14. Niebuhr, *Faith and Politics*, 8.

following William James, regarded the religious symbolism expressing human religious experience as real.

He had undertaken the same argument twenty-nine years earlier when he had attacked the rationalism of his own professor D. C. Macintosh in a *Festschrift* for the elderly professor. When he gave me permission to quote from any of his works, personal letters, and comments, he proudly said he had never misrepresented Macintosh. He had learned to appreciate symbols in his walks and talks with Tillich. Their use first appeared in his *An Interpretation of Christian Ethics* of 1935 when he discussed his debt to Tillich.

He regarded the death of God theologians' use of Tillich as better proof that Tillich was dead than that the symbol of God was dead.[15] He asserted that Tillich "would have been horrified by the proposition that 'God is dead.'"[16]

Two years after he published the essay criticizing the death of God idea, I published the essay and his earlier essay on symbols at the beginning of the book I edited with his approval. In the introduction I explained the choice:

> Many including admirers and critics have not understood Niebuhr's use of religious symbols. His utilization of such symbols combines a loyalty to the tradition with a concern for the ethical and pedagogical integrity of the tradition. Concerned with the function of religious language, his method moves beyond analysis to the reformation of traditional symbols to promote the integrity of the church in its confession and social action.[17]

JUDAISM

Niebuhr welcomed Vatican II's pronouncement on the relations among Jews and Christians. Its condemnation of anti-Semitism and the rejection of Jewish responsibility for Jesus's crucifixion were approved. Still, he hoped for a more complete confession by the Christian church of its responsibility for the persecution of Jews throughout its history. Religious differences had accentuated religious prejudice and persecution.

Protestants tended to be more prejudiced against Jews than Catholics because of their greater reliance on the Bible. The early fights between synagogue and church were enshrined in the New Testament, as was its universalism that still excluded Jews.

15. Niebuhr, *Faith and Politics*, 9.
16. Niebuhr, *Faith and Politics*, 4.
17. Niebuhr, *Faith and Politics*, xiv.

In a rare public comment on his brother, Helmut, he acknowledged him as probably the first to call for the end of missions to the Jews.[18] He recognized their own legitimate autonomy. Reinhold called for more concern about religious discrimination and the ending of it in clubs, fraternities, and residential areas. All of this discrimination was too absurd for a modern-pluralistic nation. The great moral issue of prejudice against black people needed to be met by a complete partnership between Christians and Jews in overcoming it.

The pluralism of religious groups in the nation was established, and narrow prejudices grounded in religion had to be removed. Vatican II had ignored religious texts that reinforced prejudice against Jews and this avoidance was affirmed.

Still, he recognized here and in later writings the divisiveness of Christian claims of Jewish longing for a messiah and interpretations of prophetic writings. Jesus in some ways ended for Christians the Hebrew hopes for a just-powerful ruler in his reinterpretation. The clash between Greek metaphysics and Hebrew Scripture in the church took total reconciliation of the two faiths beyond possibility. A suffering Messiah interpreted as divine was too much of a stretch for Judaism to accept. Tradition, love, cooperation, friendship between the two while remaining unique was in order, and these virtues were grounded in both traditions.

THE SEMINAR

The week before classes met, I walked to 404 Riverside Drive, and to the apartment building graced by the small park and the statue of the liberator Kossuth. Ursula met me at the open door to their apartment and showed me into the living room containing Reinhold's desk. We would hold the seminar there, crowding in ten students. We discussed the course, which was essentially the one I had taken at the seminary two years previously. Reinhold asked me to update the syllabus. Before the seminar began I added a few of the works in political philosophy and ethics from my studies in Oxford.

The overall context included the social welfare politics of the Johnson administration, and the increasing criticism of the US role in the war in Vietnam. The hot topics in theology were the secular utopianism of Harvey Cox's *The Secular City*, and the death of God theology's assault on theological education. The riots of oppressed urban blacks

18. Reinhold Niebuhr, "The Unsolved Religious Problem in Christian-Jewish Relations," *Christianity and Crisis* 26, no. 12 (Dec. 12, 1966): 279–83.

were troubling the nation. Undergraduates were discovering uncommitted sex and the worship of drugs as Timothy Leary, dismissed by Harvard, led the young into new experimentation. The walls of Protestant ethics seemed to be cracking. Even the social change led by Martin Luther King Jr. was being challenged by his former allies. The founding of Students for Democratic Society under Tom Hayden's early leadership reinforced the tendency toward moralism, utopianism, and social action without regard to the consequences of backlash. Niebuhr's reservation about importing moralism into politics, especially international politics, was under attack. It seemed like his former admirers were turning toward radical politics and even taking apocalyptic aspects seriously. Even his former journal writers drifted toward utopianism and anti-Niebuhr critiques in *Christianity and Crisis.* His liberal incremental politics and realism about the role of morality in international politics were not exciting to the new radicals. But the graduate and seminary students attending the seminar were not heavily involved in the new radical expressions, though they were politically concerned and sometimes active. The preconditions for revolution in American society were not present, but students who knew nothing of guns dreamed Marxist dreams and some of their professors encouraged them. Niebuhr had met the more radical undergraduates in his courses at Harvard, Princeton, and Barnard. He would hear about them again two years later as building takeovers and police riots shook Columbia University, followed by a sit-in at Union Theological Seminary.

He normally presented six lectures to the seminar. The second part of the seminar consisted of student papers on which he would comment. Usually the students cleared their subjects with me, and if requested, I would make bibliographical suggestions. Reinhold read and graded the final paper, a revision of their class presentation. The first lecture, "The Problem of Social Ethics in a Biblical Framework," avoided in the spirit of Ernst Troeltsch overestimations of the biblical perspective. Social ethics reflected on two moral requirements: (1) The achievement of a tolerable harmony among self-seeking men and (2) The achievement of a tolerable justice among self-seeking collectives, races, classes, families, and nations.

The biblical framework had the character of seeking to bring all of history into an ideal harmony. It refused to escape from history through denying its relevance or by escaping into mysticism. Therefore it moved toward the hope of a messianic age, rejecting idealism, leaning toward a transformed nature in which "the lion shall lie down with the lamb," or through a messianic virtue of powerlessness or alternatively the "shepherd king." He commented on the long history of the symbol of the shepherd king.

Messianism has a creative and confusing history. It is creative when the vision states the ultimate possibilities of social harmony through self-sacrifice or virtuous power. It is confusing because of its idealism of ultimate love controlling history. Social ethics on the other hand requires discriminate justice among competing claims and interests. Niebuhr understood the New Testament to present Jesus as an eschatological figure much in the manner of Schweitzer's interpretation. He spent very little time on the ethic of Jesus or Paul as he moved on to interpret the church's strategies of social ethics as it assumed responsibility.

The church has employed various strategies. The early church was an eschatological sect hoping for the fulfillment of the world in a messianic age. Schweitzer presented this well in his strategy of an interim ethics. The establishment of Christianity under Constantine and his successors claimed from the perspective of Eusebius that the reign of Christ was established. This presented the danger of the church clothing dominant power with premature sanctity. Augustine's solution of the Two Cities adjusted the church to the fall of Rome. One was governed by love of self and the other by the love of God. But in history the two were mixed. Wasn't it the case that both were mixed not only in history but within the same person? Grace maintained the power of virtue, leaving the historical city to be ruled by conflict. Niebuhr could affirm the separation of love and power, but he had reservations, as it left history to the wolves and resulted in a pretentious church. The Catholicism of Gregory VII presented Augustine without reservations as justifying the rule of the church over the world. The church could make the distinction between "natural law" and the counsels of perfection. The natural law provided the standards of ordinary justice, leaving asceticism to provide the rigorous instruction of perfectionism for the spiritual or monastic world. Perfection required the sacrifice of family, property, and parochial loyalties. It revealed the power of powerlessness as a basis for sanctity. It justified the church and allowed Gregory VII to challenge all power other than the church.

Niebuhr had no fondness for the medieval synthesis. He lacked Paul Tillich's nostalgia for the harmonies of the period, and he discussed the several reasons for its failure: morally the counsels of perfection removed the drive for transcendence from the ethics of the people, confining it to the monastery. Francis provided a new historical dynamism to the Catholic Church's morals. Neither "just price" nor "just war" conformed to the historical contingencies that arose. The combination of Aristotle and feudalism sanctified the feudal system and reinforced the sanctities of hierarchies that were crumbling.

Religiously there was the danger of using the keys of heaven to support power-seeking political authority. Gregory VII was judged differently as a saint and as an "Anti-Christ." Gregory VII's pretensions to rule as a holy Caesar were resisted; Rome's attempts to rule the world diminished its spiritual power. Niebuhr spent more time on Thomas Aquinas than on other figures he discussed in the course. Finally, for him the mixture of Aristotle, Augustine, and feudalism failed to persuade him of the viability of Aquinas's approach.

Reformation ethics proved unsatisfactory as well. Noting the possibilities of resistance to government in Calvinism, he generally found the ethics of the Reformation to be too easily captured by government on the one hand or business as interpreted by Max Weber on the other. He found his home in the revolutionary ethics of Calvinism and the Cromwellian sectarians. The further development in John Locke and John Milton provided resources for democratic government and tolerance. Basically he thought Christian ethics should remain interdisciplinary and not try to develop its own unique ethic. Christian social ethics was always relative to its time and place and the philosophical resources utilized to meet particular needs. Love, of course, remained the absolute, and it expressed itself through justice as found in the principles of equality, liberty, and order. The seminar proceeded from its glance at biblical ethics through church history and then into the utilization of political philosophy in terms of justice toward practical issues. He referred to his coauthor's book, *Religion of the American Mind*, to note the overcoming in Calvinism of religious establishment and welcomed the Great Awakening of Jonathan Edwards. With the abandonment of Calvinism's theocracy and the utopianism of Cromwell's sects, the way was cleared for the American Constitution's combining idealism and realism in its presupposed ethic. He leveled sharp criticisms at New England Calvinism's treatment of the Native Americans. By now he was really doing American social ethics from Constitutional understandings shaped by the social gospel of the twentieth century and his own additions of realism derived from his experience in war, industry, and the civil rights movement. The seminar, like most of his writing, dealt in historical themes and the development of ideas from Western and church history. Ernst Troeltsch, Max Weber, and Albert Schweitzer contribute determinative interpretations that shaped him and the course.

The second major lecture developed the themes of liberty and equality that were present in his writings and in *Faith and Politics*. It related social norms to human selfhood in terms of his study *The Self and the Dramas of History*. He recognized the historical hierarchies in economics and politics. Society was organized hierarchically. Hierarchy is necessary, and those at the top reward themselves inordinately for their roles in the hierarchy. Simple equality is an illusion, but equality understood as a regulative principle of justice helps to make the inequality less onerous. Equality becomes the ideology of the poor, but in both Communist and liberal societies the hierarchies rule. Liberty too is a regulative principle, but liberty is constantly restrained by the authorities. Chaos would be nonexistence as a society, but the principle of freedom helps to criticize the burden of order maintained by the privileged.

In the seminar he would rummage through the history of the two principles from Aristotle to the Stoics, bringing the analysis up to the French enlightenment and revolution. Personally he found the greatest contributions before the modern period in the Diggers and the Levelers and their debates during the Cromwellian revolution. He usually compared revolution and the new hierarchies in the British, French, and American revolutions, noting that none of them could establish the abstract principles of equality and liberty. America achieved a remarkable open society—except, he argued, for African Americans. Even here he saw progress, but this required black people achieving more means of power than had been won to date. Still, he treasured the American gains toward justice while rejecting the notion that either freedom or liberty had been achieved. He suggested that abstract criticisms of America in terms of equality or freedom fell short because the true picture was more complicated.

He reviewed freshly the material from *The Structure of Nations and Empires*, which was the substance of the third lecture. Other materials from his course on "The History of Christian Ethics" found their way into the lectures as he found them relevant. Students kept the course from becoming only Reinhold Niebuhr on Ernst Troeltsch, *The Social Teachings of the Christian Churches*, raising questions about the Vietnam War and race relations. He was happy to be diverted into these subjects, which he usually answered by reflecting on history rather than by teaching about abstract norms of racial justice or just war theory.

The fourth or fifth lecture in the seminar was usually on race relations as developed historically in terms of the American experience. An analysis of black movements for racial justice was included, as well as comments on different types of white response to changing racial norms. Though he served on the NAACP Committee of 100, his own preferred strategies were those of Martin Luther King Jr., whom he regarded as the most creative social ethicist in the country. Like most Americans, his thought on race evolved and judgment on this thought could most helpfully be evaluated from the perspective in 1968 following the publication of the Presidential Commission's report on the causes of urban violence.

The final lecture was on the "Morals of Family and Sex in Christian Thought." He noted the negative attitudes in the history of the church toward "eros," accompanied by the assumption of monogamy in the church. There was more discussion of biblical texts regarding this subject than in his usual presentations on other issues. The Catholic tendency to reduce requirements toward religious law was not accepted. It was a matter of relationships. He was neither conservative nor moralistic on the subject. But the tone was different; he was not so pragmatic on the subject as on other issues. When a student questioned Ursula, who was providing refreshments at the end of the session in their living room, about the missing pragmatism, she replied: "Marriage is so much fun." The protection of the bond of marriage, its "I and Thou" character, and the tradition defending marriage were satisfactory in Niebuhr's mind. Much of his argument resulted from years of counseling others in marriage troubles. He knew of those who had been terribly hurt by sexual betrayal or desertion, and while affirming sexuality he was realistic about its potential for damage as well as joy. He understood and was not prudish about sexual experimenting among the young. In one semester, we were walking on Riverside Drive and he warned me, "Ron, we are delaying the seminar with so much argument over sexual ethics. We must get on with the seminar." I questioned his possible conservatism on the issue. He responded: "Some of you young graduate students are still hot, but I am an older man with a younger wife."

The remaining sessions of the seminar were given over to discussion of student papers. Niebuhr displayed his generosity of spirit in his critiques of the student work. Even when his own positions or thought were assaulted his responses were mellow, though in a couple of cases he found it helpful to open the next session with his remarks on the previous session. The polemics were a thing of the past and not present in the seminar in his living room. Earlier versions of the seminar had contained lectures on economics. He continued the discussion of economic ethics in the first seminar, Christian Ethics 497, but it was dropped in the second, Christian Ethics 498, to allow more time to develop the framework of Christian social ethics. The first syllabus listed the collection of his economic writings in the Harry A. Davis and Robert C. Good edition of *Reinhold Niebuhr: On Politics*, pages 213–27. The subject was not present in the last seminars of 1967–68. The issues came up briefly in his reflections on "liberty." There had not been much on economics in his 1965 book, *Man's Nature and His Communities*. It usually came up in his discussion of the development toward justice for the black minority as a problem resisting change for the minority. He published his 1953 essay "The Christian Faith and the Economic Life of a Liberal Society" in *Faith and Politics* in 1968. His political identity had been tied in with the unions, and their relatively satisfactory position in 1963 led him to neglect the issues except in regard to justice for African Americans in the 1960s.

He regarded the seminar as very important. He worried about its quality and rethought most of his own presentations. He was nervous as to how it was received. A note to me soon after the seminar began in 1966 indicates his concern.

> Dear Ronald:
>
> I am concerned that I talk too much at our seminar; and that we do not have enough discussion. I must accustom myself to the shorter hour.
>
> But meanwhile would you tell the members of the seminar that in the next session we will start with a discussion on the two points elaborated in the last session: 1) The relation of self-transcendence to the capacity for moral judgments; and 2) The double character of human nature; and the historical development of social norms, which complicates the problem of drawing our norms from "nature."
>
> I hope that the members will find these questions sufficiently intriguing to start a discussion.
>
> Thanks for all your help.
>
> Sincerely yours,
> Reinibuhr

WALKS ON RIVERSIDE

After the first seminar meeting, Ursula asked me if I would like to walk with Reinhold. We arranged for me to walk with him on Friday afternoons at 4:00 p.m. On the first walk I raised the question of natural law. "If we mean by natural law, principles or regulative norms that reason has derived by reflection upon the empirical data of human personal and social nature, then are not you a natural law theorist?" I don't think you should say so, he replied. "Natural law implies just war theory, fair price understandings, and prohibition of birth control (at least in Catholic teaching), and none of those illumine the dynamic changing character of history or morality. I teach that Protestants should use norms derived from faithfulness to the love commandment and human nature. The norms change in history. Ecumenical ethics are essentially pragmatic, and I think they need to be. There is too much relativity in our norms for us to claim they are laws from either reason or history." We strolled on Riverside Drive across the street from his apartment. He could walk slowly; I was there as a companion, and maybe a little protection from the misfortunes of urban life. Usually we walked in the shadow of the trees and the normally cloudy days of the Hudson River Valley. Occasionally we would slog through the rain, but that was rare. We did not pay much attention to the trees; they were just our surroundings.

One of the legends of the earlier Tillich-Niebuhr walks was that when asked a question about Tillich in class, he had replied that Tillich was a pantheistic mystic. Now when Tillich stopped to admire a tree, Niebuhr walked on. Noticing that Tillich wasn't responding to his point, he turned and saw that Tillich was admiring a tree. "What's up, Paulus?" Tillich responded: "The damn nature-mystic is worshipping the tree!" Ordinarily they refused to criticize each other, but occasionally a student question would provoke one or the other.

I asked him about the Kenneth Thompson essay in a recent *Christianity and Crisis* essay that preceded the joint editorial statement against the war. Kenneth was a little closer to his teacher Hans Morgenthau, but he lacked the Kantian moral strands of his teacher. Niebuhr admired Thompson's exposition of Christian Realism, but he was a little softer, trying to stress the necessary mix of idealism and realism that was part of American history and character. He echoed the published statement that he didn't disagree with the editorial. John Bennett had written most of it, but he knew that Thompson had not wanted to sign it.

To a question about his plans for teaching, he replied: he loved teaching and it was good for his spirit as he had a tendency for his health to depress him. "Why don't we take it a term at a time, and see how many semesters this old man is good for? If you think I am not up to it, we can quit. The pain and discomfort leave me quite tired after a seminar, but it is better for me to continue, and as long as it is good for the students we'll make the effort."

After a walk, we would meet the doorman inside the narthex of 404 Riverside Drive, and he would take the elevator up. The doorman usually phoned Mrs. Niebuhr that he was coming up. Before we concluded our walk in the snow in 1966, he reminded me of Horace Mann's aphorism that "the best teaching takes place with the teacher on one end of the log and the student on the other." As we continued, the truth of those words became very important to me.

THE ARMY IN FORMER COLONIES

Niebuhr expressed in his post-retirement classes at Harvard, Princeton, and Barnard: "Democracy is a high art."[19] He found little reason to expect the newly released colonies to achieve it. Armies proved to be the organization of stability when new democratic governments fell apart. He knew that Americans tended to distrust military governments because of their own democracy. He believed Americans should understand the provisional virtues of armies overcoming chaos. He provisionally respected army leadership in Indonesia, Ghana, Algeria, Nigeria, and the Congo. He still deplored the Kennedy administration's pretense that the Diem regime was a democracy. He regarded the Honolulu Conference's blessing of the army junta of Marshal Ky as unfortunate, for the marshal could not secure the approval of Buddhist leadership or peasants.

Niebuhr supported reform for the Central Intelligence Agency, with more congressional control. Its efforts at the Bay of Pigs and in support of the Diems and their police revealed it operating almost as an invisible government. Likewise its secret support for journals, publishers, and universities was a mistake. He gave it credit for disclosing the placement of Russian missiles in Cuba. He praised the *New York Times* for its investigation of the CIA and called for its subordination to ambassadors and Congress. Senator Eugene J. McCarthy's work on a bill for more regulation of the agency was a move in the right direction.[20] He thought that the military was under more efficient control than the CIA. The military seemed to understand its role as subservient to civilian administration. His criticism of the military in Vietnam was mostly limited to their overestimation of their accomplishments. His critiques were of the national leadership from the president on down. Many of them were realists, but they acted like idealists in thinking they could force the quagmire of Vietnam into something resembling democracy. Their protestations of self-determination and democracy rang hollow to him.

19. Reinhold Niebuhr, "The Army in the New Nations," *Christianity and Crisis* 26, no. 8 (May 2, 1966): 83–84.

20. Reinhold Niebuhr, "The CIA: Tool or Policy Maker," *Christianity and Crisis* 26, no. 9 (May 30, 1966): 105–6.

CATHOLIC INTERVIEW

John Cogley interviewed Reinhold and published his essay before the year ended. Cogley was a skillful interviewer and he provoked from his subject some very frank views. Cogley's experience at *Commonweal* was grounded in Catholic theology, and now at *McCall's* that basic Catholic grounding fueled his questions. The interviewer started with questions about sexual ethics, but Niebuhr rejected the traditional Catholic law on divorce or birth control. He wanted to preserve the relational quality of marriage and not judge it by law. On the other hand he defined himself as a Christian traditionalist on faithfulness in marriage because he believed infidelity would destroy the marriage bond and mutuality. He rejected recreational sex without commitments of love and exhibited realism about male lust and seductive tactics. Cogley tried to pin Niebuhr down on conventional orthodox doctrine that could be associated with more conservative Protestants, and Niebuhr refused the bait, speaking about religion as a sense of meaning of the worth of human existence, and discussing the human life of Jesus. Their differences were greater in the understanding of the church. Cogley saw Jesus's life being continued in the church while Niebuhr respected the church's witness to Jesus. Cogley was sure the bishops would not deceive him any more than Christ would deceive him. Niebuhr could recognize the role of the pope in maintaining order, but he wanted more freedom in the church. He recognized the weakness in Protestant freedom, but he made himself clear in reference to the pope. He would risk anarchy rather than despotism. "My answer would be to say (I hope I'm not too irreverent) To Hell with the Pope."[21]

The interview confirmed him as a theological liberal. On a walk on January 6, 1967, he agreed that Madison, Montesquieu, and Burke could all be interpreted as liberals. Their thought should be contrasted, however, with more rationalistic idealists. The liberal is one who develops ideas and strategies for expanding human freedom. Niebuhr told me on that walk that liberalism can mean so many different things. He said that he heartily approved of being interpreted as a liberal. After all, wasn't he a founding member of Americans for Democratic Action? Going on, he said, "I don't agree with all of ADA's current policies . . . but I would appreciate being interpreted as a liberal." Cogley quoted him as saying:

21. John Cogley, "An Interview with Reinhold Niebuhr," *McCall's* 93, February 1966, 170.

> In terms of religious leadership and religious tradition my life was formed by the left-wing of the Protestant liberal movement, made up of people who extricated the Christian enterprise from the relations with a moribund Calvinism and social Darwinism, and proclaimed that the Christian doctrine of love had to be implemented by the doctrine of social justice.[22]

He still distanced himself from the unwarranted confidence in human virtue held by many liberals. He continued his liberal militancy, arguing that his realism had to be distinguished from the realism of Christian conservatives and joined to the progressive struggles for justice. If liberation meant tolerance, moderation in defense of one's own convictions, and a critical attitude toward authority, "then I think every civilized man must be a liberal."[23]

His strong positions led Cogley to ask him about the neoconservative political movement. He replied:

> I disdain it for the reasons that American neo-conservatism is nothing but moribund liberalism. That's Goldwater's conservatism. This moribund liberalism is an effort to make the bourgeois ideals of individual liberty and freedom from all social restraints, on which the bourgeois classes rose to power and created a free society, into an absolute.[24]

Sylvia Stivers, a registered nurse and wife of a seminary student, served as a practical nurse and companion to Reinhold several mornings a week when they were in New York City so that Ursula could fulfill some of her community duties. Sylvia said that her major recollection of assisting him was of his frustration. He had masses of energy to work, but his health prevented him from traveling, taking speaking engagements, or even applying himself consistently to his writing. His reach for his vocation exceeded his grasp.

22. Cogley, "An Interview," 167.
23. Cogley, "An Interview," 166.
24. Cogley, "An Interview," 166.

11.

Social Myths and Cold War, 1967

Man's capacity for justice makes democracy possible; man's inclination to injustice makes democracy necessary.

Niebuhr was quite satisfied with his 1967 essay, "The Social Myths of the Cold War." He gave me an inscribed copy when it was published in *The Journal of International Affairs*,[1] and we included it in *Faith and Politics* the next year. Writing on political, ideological myth was characteristic of the final years of his writing. Interestingly, *The Democratic Experience* published in 1969 used terms like "ideology," "dogma," "ideal," or "value" to cover the same phenomena. Of course, the 1969 volume reflected his lectures of 1961 at Harvard.

In this essay, "Myths are essentially distortions of complex historical events."[2] They are used to defend national or social interests and attach value to policies pursued by the rulers. They contain some historical truth, but are oversimplifications of complex, often ambiguous realities that general populations cannot be expected to understand. He does not make the same distinctions between true and primitive myths here as he previously explained for religious myths.[3] In this essay, he was mostly cynical about the myths of the superpowers. He concludes with UN Secretary General U Thant fearing the "Holy War" in Vietnam being cultivated by two superpower ideologies. He summarizes: "Regarding Communist myths and democratic myths: The myths underlying our

1. *The Journal of International Affairs* 21, no. 1 (1967): 40–56.

2. Reinhold Niebuhr, *Faith and Politics: A Commentary on Religious, Social, and Political Thought in a Technological Age*, ed. Ronald H. Stone (New York: George Braziller, 1968), 225.

3. Reinhold Niebuhr, "The Truth in Myths," in *Faith and Politics*, 15–31.

foreign policy seem to lead an open society into confusion."[4] He hoped debunking of the myths of the Cold War would allow for the real interests in avoiding escalation toward nuclear war to be perceived. Each superpower had power of imperial proportions and exercised hegemony within its own block of allies. The Western bloc could hardly be regarded as democratic while the Soviet bloc had tyrannical tendencies; it was also supported by consent, national pride, nationalism, and fear of the West.

Niebuhr regarded the philosophy of Marx as inadequate for governance. The work of Lenin on capitalism and imperialism was only partially true. Much of that which Soviet ideology regarded as scientific, he regarded as myth that some of the world found attractive. Marxists erred in regarding economic production as the basis of all power, as even the Soviet Union controlled economics through party apparatus. The Marxist tendency toward apocalyptic religion freed it to be realistic about the present but obscured the need for checks and balances on power. The hope for a radically new man in a new society through climactic, violent revolution was the product of a dangerous, illusory myth.

He reinforced his arguments about the importance of myth by looking at the protestations of Presidents Jefferson, McKinley, and Eisenhower, all of whom asserted American innocence from empire building. Both superpowers obscured their imperialism by virtue of their myths of innocence. On my subsequent visits to the Soviet Union in 1972 and 1980, officials continued to claim there were no ethnic tensions in this largest of empires. They would argue seriously that the removal of capitalist competition allowed all their peoples to live in fraternal harmony. Both superpowers argued innocence, obscuring the factors of power that held them and their empires together.

Lured by Kennedy's boldness and Eisenhower's precedents into the morass, Johnson, in his pride, could not lose the war. He invested more and more in aiding a succession of military juntas to resist the unification of the small nation by the revolutionary forces. Under slogans of self-determination, anti-Communism, democracy, and analogies from World War II, American treasure and lives were wasted in Vietnam. The costs to the armed forces of South and North Vietnam were staggering. Perhaps a million citizens of divided Vietnam lost their lives. The Vietcong kept up the fight, but their slaughter under American firepower nearly broke them. Political scientists could buttress the administration with data on body counts, but the difficulty of victory on the Asian continent was obscured by both data and myth. Niebuhr would speculate

4. Niebuhr, *Faith and Politics*, 243.

that the US interest might be in airfields in Thailand and the harbor in Cam Ranh Bay for a potential conflict with China. He saw some virtue in the contest in Vietnam allowing military forces in Indonesia and the Malay Peninsula to prevail while holding Thailand, but by 1967 his critique of the president who had awarded him the Presidential Freedom Medal was relentless. The struggle for power in the seas and economies of Southeast Asia continues in the second decade of the twenty-first century. Niebuhr wrote in 1967:

> Thus the confusion of myths—involving problems of prestige and power—and the fears of a conflict with a dominant power in Asia holds a great democratic nation in a grip of pitiless commitment.[5]

Neither rational-choice theory nor game theory in the newly published dissertations showed a way out of the quagmire if the decision makers believed their myths. Neither the alternate use of data nor reason, alone, provided answers. It was important for the United States to count realistically the cost of losing in Vietnam. Surely neither the president nor his advisors were correct that a victory by Ho Chi Minh would mean that the United States would have to fight in Hawaii or Seattle. More historical knowledge of Vietnam's relationship to China and less captivity to myth joined to passionate reluctance to fight unnecessary wars might have saved the United States and Vietnam from that terrible war.

Niebuhr expressed his opposition to the war in two letters to the *New York Times.* In February he wrote in support of Ambassador Edwin O. Reischauer's testimony before the Foreign Relations Committee. Reischauer's knowledge of Asian politics refuted the ambiguous justifications of the war by the administration. He argued that we must leave because of our honor, and that we were stuck because of the trust our allies had placed in our promises. In March he wrote rejecting the escalation of the war to North Vietnam in the name of resisting aggression. Niebuhr pointed out here as he had several times that aggression was in the eyes of the beholder and that our intervention in Vietnam's civil war was mistaken.

I was assisting John Bennett in the course "Moral Issues in International Relations." I responded to his concern about the quietism of the Union Theological students on the Vietnam War, suggesting we ask Reinhold Niebuhr to address the students. I made arrangements to have Reinhold speak in the social hall on an afternoon. Niebuhr was delighted. I drove him to the seminary. It was almost like shoveling him

5. Niebuhr, *Faith and Politics*, 242.

into my low Mustang for the short drive. He supported himself on the podium. He spoke without notes and used his humor to great advantage with the students, who roared with laughter as he satirically criticized the recent imperial venture of intervention in the Vietnam civil war. He began by quoting Gunnar Myrdal's criticism of the war at the expense of the urban black minority. He traced current American imperialism through the two world wars and into its third period of anti-Communism. Communism was no longer monolithic, and the leaders in Hanoi had their own form of Communism independent of Russia, China, or Yugoslavia. It seemed unlikely that we would have to fight Ho Chi Minh in Hawaii or on Cape Cod, which various members of the Johnson administration had suggested. He traced the history of the war, admitting that historical analogies were dangerous as they were not exact. He suggested history repeated itself, but never in the same way. His history showed the unlikely success with former French Vietnamese allies supporting the successive juntas in Saigon. He hoped for political figures to develop alternative strategies for ending the conflict, but he refrained from producing any plan of his own. He admitted it was difficult for superpowers to admit their mistakes or to withdraw from such costly conflicts. Still, his major argument from just war theory was that the cost was disproportionate to the desired end. The war was too costly to the United States in funds and lives. It had very little chance of success, and the cost was disproportionate to the hoped-for goal.

This 1967 address would be Niebuhr's last speech at the seminary, though, maybe, only he knew it was the end. From his earlier speeches in the 1930s urging preparation for conflict with the Nazis, he was now arguing for the leadership of the country to end the war. Student activity against the war developed soon after the address, and it swelled into deep participation against the draft and the war. A couple of years later President John Bennett would himself be arrested protesting the war and the draft. He founded Clergy and Laity Concerned about Vietnam, the leading ecumenical group working against the continuation of the war. Reinhold Niebuhr served on its executive committee as he could. Eventually it would be joined by Martin Luther King Jr. and Abraham Heschel.

We walked on March 6 in the warmer weather. He felt unwell, as the warm weather had rather taken him aback, though he had wished for it to come. After a coffee and a chat with Mrs. Niebuhr talking about Christopher, we went out on the mushy sidewalks of Riverside Drive. He opened the conversation with remarks about Morgenthau. The differences between them now seemed insignificant. Morgenthau rejects

Niebuhr's theology, but Reinie rather suspects he is borrowing from Christianity without affirming it. He remarked how East Coast empirical social scientists had distrusted Morgenthau and regarded him as something of a Machiavellian devil.

We went on to discuss the problem of judging between Nazis and Communists and how Communist power drives were often qualified by ideological factors and also ethnic factors. He agreed that power-political factors would continue to poison US and USSR relationships even if Russia becomes bourgeois.

He was having several interviews next week in preparation of his seventy-fifth birthday and was also writing an article. He was quite troubled over not being able to accomplish that which he wanted to do.

We argued a bit over the relationship of theology to politics. He said it is really the doctrine of man that is determinative. Christianity's contribution was its resources for understanding both his creativity and evil. He also made his usual claims for the historical evidence of claims for theology's influence on political thought. But, he refused to claim that Morgenthau's thought is weaker for being nontheological. Most other schemes (particularly forms of pantheism) try to escape history. Christianity, thanks to Judaism, takes history seriously. He expressed again appreciation for Martin Buber's thought.

He indicated that his dropping of original sin in his recent book was only for pedagogical reasons. When I joked as we entered his apartment that this seemed to be quite an admission for a professor, he replied, "Why should professors be so proud?" I did not usually record a memo about our walks, but I did that day when neither one of us was feeling our best. "Talking with Reinhold," I wrote, "is a rich experience even if we both are off for some reason. What a teacher!"

WARS

General Westmoreland asked for another 100,000 troops as 1967 opened. He also required the further bombing of North Vietnam. Niebuhr had seen some hope in the cooperation of Ambassador Goldberg and Secretary General U Thant lobbying for peace. The renewed armed efforts pointed to the United States wanting both peace and the defeat of the Vietnamese enemies. The contradictions were obvious, and both goals were unachievable. Both democratic leaders and Cardinal Spellman wanted an early victory in the war.

Niebuhr pushed Gunnar Myrdal's thesis that we could not fight the domestic war on poverty and racial oppression while warring in

Vietnam. Myrdal's argument fit Niebuhr's frequent refrain that there are limits to a nation's great wealth and power.

The new element in his critique of the government was his raising the claim that "the Pentagon calls the tune."[6] Despite the claim of decades of civilian control, the "Defense establishment still is dominant in our foreign policy."[7] So once begun, military victory was required without counting the cost. In September, Governor Ronald Reagan urged the full employment of technological resources to win the war quickly, endorsing the threat of nuclear weapons. In the case of Vietnam, Niebuhr responded that such recklessness would wreck both the presidency and the morale of the army. His other three essays on Vietnam of 1967 in *The New Republic*, *Christianity and Crisis*, and *The New Leader* echoed the critique, as did his letter to the *New York Times* in February.

Opposition to the war increased in 1967. Some 50,000 tried to storm the Pentagon in October. Muhammad Ali refused to serve in the draft. Jane Fonda, Norman Mailer, Joan Baez, and Benjamin Spock accepted arrest in protesting the war. President Johnson made another trip to troops in Vietnam. The vice president and the secretary of state both promised US victory in the struggle. They were both met by large protests against poverty, war, and oppression in New York City where they spoke.

Niebuhr's support for Israel's Six Day War was as strong as his critique of the US war. He compared it to David's vanquishing Goliath, revealing his pro-Israel leanings. According to both Bennett and Niebuhr and other following essays in the journal, Egypt had prepared for war with its allies and Israel was justified in striking the first blow. Israel had fought against foes that according to their propaganda broadcasts sought the destruction of Israel. Niebuhr hoped the offices of the United States could assist in the necessary Arab-Israeli reconciliation process, and Bennett concurred, hoping that the refugee problem would not be exacerbated by Israel's victory. Bennett still advocated that the UN could help resolve the Vietnam issues and that a too-easy UN resolution condemning Israel would not materialize. Niebuhr's strong support for Israel during the 1960s was consistent with his postwar arguments for the creation of a Jewish homeland in Palestine.

6. Reinhold Niebuhr, "Our Schizoid Vietnam Policy," *Christianity and Crisis* 26, no. 23 (Jan. 1967): 313.

7. Niebuhr, "Our Schizoid Vietnam Policy," 314.

DIALOGUE WITH HANS J. MORGENTHAU

Reinhold and I had often discussed the political philosophy of Hans J. Morgenthau on our walks. The interview conducted by the *War/Peace Report*[8] editor, Richard Hudson, is the best recorded dialogue between them. He focused on the ethics of international relations, introducing them as the most famous thinkers in their respective fields of theology and political science.

Niebuhr denied that he and Morgenthau were "somewhat different." He thought they basically agreed, with only peripheral differences about ethics and international affairs. In most cases national interest prevailed, but morality had an influence through those making the decisions. They essentially agreed that moral action emerged through defining national interest and the means to be used in pursuing it. Niebuhr expressed concern that ethics of politics should not be expected to be self-sacrificing whereas the Jewish realist, Morgenthau, did not raise the question.

Neither thinker argued for the achievement of equality because the means of effecting it were not present. Rather it remained a regulative principle and a guide toward justice. But self-interest gets in the way of achieving justice if its meaning could be determined. Even justice is a corrupted instrument. Niebuhr expressed, as he often had in this decade, Pope John's formula: "Love must be the motive, but justice must be the instrument."[9] Morgenthau agreed, but with the proviso that humans seeking justice were limited in power and understanding.

Niebuhr turned the conversation to the ethics of wars and particularly Vietnam. Both philosophers agreed that the means of warfare had to be proportional to the ends of the war. Nuclear war was ruled out of moral bounds. The Vietnam War derived from a series of mistakes and illusions, and the American role could not be justified. It was a losing effort and needed to be ended.

Morgenthau thought that imperial presence in Southeast Asia could be justified, but that the claims to defend freedom in Vietnam failed to make sense. He pushed hard that wars had to be justified morally, as the deciders were human beings and therefore moral actors. As opposed to some of his earlier emphases, he insisted on the moral dimension of policymaking.

Niebuhr referred to his discussion of Morgenthau in *Man's Nature and His Communities*. Often the reasons given for national actions

8. Richard Hudson, "The Ethics of War and Peace in the Nuclear Age," *War/Peace Report* 7, no. 2 (Feb. 1967): 3–8.

9. Hudson, "The Ethics of War and Peace," 4.

are hypocritical. But still, the moral arguments point to the need for morality. Morgenthau referred to the point often made by each of them that "hypocrisy is the homage that vice pays to virtue."[10]

Hudson interjected his hopes for world government. Both thinkers rejected his arguments point by point. For Niebuhr, the goals of foreign policy were to "avoid hell and nuclear disaster." The point is central in understanding Niebuhr. The central question is stabilizing great power competition and preventing nuclear war. Morgenthau let Niebuhr carry the argument against the relevance of arguing for world government and then concurred: "I fully agree with you."[11] Both regarded intelligent diplomacy as the best hope of mitigating the anarchy of the nation-state system and avoiding major war. For Niebuhr, "coexistence should be the first order of value."[12]

Neither Niebuhr nor Morgenthau regarded the goal of imposing Western democracy in the world as viable. The old ideas of Wilsonian idealism and Marxist world revolution were dismissed by Morgenthau as dying secular religions, and the last echoes of them were fading.

Niebuhr repeated his formula: "Man's capacity for justice makes democracy possible; man's inclination to injustice makes democracy necessary." So for him, "the consent of the governed" was a legitimate goal to achieve, but it had been corrupted by its elaboration in European culture.[13] Morgenthau regarded democracy as too dependent on Western ideas of individualism, and he remained even more restrained than Niebuhr who here as elsewhere used his normative ideas as forward thrusting, whereas Morgenthau was more inclined to use them as limiting action. Neither was utopian, both were anti-utopian, but Niebuhr's Augustinian realism was a little more positive in interpretation than Morgenthau's Aristotelianism. Of course, Morgenthau as a European Jew had been subject to persecution that Niebuhr had only fought against.

MARTIN LUTHER KING JR.

Though King and Niebuhr never met, there was a deep intellectual and moral bond between them. As a student, King had read Niebuhr and written papers on his thought in which he regarded Niebuhr as too pessimistic. The Boston personalism that King was taught was more opti-

10. Hudson, "The Ethics of War and Peace," 5.
11. Hudson, "The Ethics of War and Peace," 6.
12. Hudson, "The Ethics of War and Peace," 7.
13. Hudson, "The Ethics of War and Peace," 8.

mistic than Niebuhr. Later as an activist, to rally his supporters King had to believe the civil rights movement would succeed. King was influenced by Niebuhr's *Moral Man and Immoral Society* arguments, that the way forward for black justice was through nonviolent action. Niebuhr had suggested the ways of Gandhi might be the most practical for the minority black population. Gradually King became more realistic as whites resisted justice for the black population. He began to see that moral argumentation required more power to force whites to change the structures. Andrew Young wrote that the Southern Leadership Conference was realistic in its later days following the thought of Reinhold Niebuhr, John Bennett, and *Christianity and Crisis*. The social thought of the movement owed more to generations of black church activists than it did to Niebuhr, but King, Young, and others were also aware of the Niebuhr influence in the strategy.

King's trip to Union and to Riverside Church in April 1967 could have been a time for their meeting, but no one arranged it. Niebuhr was too ill to attend the evening lecture at Riverside Church in which King announced his deep criticism of the American role in the Vietnam War. The lecture was bracketed by calls for decision. The conclusion to the Christian hearer sounded like an altar call to decide against the government and for peace. After the first paragraphs, King noted that many were objecting to his denouncing the war because they insisted he should remain a civil rights advocate and not endanger the movement by criticizing the war effort of the United States. He argued that his role was appropriate because the war was destroying the hopeful war against poverty. The United States was joining black and white boys together in burning Vietnamese villages even though those boys could not sit together in America. Young men were challenging nonviolence's relevance for social change while their own government was the largest purveyor of violence on earth. King's commitments to the life and health of America forced him to object to this war that was destroying the moral fiber and reputation of the United States. Then he laid out his narrative of the war reaching back to Truman's support of the French colonists and continuing through Kennedy to the Johnson administration. It was a sorry history of twenty-two years, and to my ears the sad narrative sounded very much like Reinhold Niebuhr. He even echoed Niebuhr's terms like "ambiguity" and "tragedy." He tried in the spirit of his movement to hear and truly listen to the voices of the perceived enemy, and his words convicted the United States without apologizing for the Vietnamese opponents. He spoke, also, on behalf of the young Americans who were being brutalized by the war. In his moments of vision he called for a transvaluation of American values so that the country could support the needed peaceable revolutions. The whole system of colonial exploitation needed changing, and that would require a fundamental change in American values. He explained his arguments that the times were revolutionary and that America had to change. The spirit of a realistic love that could change structures was required as America changed its values. He held firmly to his commitments to nonviolence while stressing the need for radical change. In conclusion he called for a commitment to the struggle for a new world. "The choice is ours, and though we might prefer it otherwise we must choose in this crucial moment of human history."

The speech was arranged by Clergy and Laity Concerned about Vietnam. It had been founded at Union Seminary with the leadership of John Bennett and others. The precedent of founding parachurch organizations for social justice was well established at the seminary. The organization put together King's Los Angeles speech of February 25, 1967, the Riverside Church speech, the comments by John Bennett, Henry Steele Commager, and Abraham Heschel on the speech, King's *New York Times* interview of April 2, and letters to the editor of the *New York Times*.[14] Both the *New York Times* and the NAACP opposed King's criticism of the war on the grounds that civil rights activists should not criticize the war and that their efforts should be confined to the domestic front. King, I thought, had more than adequately overcome the criticism, but the critique threatened the SCLC's work.

Niebuhr's foreword to the publication by Clergy and Laity Concerned about Vietnam picked up the argument in two points and placed his prestige behind Martin Luther King Jr. in the debate. He argued that both causes must be pursued and that "Dr. King has the right and a duty both as a religious and civil rights leader to express his concern in these days about such a major human problem as the Vietnam War." He noted that journals confused King's position with absolute pacifism, which they rejected. It was rather the case that "Dr. King's conception of the nonviolent resistance to evil is a real contribution to our civil, moral and political life." He called the war futile intervention in a civil war and regarded it "as an example of the illusion of American omnipotence."[15] Even Pittsburgh's famous African American newspaper, *The Pittsburgh Courier*, condemned the civil rights leader for taking on the protest against the

14. *Dr. Martin Luther King, Jr., Dr. John C. Bennett, Dr. Henry Steele Commager, Rabbi Abraham Heschel Speak on the War in Vietnam* (Clergy and Laity Concerned about Vietnam, April 1967).

15. *Dr. Martin Luther King, Jr., Dr. John C. Bennett, Dr. Henry Steele Commager, Rabbi Abraham Heschel Speak on the War in Vietnam*, 3. *Foreword by Dr. Reinhold Niebuhr.*

futile war. Niebuhr and King were one in their opposition to the war. Both were under the administration's watch because of their criticism of American involvement in the war. They both pleaded for stronger church support for the integration of American society and in opposition to the war. By 1967 the differences between them were incidental, and Union Seminary students were influenced by both to join in protests in New York City and Washington, DC. Niebuhr's defense of King's speech helped in progressive circles, but the criticism of him was predominant for a while. The Johnson administration turned against him, and the FBI withdrew its protection from him. The attacks on him continued until his murder. Before his assassination King was preparing the strategy for the "Poor People's" march. He and Niebuhr both recognized in their publications the need for subsidized income for African Americans and others unable to find employment. When I asked him, during one of our walks, about Roosevelt's "New Deal" and whether he would call it "state capitalism" or "socialism," he replied that he preferred "mixed economy" to "welfare state." The black civil rights movement needed to add more economic rights to its agenda.

LIFE AND DEATH

Thirteen years after Reinhold's death, Ursula published a previously unpublished essay he had written in 1967. It was titled "A View of Life from the Sidelines."[16] Without detailing the illnesses he had been subject to, he described the anxieties and depressions of being forced to abandon the activist life he had led prior to his 1952 stroke. By this time several minor strokes had followed upon the major one in 1952. His left-side paralysis had hardened, and he required therapy twice a day. He had gone through prostate surgery and a broken tailbone, and that pain added to his colon pain. So pain distracted him from work, but he understood the importance of work to his health.

The first stroke, caused by cerebral vascular thrombosis, he recorded as "not too severe." His left side was lame, and his typing was restricted to his right hand and in practice to one figure. An electric typewriter provided by his friends allowed him to continue commenting on events and ideas of the time. Further ancillary illness led to dependency.

The natural depression of such events was exacerbated by the continuing questioning of his authorship of the Serenity Prayer, which was only resolved post-death. By the age of seventy-five he became aware

16. Reinhold Niebuhr, "A View of Life from the Sidelines," *The Christian Century* (Dec. 19–26): 1195–98.

of his own inability to reflect the serenity or Stoic quality of the prayer. A medical doctor assured him that neither preachers nor doctors were expected to follow all of the counsel they provided. Years later the scholarly community recognized the prayer as genuinely Niebuhr's.

> God, give us the grace to accept with serenity the things that cannot be changed, courage to change the things that should be changed, and the wisdom to distinguish one from the other.

He noted that from the "sidelines" he was less polemical. Furthermore he came to appreciate the sense of divine mystery communicated by the Catholic mass. He also became less critical of Catholicism because he appreciated its sense of human solidarity and its political wisdom in many cases. He also found the common moral commitments of Protestants, Catholics, and Jews on the great issues of the Vietnam War and the improving of the conditions of the black minority heartening. Still, 1967 was a year of the war's intensity increasing. Hubert Humphrey declared the United States was winning, and Rusk said winning was the only solution. President Johnson told the troops at Cam Ranh Bay not to be troubled by the protesters at home against the war.

Reinhold found grace and goodness among the people that helped him. He learned how Ursula was his chief source of spiritual strength and one on whom he increasingly depended. She increasingly helped with editing and contributed to the substance of his thought.

He concluded the essay by commenting on the correspondence with his friend Bishop Scarlett. Both were ill and aware of their mortality. Niebuhr's anxiety about his life is revealed more in his correspondence with the old bishop and partner than elsewhere. The anxiety in the correspondence is such that Ursula has urged interpreters not to overestimate the fears in the letters as the old men dialogued with each other. Both writers knew that the contents of their letters were private and would not trouble those working closely with them. He reflected on the persistence and confusion between the two symbols of life after human death of resurrection and immortality. He could not resolve the issue that had occupied him a half-century earlier in his MA thesis at Yale. The human self is mortal, but in faith, hope, and love it relates to the eternal, and he concludes it is best to leave the mystery of the divine and human self in symbolic terms. The individual remains mortal but related to the immortal "by personal relation to the divine. He cannot claim more for himself or his loved ones as I face the ultimacy of death in the dimension of history which is grounded in nature."[17]

17. Niebuhr, "A View of Life," 1198.

By the summer of 1967, he was worrying about continuing his seminar at Union. These doubts affected him, as a dedicated teacher, deeply. He wrote:

Yale Hill
Stockbridge, Massachusetts
July 2, 1967

Dear Ronald:

I promised you and President Bennett that if the probability of our staying here till Christmas for the sake of my therapy, pure air for Ursula's epicene of the lungs and the chance of her having a seminar in a local college for a short semester, I would let you know.

Negotiations have now been completed for our fall tenure. President Bennett is in Europe, so I will count on you to pass the word along. I hope one semester for the old man will not seriously disarray the program of the Seminary.

Braziller Inc. has asked for a book of my occasional writings. I told them it would be better to wait a year because a book by Paul Sigmund and me on democracy in world affairs is scheduled for 1968. But I told them that you might consider and offer to select those writings. I thought I would trust your judgment implicitly.

Thanks for your nice letter. We are getting along as well as a senile man in his 76th year has any right to expect. Our affectionate greetings to your charming wife.

Gratefully yours,
Reiniebuhr

By late 1967, Reinhold was taking an interest in where I would go after completing the dissertation. We were also working out our contract for the book of his essays I would edit.

Yale Hill
Stockbridge, Massachusetts 01262
Nov 25[18]

Dear Ronald:

Thank you so much for your nice letter. We spent thanksgiving here with our son, Christopher. It was a pleasant day though I now know that my doctors were Pollyannaish in predicting that my coccyx would heal in six weeks. My friends, who have had the same experience, assure me that six months is more probable.

I am glad you have had a bid from Claremont. You will see for yourself on your trip there. I do not know the challenges there, but I suspect that you will be negative on inspection.

So glad you conferred with Mr. Seaver of Braziller, Inc. Anything you decide will be satisfactory to me. He originally offered me an advance of a thousand dollars. I accepted it, with the idea that it would go to you for your editing. But you probably are entitled to a percentage fee. Anything you decide will be satisfactory. I am deeply appreciative of your willingness to accept this chore.

Hope we will be back at year's end. Ursula and I send holiday greetings to the Stone family, your charming wife and son.

Affectionately yours,
Reinbuhr

18. The appearance of the year in the dating of his letters usually means it is typed by someone else. Another clue is the greeting; "Ron" implies typed by a secretary while he usually retains "Ronald" in his own typing.

12.

Faith and Politics, 1968

> God, give us the grace to accept with serenity the things we cannot change, courage to change the things that should be changed, and the wisdom to distinguish one from another.

Niebuhr opened 1968 with an essay on race and the Vietnam War. "A Question of Priorities"[1] attacked the reluctance to aid black people, who had existed from the country's early colonization in slavery and poverty, while expending billions of dollars and thousands of young lives in Vietnam. The Civil Rights Act of 1968 revealed the weakness of law and moral righteousness in overcoming folkways fueled by prejudice. Even the Supreme Court's 1954 decision for equal rights in education was widely ignored. Weighing the American debt to black people outweighed any funding obligation the American nation owed to the government of Vietnam on the scale of justice.

The essay reviewed, as Niebuhr often did, the miserable fate of black people who were left without quality education or the skills for the technology of the present. Without economic power they had only the weaker resources of boycott, demonstrations, and law to advance their case. These instruments were insufficient for a minority to win a fair deal. The war in Vietnam was ruining the administration's attempt to fund the war on poverty. Niebuhr recognized the US imperial interest in maintaining bases for a contest with China, but he harshly attacked the Johnson idealism of Wilsonian self-determination for the divided land of Vietnam. The odds were against the US fight in the Vietnam "civil war."

1. *The New Leader* 51, no. 2 (Jan. 15): 9–11. Reprinted in *Faith and Politics: A Commentary on Religious, Social, and Political Thought in a Technological Age*, ed. Ronald H. Stone (New York: George Braziller, 1968), 261–68.

Two weeks after the essay's publication the Tet offensive threatened to overwhelm US and South Vietnamese forces. However, the Vietcong forces were decisively repulsed in Saigon and within a few weeks driven out of Hue. General William Westmoreland claimed victory after Hue was retaken in late February. But the severity of the attacks in the cities was broadcast over television into most American homes. The country lost its heart and its idealism for the war. Before the year 1968 concluded, both the church-led civil rights movement and support for the war would collapse. Johnson would increase the US troop level to over half a million, but the American populace gave up on Johnson's war. The murder of Martin Luther King Jr. defeated the civil rights movement along with its politically ambiguous support by President Johnson and Vice President Humphrey. The urban riots, which Niebuhr recognized as the politically futile cry of the oppressed, combined with the war to doom prospective Democrats to defeat. The essay, "A Question of Priorities," also reflected his priorities for the remainder of his writing on civil rights and the Vietnam War.

In April, Niebuhr repeated in print that which he had said in the seminar when the students lured him into discussing Vietnam. It was "A Time for Reassessment."[2] Three events were forcing a reconsideration of US policy. The Tet offensive with US casualties over five hundred per week refuted the Johnson administration's promises that things were going well and victory in the war was near. Secretary of State Dean Rusk could not refute his critics in the Senate Foreign Relations Committee. Finally, the results of the New Hampshire primary and Robert Kennedy's announcement promised to split the party or defeat President Johnson. It was time for fundamental reconsideration.

Niebuhr wrote to his friend, Bishop Scarlett, that he could not vote for Johnson. He could not vote for Nixon either, and he asked his old friend for advice. At the same time he admitted the seminars had not gone as well as he had hoped. He wondered if he would repeat the course or maybe it was time to end the tenuous relationship with the seminary. He appreciated George Kennan's memoirs, and hoped some of his wisdom could be taken seriously enough to desist from this disastrous waste of lives and resources in Vietnam. He suggested he might vote Republican for the first time if Nelson Rockefeller and his advisor Henry Kissinger would propose a policy for the United States to exit from Vietnam. Otherwise he might not vote. Neither option was a likely choice for Niebuhr. The suggestions, made only to Scarlett, were not plans but expressions of disgust. After Robert Kennedy was assassinated

2. *Christianity and Crisis* 28, no. 5 (Apr. 1, 1968): 55–56.

in California, he nodded kindly at my working for Governor Rockefeller as an alternative to Richard Nixon. In March, Eugene McCarthy won 41 percent of the votes in New Hampshire and shortly thereafter President Johnson announced he would not run again. The announcement claimed that full attention must be given to winning the peace in Vietnam. The president did not want to be distracted by domestic politics. The health issues of the president were not generally known by the public. Niebuhr's early endorsement of McCarthy prevented him from openly supporting Robert Kennedy, whose ruthlessness gave him pause.

We finished the seminar in the spring of 1968 without realizing it would be our last seminar together. Health issues and teaching opportunities for Ursula at Simon's Rock College by June conspired together for his final retirement from teaching. The decisive paragraph of his letter was:

> Dear Ronald:
>
> I waited with this letter to thank you for all you have done for me, until some definite decision could be made about our stay in the Berkshires till December, to allow Ursula to teach a seminar at a local junior college named Simon's Rock. The offer has been made to her; and we are going to make a decision sometime this month. In favor of our staying is the double therapy I can have here morning and evening from our faithful friend, Mrs. Burrington who helps both Ursula and me in many ways. Also the cleaner air offers no threat to Ursula's emphysema. Also, as she gave up her career for me though she loves to teach, I am anxious that she should have this college teaching experience. So the chances are we will accept.
>
> If we do I will write you and President about it in due time. But there is no reason to delay any longer the expression of my gratitude for what your friendship and intellectual vigor and help in the Seminar has meant to me.[3]

In late October, Humphrey was narrowing the gap between Nixon and himself. Johnson was negotiating with the Russians to stop the bombing so that Russia would pressure Hanoi into peace negotiations. Still, the balance depended on Thieu agreeing to include the Vietcong and North Vietnam in the negotiations. Richard Nixon, fearing peace negotiations, urged Thieu not to agree to negotiations. The H. H. Haldeman papers released in 2017 indicate the Nixon campaign worked through Rose Anna Chenault and Mary Woods to urge Thieu to hold on and to prevent peace negotiations from beginning. Pressure was also put on

3. Letter to Ronald Stone from Reinhold Niebuhr (June 15, 1968). Original in Reinhold Niebuhr Papers, Library of Congress.

the CIA and FBI not to reveal the plot. Nguyen Van Thieu feared that Johnson would appease North Vietnam and sell him out for peace. He perceived Nixon on the other hand as willing to continue the war to victory. Thieu stalled, and Nixon won the election. Nixon repeatedly denied the plot, which President Johnson called "treason." The Haldeman papers according to his biographer, John A. Farrell, report Nixon's instructions to Haldeman to wreck the negotiation potential.[4]

FAITH AND POLITICS

In the early months of 1968, I collected essays to publish the book that George Braziller, on the recommendation of Reinhold, had asked me to edit. I chose to structure it in three parts: part 1 contains sources of his thought and his use of symbols; part 2 represents long essays in the substance of Christian social ethics; and part 3 represents political philosophy and international relations thought, mostly from the 1960s. I chose the title *Faith and Politics* and he added the subtitle: *A Commentary on Religious, Social, and Political Thought in a Technological Age*. Ursula chose one of the essays and Niebuhr approved others I had chosen. We were all pleased with the result, and I received comments as late as 2017 about its usefulness. The first review was from an old critic, Paul Blanshard in the *New York Times*.[5]

The first part introduced his criticism of the death of God theologians. The main point was that they provided no alternative framework of meaning. Faith for Niebuhr means trust that beyond all human misunderstanding there are signals that human life is meaningful in relationship to the variety of ideas circulating about the meaning of God. Humans probably see only dimly, but they usually glimpse a sense of being part of a universe that creates them and nourishes them for their time. Niebuhr falls back on myth, the ancient stories of meaning that protect and nourish the human condition. Some myths are primitive and need to be forgotten; others still have meaning that locates those who follow the myth in a discourse of symbols to guide their lives. Niebuhr reveals his use of Tillich's language when he argues for the relevance of myth. In his thought, the myth is subject to scientific and rational explanation, but the human reality cannot be completely covered by either science or philosophy. He questions rationalism, idealism, naturalism, and in the end accepts some religious myths as the best guides

4. John A. Farrell, "Tricky Dick's Vietnam Treachery," *New York Times Sunday Review*, Jan. 1, 2017, p. 9.

5. Reinhold Niebuhr, *Faith and Politics*.

to human existence. They are best understood by poets and prophets; however, neither poet nor prophet is a completely trustworthy guide. Human experience explored by all the complementary disciplines gives the best guide as to which myths to live by.

The essays following the two chapters on myth explored Walter Rauschenbusch and Karl Marx's contribution to his thought. The social gospel of Rauschenbusch provides the more important stream of thought after he had shed his Marxist illusions of the late 1920s and 1930s. His realism both criticizes and absorbs the social gospel improvements over traditional Christianity. The realism he learned from the prophets, Augustine, the Reformation, and the experience of the twentieth century. The first chapter of the second part affirms the Christian pragmatism or realism of his thought and of the ecumenical movement. His introductory chapter to William James's *The Varieties of Religious Experience* could have introduced his pragmatism in the first part, but it failed to focus on the social dimension adequately for my purposes. The essays in this part support the interpretation of Niebuhr as a pragmatist of the William James type and not that of John Dewey. However, their value in this book is to illustrate his social ethics before turning to the political philosophy and critique of politics of the third part. The book shows him as the liberal theologian of his own creation that he was in these last years with an earlier beginning. It reveals the type of light-theology that was important to him in this last decade. It reasoned from Christian mythology in light of his realistic interpretation of experience for the development of a social ethic-political philosophy to guide the republic through the Cold War.

CIVIL RIGHTS

He produced his most powerful piece on the oppression of the black community for his denomination's publication on church and society.[6] It was published in the joint election issue combining the United Church of Christ's *Social Action* and the Presbyterian *Social Progress* in October 1968. "The Negro Minority and Its Fate in a Self-Righteous Nation" began by referencing the urban riots of the 1960s. He praised the report of the National Advisory Committee, which studied the facts of the urban ghetto and police actions that sparked the riots. Poor education and discrimination in the workplace and wages kept African Americans in a cycle of poverty. The commission did not explain the tardiness of

6. "The Negro Minority and Its Fate in a Self-Righteous Nation," *Social Action* 35, no. 2 (Oct. 1968).

societal reforms to overcome oppression. Niebuhr responded to the issue with his old enthusiasm.

Yale Hill
Stockbridge, Massachusetts 01262
July 15

Dear Ronald:

I am glad you, and your wife and Randy found your visit to us enjoyable. We all enjoyed it so the pleasure is mutual. . . . Glad you like my article on the Negro minority. It was a second version, designed to avoid a conventional approach to the theme without neglecting the splendid report of the National Advisory Commission on civil disorders. I'll write to President Bennett in late August and report to him on our visit and tentative plans. I am not at death's door; but certainly below par. Age is creeping up on this old man. Glad to see that Rockefeller has finally come up with a war solution of some persuasiveness.

Affectionately yours,
Reinie[7]

Niebuhr found the tardiness of social reform movements regarding race due to the complacent self-righteousness of the nation and the church. The idealism of the Declaration of Independence, the Constitution, and the Gettysburg Address obscured the reality of the evils of slavery. Even when emancipated they were given few opportunities to succeed. While white labor organized and managed to wrest middle-class livings from their overlords, blacks were not allowed into craft guilds, and they were shut out of prosperity. The mechanization of agriculture in the South drove them into deeper poverty and provided motivation for migration to Northern urban ghettos.

The few gains won by legislation, court decisions, boycotts, and demonstrations were not adequate to join regained civil rights to economic power. In presenting the history he hoped to present a view of our "moral crisis." The churches ought to be interested in reforming the welfare system. It too often helped fatherless families only, creating a matriarchal system that encouraged fathers to leave or to pretend to not be present in the home. Such a system drove young black males into a mistaken, dysfunctional lifestyle.

He supported the establishment of a poverty minimum and a negative income tax to support the poor. More important, he thought, would

7. Letter to Ronald Stone from Reinhold Niebuhr (July 15, 1968). Original in Niebuhr Papers, Library of Congress.

be a program of college scholarships to alter the educational disparity between African Americans and whites. Other recommendations to relieve the poverty needed to be reviewed and enacted. The riots of 1968 were more ominous than the 1967 riots, and the new Congress needed to act to relieve grievous injustices. The Commission, he said, had shown the way and a prosperous nation needed to reform itself to break poverty. The billions could be afforded if the expenditures for war in Vietnam were ended. Two hundred years of broken promises and pledges in the name of American idealism needed to be overcome. The frustrations of hopeful programs and legislation leaving the poor oppressed produced riots that were not part of the civil rights reform movement. Hopes were raised and then dashed. Only significant redress could ameliorate the pain of urban ghetto life.

The cover for the issue was a drawing of the US Capitol building immersed in the flames of the red stripes of the American flag. It represented the view from the streets of the capital perceived through urban fires in Washington, DC, the repository of democratic hopes. Niebuhr's essay was preceded by Roger Shinn writing about election issues with comments by Paul Ramsey, George A. Chauncey, Steven Rockefeller, and Walter Mondale. Lewis Maddocks presented a long essay and data about the voting records of senators and representatives in 1967–68.

Most of the essays commented on race, war, legislation, and poverty. Niebuhr's piece on race and the priority given to war was the climax of the issue. Other issues of the journal in that year on race were: apartheid in South Africa, tensions and violence between blacks and the police, and reforming education for racial justice. Fifty years later, only apartheid has been tenuously overcome. Shortly after the issue's publication he wrote:

Yale Hill
Stockbridge, Massachusetts
October 22

Dear Ronald:

You are, besides your various accomplishments of genius, a genius of an editor. Your pamphlet: "Election Issues," six copies of it, has arrived. It is superb. [I appreciated] your introduction, Roger Shinn's general analysis, with no prejudice or partiality, to the candidates and their causes. I have never seen Roger in better form, perhaps because I agree with him in every instance.

The commentaries were also superb. Steven Rockefeller's commentary heightened my distant admiration of him; and caused renewed regret that he came to Union on the year of my retirement which permitted only one brief visit in my office. It also made me regret that his father entered the race too late to defeat that insignificant careerist, Richard Nixon. Thus history may have been changed; for it robbed many of us the chance to get rid of the Viet Nam Albatross by voting for a type of progressive Republicanism, which has come to terms with both the industrial and the Negro revolution, which had the support of both the industrial workers and the Negro minority. Now we must reject a new Republicanism, representing the southern whites and the wealth of the suburbs. It is one of the tragedies of the war's election.

I found Senator Mondale's commentary also very interesting. I congratulate you on securing this promising young Senator, so rich in Christian political insights.

I doubt if any church has produced a more mature study of our election issues and of the problems occasioned by our long neglect of our Negro minority, and by LBJ's tragic Viet Nam involvement.

My congratulations to you and best wishes, from our whole family, to you and your wife. I only had the belated news from my doctor that I was in the hospital, not only for the urinary aliments but for a mild case of coronary thrombosis. Thus the old machine, my body, creaks at every joint, and my future, including that seminar, must remain uncertain.

Affectionately yours,
Riniebuhr[8]

8. Letter to Ronald Stone from Reinhold Niebuhr (Oct. 22, 1968). Original in Niebuhr Papers, Library of Congress.

The tumult of 1968 was fueled both by youth attacking their universities and by losing themselves in music, sex, and drugs. The mistaken war erupting in the Tet offensive paralleled the assassinations of Martin Luther King Jr. and Robert Kennedy and in the burning of the cities in racial riots. Tom Hayden's charisma and the city's police overreactions incited the riots at the Democratic Convention in Chicago. The Students for a Democratic Society could bring a great university like Columbia to its knees. Adult reactions whether at Columbia or Berkeley were usually not wise. Both in political and educational institutions the leaders failed to reform, and the stress continued. The turmoil hampered the parties from finding a way out of the war. Humphrey broke from Johnson's war policies too late, and Nixon's promises were not believed by the war protesters or the Vietnamese. Niebuhr maintained a cool rationality through the terrible year. He was, as he said the previous year, "on the sidelines." Nixon's treachery regarding the war was more evil than the Watergate scandal that would dislodge him from the presidency a few years later.

The suppression of the 1968 Czech Revolution by Russia and the Eastern European invasion did not attract his publication as the 1956 Hungarian repression had. Perhaps the war in Vietnam denied him moral ground to stand upon, and his recognition of the Russian domination of Eastern Europe made him less critical than before. But also by 1968 his publication production was slowing down; he no longer could work as he had earlier.

We postponed the seminar until the spring of 1969, but as his health declined that possibility receded. As we moved into the autumn of 1968 the realization that he would not be coming back to teach slowly dawned in his letters.

Yale Hill
Stockbridge, Massachusetts 01262
Oct 24

Dear Ronald:

On my doctor's advice I wrote to President Bennett yesterday, to inform him that the doctor doubts my ability to make the trip to NYC in the aftermath of the coronary thrombosis. He will give his verdict in November, but I thought it wise to give Union advance notice.

I dread the New England winter, and if I must stay here I want you to know that I would miss most my talks with you and my seminar in which you kindly offered once more to help, though I have my doubts whether your increased duties would again make our partnership possible.

To tell you the truth, my weakness is such that even an hour's seminar would prove too much. In short I am an old has-been ready for the pasture.

I neglected to write you in my enthusiastic letter about your "Election Issues" that I was pleased that you included my essay on the Negro minority. I owe you so much for many things.

Affectionately yours
Reinbuhr

P.S. from U.M.N.

Dr. sensed as we have done (we—the nurses, friends, etc.) that R. was (unconsciously) apprehensive about any return to N. York. Who would want to return to N. York?? So we proceed on the supposition that we might stay here—only "might."

So—we shall see. He is doing quite well, but progress is slow. Trying to seal this letter, he stood up and fell over—plonk—on the floor. Luckily I was nearby & the remarkable nurse, but it shows we cannot leave him—unwatched. (Mrs. Burrington is off on a short holiday—which means she is going to let a daughter or son go away so she will baby sit!!)[9]

9. Letter to Ronald Stone from Reinhold Niebuhr (Oct. 24, 1968). Original in Niebuhr Papers, Library of Congress.

Yale Hill
Stockbridge, Massachusetts
November 8, 1968

Dear Ron:

Thank you so much for your letter. Meanwhile, the doctor raises some questions about whether I will have enough strength to go down to New York or to teach that seminar, so I am afraid that my relationship with the Seminary and to you will be minimal. I regret this very much since my attraction in New York is chiefly my relationship to you, and I am afraid that even if I should be able to come to New York, your main duties will prevent you from being my valued assistant.

In regard to the offer (Sic.) from Yale Divinity School, I am afraid I have an egoistic reason for saying that I would quite understand it if you were favorable to this offer providing they gave you a very good course to teach. As one who was on the original committee to set up an undergraduate religion department at Columbia, I realize the Columbia department is not ideal as it has been messed up by Bishop Pike when he was Dean of the Chapel and insisted on being the Head the Department despite the fact that our Committee warned against this. Other personalities messed it up even more. Perhaps my loyalty to my alma mater rather than my loyalty to my position at Union persuades me to have this favorable attitude toward the invitation from Yale.

Yours affectionately
Reinbuhr[10]

10. Letter to Ronald Stone from Reinhold Niebuhr (Nov. 8, 1968). Original in Niebuhr Papers, Library of Congress. He had misunderstood the situation regarding Yale Divinity School. I visited there because Jim Gustafson wanted me to join the school after Joseph Hough had opted to remain in Claremont (the other position I visited that year to possibly replace Professor Hough). At Yale, it was the rainy post–election day victory of Nixon. My interests in teaching political ethics and international relations ethics were not exactly the school's needs, as David Little was teaching in those fields. The dean at Yale, Bob Johnson, forwarded my interest in moving from Columbia to Pittsburgh Theological Seminary, which soon made me an irresistible offer where I could teach my special subjects and also have plenty of time to write and travel. Ironically, both Niebuhrs opposed the move to Pittsburgh. The move gave me the time I needed to write from my dissertation my first book on Reinhold and to offer courses on his thought while developing as a scholar-writer.

13.

Democracy, 1969

> Somebody ought to quote Aristotle on the standards of just war. One of the standards of a just war is that it must have a good prospect of success. This is very cynical, but the Vietnam War failed to meet the test, and second, the means must be proportional to the ends. Well, the means were not proportional to the ends, either in blood or in money in Vietnam.

By 1969, Niebuhr was faltering. Still, he could work on a limited schedule and there were significant publications. We had prioritized the publication of his last two books. Originally we assumed *The Democratic Experience* would publish in 1968, and *Faith and Politics* in 1969, but the pace of the publishers reversed the plan and *Faith and Politics* appeared first, in 1968. Significantly then, his final book was on the theory and practice of democracy and its relevance for the world. However, the volume on democracy is taken from his 1961 lectures from Harvard. Paul Sigmund, the coauthor, was coteacher and master of the house in which the Niebuhrs resided during the academic year. Reinhold repeated the lectures at Princeton in 1962 and at Barnard College in 1963.

Beyond the book, his essay "The King's Chapel and the King's Court" was one of his more significant contributions of his last years. Our interview, "An Interview with Reinhold Niebuhr," was the last interview published in his later years, and it covered the topics we had discussed over two years of walks on Riverside Drive. The walks had been largely dialogues on politics and political philosophy. He usually started the conversation with a question about what I thought concerning a particular question like the developments in apartheid or a relevant political problem. The late reflections in the series "How My Mind Has Changed" evince his mellowed ecumenical spirit.

THE DEMOCRATIC EXPERIENCE

The argument of the book is based on a realistic assessment of democracy as it emerged in North Atlantic civilization based on national unity, individualism, and the need for conciliatory governments to balance internal forces. Given its success in Western Europe, its future relevance to developing nations was examined.[1]

The first half of the book repeated Niebuhr's themes and revised some prepublished chapters. The second half of the book contains introductory sentences by Niebuhr in most chapters, but it largely represents Sigmund's writing from his knowledge of developing nations. The final chapter, "A Review of the Literature," is by Sigmund.

The opening chapter on the utopian illusions of Communism and democracy had been published before, and it was a standard theme in previous writing of Niebuhr. The utilization of the earlier elections meant that the chapter failed to take seriously enough the cynicism of the Nixon-Kissinger administration or the idealism-moralism of the student protests.

The argument in brief was that the Marxist illusions of the monolithic power of the economic production system neglected to provide an adequate account of ideological and political power factors. Their vision of the free-prosperous person in a socialist system was utopian. The bourgeoisie illusions of individual freedom to the neglect of social and governmental reality were also illusions that needed correction. The social-historical realities were more influential factors than either theory recognized. The authors hoped to maintain democratic strength without illusions. With Churchill, they understood the argument for democracy as inadequate but better than the alternatives. Democracy itself was threatened in the tragic year 1968 in the losses of Martin Luther King Jr., Robert Kennedy, the soldiers in Vietnam, and the casualties of the burning American cities. Niebuhr was saddened by threats to democracy in America, and his sober book about its prospects was relevant to the late 1960s.

The second chapter briefly analyzed how the late emergence of the nation-state could overcome diversities in race, language, and religion to achieve government out of which democracy could eventually arise. All of these factors, more organic than rational, could tear nation-states apart or prevent their development.

National unity needed, in their view, to precede democracy, and

1. Reinhold Niebuhr and Paul Sigmund, *The Democratic Experience: Past and Prospects* (New York: Prager, 1969), 5–6.

many of the new states lacked national unity. A united India was impossible due to religious factors, and thus Pakistan was established. Unity in Belgium was difficult, and in Nigeria or the Congo it could only be tenuously achieved through armed force. So pluralism in important organic factors made democratic government difficult to achieve. Even in Europe it was only slowly achieved through force and compromise. Furthermore it was unable to achieve racial or social justice in the United States. In Europe, democracy emerged and collapsed due to depression and war. Its emerging strength in India and Japan had depended upon British or American occupation.

Niebuhr used class analysis in the chapter on the impact of industrialization upon democracy. He noted the interplay of four classes: the landed aristocracy, the industrial owners, the working class, and the people of the soil as peasants or free yeomen. He faulted Karl Marx[2] for focusing too much on the Second Republic of France, which Niebuhr regarded as a fraudulent republic that soon gave way to the second Bonaparte empire. Niebuhr based his work on the interaction of the classes in England and America to show the slow progress toward democracy. The development in England from feudalism through the Reform Acts of 1832, 1867, and 1895 conceded the right to broaden suffrage and to permit industrial organization of the workers. The more consistent developments in America's dependence on John Locke moved toward universal suffrage earlier but postponed the right for the workers to organize. Both Marx and Trotsky's predictions of industrial revolution by the workers were overcome by the broadening of democracy and the slower workers' organization.

The United States under the influence of individualism, without an aristocratic sense of social solidarity, was beset by Calvinist religious individualism mixed with social Darwinism to postpone collective bargaining until the Depression and the New Deal. The achievement of partial social justice was due to a government recognized as legitimate and from moral development in the ethos of a country.

In the struggle over the interpretation of Niebuhr's democratic theory it is worth noting that while class analysis is joined to complex historical explanation, there is no reliance on Edmund Burke. More credit is given to evolutionary socialism joining with religious socialism to push Britain toward social justice, and to various strands of the labor movement in the United States.

The chapter on Italian and German democracy flows from Niebuhr's previous writing and a couple of standard historians, without entering

2. Niebuhr and Sigmund, *The Democratic Experience*, 30.

into detailed analysis of the historians of the two countries. Both are cases of unification, revolution, some overcoming of aristocracy, and emerging democracies with differing political organizations. The democracy in both was killed by Nazism and fascism, creating fertile ground for renewed Catholic and Socialist parties to reorganize democracy after their defeat in war led by American influence. The American pressure in both cases seems more heavy-handed to me than Niebuhr and Sigmund detail. The democratic socialism that Niebuhr preferred at the end of the war was compromised by contending social forces in both countries. The welfare state of Germany was successful by the time of the book's publication, and the Italian situation has improved in the years following 1969.

The modern history of each state indicates the contingency and precariousness of democracy and the need of democratic interests to use force to preserve it in difficult times. More than a democratic constitution is required to maintain democracy in times of stress. Catholicism's adjustment to democracy has been a vital force in its development in both Germany and Italy despite its earlier Concordats with Nazis and fascists.

Even in Western Europe, democracy has been unstable. The authors summed up its Western history by noting: "Three constant prerequisites of free government":[3] (1) Unity and solidarity of a geographically defined community; (2) Appreciation of the individual worth of each person possessing rights; (3) Enough harmony and belief in a system based on balances of power adequate to maintain the governing structure. The authors recognized that democratic governments may suffer from instability and become tyrannical or authoritarian. The exact form of democracy depends upon the historical contingencies of particular societies.

These conditions are further dependent upon the competence of ruling elites and the degree of literacy among the citizens. The relative freedom of the individual in Western society depended upon the historical contingencies of Western history and eventually upon the myth that the people consented to be governed democratically. Individualism, which may in combination with other ideas be neglectful of social justice, has its own value. It recognizes the need of the citizenry for veto power over the acts of the rulers. Alternative systems of meaning to the ideology of the rulers must be respected. Culture maintains integrity beyond the contingencies of ruling groups.[4] Democracy preserving the above values

3. Niebuhr and Sigmund, *The Democratic Experience*.

4. Niebuhr and Sigmund, *The Democratic Experience*, 81.

depends upon a balance of power more than it does upon reason. Different groups compete for their own interests, and a democratic structure guarantees that the competition can proceed without too much violence or the overthrow of an approximation of social justice. Niebuhr argued that political legitimacy in the Western world depends upon more than order. The relevant actors must be persuaded that policies are promoting welfare and social justice.

Industrialization reinforced undue power among successful owners of industry until government and organized labor power could establish a strong middle and working class. The increased power of the wealthy managers and owners under globalization and technological development upset the balance in the West. Still, while Niebuhr's lectures were being heard and refined by Sigmund, the full effects of globalization, the information age, and robotics were not perceived. The increased power of industrial managers was seen as dislodging owners from control, to the benefit of the managerial class. However, they did not see the resurgence of the oligarchs to power as understood by analysts in the twenty-first century. Niebuhr believed a tolerable social justice had been achieved in the years between 1952 and 1960. Democratic institutions, combined with union power, achieved a rough justice of the kind he had struggled for since the 1920s. That postwar prosperity for workers was destined to be short-lived, as new forces increased the power of the oligarchs.

The second half of the book focused on the unsure future of democratic governments in Africa, the Middle East, Asia, and Latin America. Their histories were so unlike the North Atlantic community that the Western models should not be expected to be replicated. On the other hand, the democratic ideal was very attractive. Often the forms of democracy would be inhabited by authoritarian governments. In the long run the authors thought democracy might prove as likely to encourage economic development as one-party governments so popular in Africa. Military-led governments that alternated with more democratic forms were common in Latin America. Cheered by the possibilities of democracy in India, as led by the Congress Party and the Nehru dynasty, they remained dubious about democracy in the large nations of Indonesia, Pakistan, and China.

Their negative judgments about democracy in Vietnam directly refuted the necessity of pursuing the war for its sake. Their whole philosophy and survey of the world made fighting for democracy in Asia a nearly impossible goal.

Still, given the failures of Communism economically and authoritarian government's record on social justice, the prospects for development toward democracy were not impossible in Africa. Fifty years later the future of Africa under climate change and population surge seems even less certain.

The Middle East was not moving toward democracy. The possibilities for democratic government in Latin America were higher than elsewhere. The ideal of democracy had a relevance to developing countries in Asia, and its influence could grow if the ideal were realized more in Western society. The call in Asia seemed to be more for efficient, honest government, and social justice rather than the liberal, democratic forms of government. The authors concluded that even in the West the ideal of democracy was more often articulated than achieved. Here in his last book Niebuhr was using the dichotomy of the ideal and the real that had characterized his first work forty years earlier. The power of the real to resist the ideal was now more pronounced.

THE 1969 INTERVIEW

Relations between Reinhold and the editors of *Christianity and Crisis* were strained in 1969. I was more impressed with his general wisdom and perspective on foreign policy than was the editorial staff. I was happy to interview him in his home in Stockbridge on foreign policy.[5]

Most of my questions were not new to him. We had been discussing foreign policy issues for almost three years, but he was never without surprising answers and insights. His eyes twinkled, and his good humor showed through his pain. There was still a very strong critique of the president to appear later in his former journal. Expecting Nixon, at this date, to resolve the Vietnam War, his thought moved beyond the Cold War to the management of nuclear weapons and terror with the Soviet Union.

Professor Niebuhr, in the post–World War II planning of the State Department Policy Planning Staff with which you had some connection, two emphases were American responsibility for world order and the containment of Communism. Are those emphases valid today?

The changes since 1947 in Communism and the proper American response to it have been dramatic. Rather than containing Russia we are now seeking to maintain a precarious nuclear peace. By the way, I was only

5. Ronald Stone, "An Interview with Reinhold Niebuhr," *Christianity and Crisis* 29, no. 4 (Mar. 17, 1969): 48–52. The interview here is complete except for a few paragraphs that repeated material available elsewhere in the chapter, and one paragraph inserted with permission by his son is also dropped.

on an advisory committee of the Policy Planning Staff of the State Department and didn't play any significant part. It was the chairman of that group, George Kennan, who first formulated the policy of containment of Communism in the famous Mr. X article in *Foreign Affairs* (July 1947), but I think we've all followed him in shifting subtly from the containment of Communism to the prevention of a nuclear war. This is the change that history has wrought, so that Kennan would be the first one now to disavow any simple containment of Communism.

Has the idea of American responsibility for world order become a dangerous symbol?

Well, it can be a dangerous symbol if you think that we are one superpower with superiority in nuclear weaponry, which is the significance of a superpower today. We don't have responsibility for world order except in partnership. We and the Russians together have the responsibility for world order in the sense of maintaining a precarious nuclear peace.

Of course, American responsibility for world order is also a danger if it is taken to mean, as some have interpreted it, a responsibility to impose an American order on the world.

Is the present disenchantment of the intellectual community with US foreign policy due to the debacle of Vietnam or to a more general failure?

I would say the debacle of Vietnam is the ultimate symbol of the general failure. For instance, the involvement in Vietnam was motivated by a utopian idea of democracy and freedom for the whole world and by a simple anti-Communism. The anti-Communism lost its credibility in Southeast Asia when it became clear that China and Russia were more rivals than allies. The Chinese were real revolutionaries whereas the Russians did not want to risk major international conflict. The Russians wanted to maintain their new technocracy. The argument that the US presence in Southeast Asia was to protect Asians from China was weakened by the inability of the Chinese to assist their comrades in Indonesia. The Communists had tried to have a *coup d'état* in Indonesia under Sukarno and they were absolutely beaten. China was unable to intervene to save the Communists from the tragic blood bath that destroyed them. So our mistake in Vietnam was the symbol of our stupidity as one of the two hegemonic nations of the world.

How long should Americans grant the new Administration the benefit of the doubt and refrain from the level of criticism that routed the Johnson administration?

Well, that's an interesting question. How long should we give them the benefit of the doubt? If you make a big mistake, and I think this was a tragic mistake in Vietnam, only an opposition party can correct the mistake. The party that originally made the mistake wants what it now calls an honorable peace, i.e., partly a peace of prestige and partly a peace that will do justice to the tremendous treasures of blood and money that were spent. It now seems apparent that this peace can never be effected without a united front with the Communists and with terrorist Communists at that. So the peace that we'll desire will result in a Communist united Vietnam. If the Democratic Party under Johnson or under Humphrey would have accepted that peace, it would be subject to impeachment. The only possibility (and this is the virtue of the alteration of politics) is that the Republican Party must say, "This is a damned peace, but the Democrats got us into this, and we have promised to get you out of it." So I would say in foreign policy we've got to give the Nixon Administration a chance to accept the peace, honorable or not. . . .

It's rather strange, also, isn't it, to posit that the peace of the entire world hangs upon one particular conflict, as the president argues?

Oh, that's a very important question. The peace of the entire world doesn't hang on one particular conflict, although one might say that this conflict disturbed the potential partnership of the two superpowers, and the peace of the world depends upon that potential partnership. This partnership needs expression in the Middle East where our championing of Israel and the Russians' championing of the Arabs has created a potential source of great danger. The case of the antiballistic missiles (ABM) is also a matter of partnership between us and the Russians. We should have enough confidence in each other or if not confidence, at least concern for our self-interest that we could say we must stop this terrible military expenditure to meet the needs of our people for social justice.

Dr. Niebuhr, why should our country have made such a great mistake as to involve itself in this disastrous foreign policy in Vietnam?

Vietnam proves what many people, including George Kennan said: "Foreign policy is the Achilles' heel of democracy." You can show this in various ways. Democracy is social wisdom in domestic politics because the common man, who may not be as wise as the representative, is wise enough to know that his shoe pinches him: and he knows something is wrong because the shoe pinches him even though he is not the cobbler. But in foreign policy, who is to represent the soldiers, and the Vietnamese and the foreign peoples? Who, by the way, in foreign aid is to represent their needs? The foreign policy of England was on the whole consistent because it was relatively independent of the House of Commons or because shoes were not pinched as A.D. Lindsay has reminded us in his book, *The Modern Democratic State.*

The voters did not have a conception of the absolute corruption in Vietnam. We had made the mistake of being residuary legatee of the French empire. South Vietnam was incapable culturally of either integral nationhood or democracy. Now the common man cannot know this. But one can say, "Why the devil didn't some of our leaders, some of our generals, some of our ambassadors, know this?" Then, we have another problem: what about the people who did know? After the leader of the nation had made up his mind that he was not going to be the first president to lose a war, many men in his Administration who knew better were silent.

An English friend of ours says the trouble with american politics is that nobody in an administration ever resigns over questions of policy. McNamara did not really believe in the bombing of North Vietnam. He believed that we ought to have land reform in South Vietnam, not bomb North Vietnam. We don't know exactly why, but we do know that somehow or other McNamara was kicked upstairs into the World Bank. These are mysteries that only history will divulge. We know there were other cabinet ministers that were not directly involved who privately expressed their dissent and supposedly were informed that if they would resign, this would not be made an issue. Now there's a whole series of these people.

Democracy depends upon a certain degree of honesty of our representatives. And we have to ask ourselves the question, did they all shade their honesty too much? With the exception of the students and certain obvious and outstanding critics, both academic and religious, many ask the question, did we criticize the war rigorously enough?

And incidentally, somebody ought to quote Aristotle on the standards of the just war. One of the standards of a just war is that it must have a good prospect of success. This is very cynical, but the Vietnam War failed to meet this test. And second, the means must be proportional to the ends. Well, the means were not proportionate to the ends, either in blood or in money in Vietnam . . .

You are generally thought of as the father of Christian realism. To what extent do you think your political thought is applicable to the needs of the revolutionaries in Latin America and also in Southern Africa?

Realism is applicable if you admit that justice, particularly collective justice in any society, depends not on pure love or on pure self-sacrifice but upon equilibrium of power and perhaps on a conflict of power. Now realism emphasizes justice through either conflict or equilibrium because of the perpetual character of human self-interest, particularly collective self-interest. That is the basis of all realism. We've had this long history of realism, Christian and non-Christian, and it's an interesting thing to me that many of my non-Christian realist friends like Hans Morgenthau were particularly anxious to say that they have agreed with me though they did not share my "theological convictions."

The fact was, and this was my great offense, my theological convictions to them were positively irrelevant. I used the doctrine of original sin as a symbol of the perpetual, universal character of self-interest. Others in my generation, such as T. S. Eliot, for example, likewise had emphasized the same orthodox symbol over against the liberal rationalism of the eighteenth century. I thought in my Gifford Lectures that I had made the doctrine of original sin acceptable both by disavowing the historicity of the garden of Eden story and by disavowing Augustine's rather horrible doctrine of the transmission of original sin through the sexual lust in the act of procreation. I thought this cleansed the doctrine for the modern mind, as well as making it relevant, but it didn't.

Intellectual life as well as political life uses all kinds of symbols and myths, and for good and bad reasons people accept or reject these symbols and myths. In other words, I think that I was right in my realism, and in my theology, but wrong in my pedagogy.

That's quite an admission for a professor to make.

I wouldn't say so. Why should professors be so proud? Professors are necessarily interpreters and in their interpretations they may fail.

Do revolutionaries necessarily require a certain number of illusions that realism might expose and thereby stifle revolutionary fervor?

All revolutionaries have utopian illusions, but nonrevolutionary political leaders also have utopian illusions. Here's our new president, Mr. Nixon, in his recent inaugural address. He talked about the dark night of injustice and war, but thanked God for the new day. The new day was in him. Now the new day may be peace in Vietnam, but it takes a lot to have a new day. The idea of illusion in political conflict is very interesting. Here was FDR who was certainly no utopian, but you remember he had the Four Freedoms. Two were the classical freedoms, the freedom of thought and the freedom of religion. The other two were absolutely utopian: freedom from want and freedom from fear, not only here but in the whole world. And this was stated at the precise moment when we were at the beginning of a nuclear age.

There is much current discussion of the relevance of eschatology to Christian ethics. How useful is it for Christian ethics to concern itself with or to rest its methodology upon a problem which admittedly we have no way of resolving?

Well, I wouldn't say admittedly no way of resolving. I would quote Browning, "Ah, but a man's reach should exceed his grasp, or what's a heaven for?" Let us say that all human aspirations transcend the possibilities of history. So the messianic prophets assumed that history could be good only if it rested in a transformed nature—the lion will lie down with the lamb. And you would say that most modern utopianism has neglected this prophetic insight, that a heaven on earth is partly dependent upon a transformed nature.

No, I think that these eschatological notions, provided we don't take them too literally, ought to be discussed in Christian pulpits and in Christian theology in terms of the character of human nature itself. Because man is on the one hand a creature of nature and a creature of history, which he has created above nature. On the other hand he has an additional quality of self-transcendence which transcends the whole of the historical process. This is, I think, the mystery and the meaning of the Christian faith in regard to all these social and ethical problems.

He wrote short notes after the interview:

Yale Hill
Stockbridge, Massachusetts 01262
Feb. 28

Dear Ronald:

Thank you so much for your letter. I am glad the revised copy of our interview proved satisfactory. . . . We will split the typing fee only in case my royalties [from *Faith and Politics*] are less than your thousand bucks. OK?

We will be delighted with a visit from you on any project which you and I dream up. We crave your company. It proved right not to go back to NYC. New complications, Neuritis, plus arthritis have laid me low or made me weak. But I am not dying.

Affectionately yours,
Reinbuhr[6]

Yale Hill
Stockbridge, Massachusetts 01262
March 13

Dear Ronald:

I am beholden to you for so many things; but this time for your work and trip for that interview. I hope you are satisfied with it. Our family and friends are highly satisfied.

I have a residual modesty which makes me embarrassed by that extravagant introduction. I am not that important in the scheme of things.

Ursula reports a delightful visit with you [in New York]. Thanks for carting off some of those books.

I am so sorry about your experience with that drug-addicted student. I confess that this student generation baffles me completely; as much as the policies of the new President who was supposed to stop the war. It seems now

6. Letter to Ronald Stone from Reinhold Niebuhr (Feb. 28, 1969). Original in Niebuhr Papers, Library of Congress. The signatures on the letters reflect the hastily scrawled actual spellings on the letters, though most were intended to represent Reiniebuhr.

that we have chosen a Nixon war for a Johnson war. So, political providence gradually unfolds its ambiguous details.

With love from both of us to you both,

Yours ever Rienie

R. seemed very lively or relaxed when I got back (Perhaps I should disappear more often?) I gather he had a bad day.[7]

"THE KING'S CHAPEL AND THE KING'S COURT"

While we were producing the interview with Reinhold, Ursula told me frankly how disappointed she was that I was accepting the offer for associate professorship at Pittsburgh Theological Seminary. Her concerns were for me as well as they were for my support for Reinhold. The reasons I gave for moving were not strong enough to convince her. The academic community at Union and Columbia was important for me. She knew better than I how important a fine academic community could be to one's thinking and vocation. While recording the interview in their home a phone call reached me from Pittsburgh Seminary. She notified me that it was for me by saying: "Mammon's calling, Ron." She had told me of the marital counseling she and Reinhold had done for one of their students, who later was one of my professors and a world-famous theologian, by 1969. Still, I was too guilty and vulnerable to discuss marital reasons for moving to Pittsburgh. By the summer of 1969, we had all accepted my moving to Pittsburgh after finishing the Columbia University summer school. Reinhold responded to my critique of *The Democratic Experience* in May and noted the end of our working directly together.

7. Letter (Mar. 13, 1969). With note from Ursula Niebuhr.

Yale Hill
Stockbridge Massachusetts
May 27, 1969

Dear Ronald:

Thank you so much for your letter. You are right: in the light of Vietnam my confidence in the subjection of military to political authority is too simple;

Paul Sigmund, of course, worked with my outline and general concepts when my health prevented me from finishing the book. But he was more expert in the non-European cultures than I; and I thought he did a splendid job in keeping up with the catastrophic changes in Asia, Africa, and the Middle East.

Your acquisition of a house in Pittsburgh means the finality of your separation from UTS. So we will both be separated from our original habitat. I thank God for our partnership.

My health is not too good. The last stroke did me much damage. Even writing a letter exhausts me. I wonder whether I will ever write another article. But I had a good run for my money before the Nunc Dimitis sets in.

Love from us both to you both,

Affectionately yours,
Reinbuhr

Reinhold sent me a copy, it appears to be the original, of "The King's Chapel and the King's Court," in July. It had a few minor editorial marks and some spelling corrections by Ursula. Reinhold's one-handed typing usually produced very rough manuscripts. He was simply sharing it; he did not ask for any editorial corrections or comments, which I had occasionally provided for other manuscripts. I think he was rather proud of it. A week later he wrote me again:

Yale Hill
Stockbridge, Mass 01262
July 17

Dear Ronald:

Thank you so much for sending me the reviews of our book. I had seen Blanshard's Times review; and was not surprised by the criticism of that consistent rationalist. But all the criticisms of the other reviews were helpful and instructive.

We so enjoyed yours and Joan's visit. I told Ursula all about the good gossip we had about many problems and persons.

Ursula arrived back last week from Jerusalem and her relatives and friends in England.a She was brimming with news and greetings from some of my friends on the commission.

President Bennett called up with Wayne Cowan about the Nixon Ed. "The King's Chapel and the King's Court." Both seemed pleased with it. Ursula did her usual editing job, clarifying my obscure phrases.

Our love to Joan, Ursula wishes you both well in Pittsburgh.

Affectionately yours
Rhini[8]

Ursula added three notes as she usually appended a message or two to Reinhold's letters to me:

a) Jerusalem is marvelous, I want to go & live there; b) No—I hardly did anything—The piece is absolutely his & Wayne hardly changed a thing. I was very pleased—with R's state of mind and health. c) There is a pro-Arab Biblical man Lapp?—at you place. ??!?

The significance of Ursula's point "b" is that the essay was later taken as evidence that Ursula should have been recognized as coauthor of the piece by Rebekah Miles in "Was Ursula Niebuhr Reinhold's Coauthor?"[9] I sent a copy of Ursula's denying even editorship to Dr. Miles, but so far as I can determine this demure by Ursula has not entered Miles's scholarship. The case to make Ursula coauthor of this piece is far from proven. What is well known among Niebuhr scholars is that Ursula had

8. Letter (July 17, 1969).

9. Rebekah Miles, "Was Ursula Niebuhr Reinhold's Coauthor?," *The Christian Century* 129, no. 2 (Jan. 25, 2012): 30–33.

various plans to write about her husband. Reinhold said that she had hoped to produce a posthumous biography. That explains the bitterness Ursula directed toward June Bingham over her biography. Years later she hoped to produce a book of their conversations, and she began recording conversations between her husband and herself for this project. The recording transcripts for this project are in the Niebuhr papers in the Library of Congress as Miles notes. I wish the project had been brought to culmination and the conversations published. One of those transcripts contains phrases that also appear in the essay "The King's Chapel." I'm not surprised that Reinhold used portions of that transcript to type the essay he published. The transcript was joint property, and Ursula was responsible for placing both the transcript and "The King's Chapel" in the papers. I think a better explanation given Ursula's denial that she was responsible for the essay is that Reinhold used that joint conversation when he wrote his own essay. So Ursula's denial of responsibility for the essay is true. The piece Dr. Miles refers to is only a page and a half long, double-spaced, and there is nothing in it by Ursula of significance used in the later essay except for possibly the title on established and disestablished churches. There are at least two examples where Reinhold and Ursula assumed joint responsibility for authorship. Both are in the *New York Times*. One denounces the war in Vietnam, and the other praises the work of their friend W. D. Davies as they review his major book, *The Setting of the Sermon on the Mount*. Reinhold would in his later years credit Davies's study for saving him from earlier misunderstandings of Jesus's perfectionism. Davies told me in 1969 at the Festival of the Gospels that he regarded "Reinhold Niebuhr as a Saint." So on at least two occasions they published jointly authored work and recorded it as such. This failed project of Ursula's to publish conversations with Reinhold was well taken, but it provides inadequate evidence for Miles's claim:

> This conversation makes it clear that they had a familiar pattern of working and writing together, and it points to her significant role as editing, and in this case, I believe, coauthor.[10]

Very early in her career she had published in journals edited by Reinhold under her own name. Much of this work was on liturgy for Christian social activists who were in Reinhold's organizations. My favorite picture of them is with Paul Tillich at a retreat for the Fellowship of Socialist Christians in the 1930s.[11] Her writing on their friendships with Auden

10. Miles, "Was Ursula Niebuhr Reinhold's Coauthor?," 31.

11. "Frontispiece" to Ronald H. Stone, *Politics and Faith: Reinhold Niebuhr and Paul Tillich*

and Heschel is among the most sensitive personal writing on their life together.

The power of the essay rests in Reinhold's incorporation of themes that were standard to his work. The need to keep contemporary politics at a distance from perennial religion was standard argument for one who often polemicized against the prayers at the inauguration, and who insisted on a rigorous separation of church and state. His contempt for Richard Nixon is clear in the essay. He had hoped the president would lead the United States out of the war, but instead he had directed it into more countries. He understood how presidents tried to capture religious culture to defend them. With Nixon's victory he warned his daughter, Elisabeth, that now she would have to learn just how bad it was to have a Republican administration. His text was taken from Amos and applied to the present as he had learned to do in a seminary research course with Samuel Press at Eden Seminary. His respect for Martin Luther King Jr. shows through in the essay. He dragged in Billy Graham, whom he had fought with over Kennedy's Catholicism in 1960. Hoover had led the FBI to harass Niebuhr since his service to Franklin D. Roosevelt on religious freedom. Now Niebuhr would compare him to the court priest, Amaziah, who defended the corrupt king from the prophetic critique of Amos. The one theme I assume came from Ursula, which was the title of the dialogue in the Washington Niebuhr papers, is that of established and disestablished religions. After he quit preaching, Niebuhr found more comfort in higher liturgical services than he had previously. This development and his preaching at Episcopal churches and worshipping at the Cathedral of St. John the Divine in New York City pointed to Ursula's influence. "The established and disestablished" sounds more like Ursula than Reinhold. In my presence they would sometimes discuss their preferences in services or churches. Reinhold would playfully refer to his denomination the United Church of Christ as "the one true church." Without the recorded dialogue between Reinhold and Ursula intended for other purposes, I cannot imagine Niebuhr scholars thinking this was not standard Reinhold writing, as Ursula seems to have indicated with her comment in her letter to me. In a letter from 1973 to her publisher, Ursula mentioned that in conversation with her husband she had contributed the titles of his books of *Moral Man and Immoral Society* and *The Nature and Destiny of Man.*[12]

The essay moved from Roger Williams and Thomas Jefferson's work

at Union Seminary in New York (Macon, GA: Mercer University Press, 2012). Contributed by Mutie Tillich Farris.

12. Letter from Ursula Niebuhr to Mr. Shopp (Sept. 16, 1973). Niebuhr Papers, Library of Congress.

to disestablish religion to Amos's critique of unjust government. He accused Nixon and Graham of trying to establish a religious cult of complacent religion that had no word of justice. Religious conformity and invitations to preach in the White House promote soothing words for the president, whereas even the rabbi from across Broadway from Union forgot himself and regarded President Nixon as the savior of the world. The individualist religion nurtured by the White House was silent on the war and on questions of nuclear weapons threatening humanity. Graham believed in addressing problems by individualist religious experiences without realizing how little race relations had been served by the most converted portion of the country, its southland. The Graham belief that individual conversions would produce morality seemed sadly inadequate to address the great moral questions of the 1960s. Reinhold deplored the absence of Martin Luther King's favorite text:

> I take no delight in your solemn assemblies. I hate and despise your feasts. . . . Take away the noise of your songs. To the melody of your harps I will not listen. Let justice roll down like waters, and righteousness as a mighty stream. (Amos 5:21–24)

But, he questioned whether King would have been invited if he had lived. Without mentioning the investigation of himself, he referred to the FBI investigating and attacking King. Then he concluded by attacking complacent religion and connecting J. Edgar Hoover, who had an unusual fear of religious critique, to Amaziah the protector of the unjust king.

Niebuhr was very aware of the dangers of relating theology and politics, or in this case sermons and the official White House chapel. But he waded into the fray. It was a very powerful indictment of the Vietnam War and its religious cover-up. I hope it will appear among whatever future collections of his occasional essays are published. Though recent biographers Richard Fox and Charles Brown mention the essay in the pages they devote to Niebuhr in the 1960s, recent collections of Niebuhr's writings have not included it yet. The United States still has a lot to learn from Reinhold Niebuhr on the relationship of worship to politics. We exchanged letters about the fray over the chapel. He wrote:

Yale Hill
Stockbridge, Massachusetts 01262
Sept. 5

Dear Ronald:

Thank you so much for your letter with the enclosed defense of me. I needed the defense because the converts of Billy Graham sent me hate mail by the bushel.

I am so glad you are immersed in union politics and that Joan is quite pleased with the pace of Pittsburgh.

The doctor now thinks my ulcers are chronic, so I suffer much pain and spend sleepless nights. But fortunately dear Ursula is patient as she has always been. Bless the Lord for loving wives.

When I wrote you the letter about the biographer Turnbull, I merely wanted to emphasize that he was a professional biographer, interested in my personality, but promised he would read all my books before he wrote a word. Scribner's did not "order!" the biography. Bill Savage, the publisher of all my books, merely suggested it in a letter of introduction.

Write me if you think we made a mistake. Our affectionate regards to Joan. We miss you very much.

With love, your ever
Reinibuhr[13]

A few days later, he celebrated in a letter to the *New York Times* the landing on the moon. He refused to equate it with a journey discovering for Europe a new continent. After all, the moon was barren and desolate and incomparable to the Americas. It was a great technological achievement. His reservations about celebrating it lay in the ambiguity of technology that had led Americans from the fields to the cities. Now the poor of the country huddled in the cities, which could not care for them. The black minority became increasing resistant to a society that failed to educate

13. Letter to Ronald Stone from Reinhold Niebuhr (Sept. 5, 1969). Niebuhr Papers, Library of Congress. In my own experience, a local Pittsburgh paper criticized Reinhold's piece in an editorial. The essay had ignited a debate in the country about the use of religion and its misuse in the country. A book was being prepared by Stephen Rose titled *Sermons Not Preached at the White House*, beginning with the essay. Nixon's staff was consulting the FBI report that Hoover had furnished to the White House. I responded to the editorial in a published letter that elicited about a dozen responses. Among the letters I received was one anonymous Christian suggesting I should be machine-gunned. I also received anti-Semitic diatribes, but it was my first Christian death threat.

them for the technological work and segregated them in failing neighborhoods. Even the necessary food to equip African Americans for full citizenship was lacking in the cities, which could not receive the aid they needed. "We are betraying our moral weakness in our very triumph in technology and economics."[14]

Niebuhr was distraught over the earlier occupation of the Columbia Campus by students led by the Students for Democratic Society. But the occupation of Union by students demanding reparations for earlier black servitude and other issues bothered him more fundamentally. He often reflected on these issues in terms taken from the radical calls for change of the 1930s. He would write publicly about it in 1970. He knew that I had opposed "takeovers," continuing to use my Columbia classroom and my Union office in 1968–69 while serving as assistant professor at Columbia and lecturer at Union.

Yale Hill
Stockbridge, Massachusetts 01262
May 17

Dear Ronald:

Thanks for your good letter. I confessed that I was completely dismayed when it was reported that radical students occupied the administration building to coerce the trustees to contribute hundreds of thousands of dollars toward the "Reparations" demanded by Foreman.

My old friend President Bennett joyously reported [the action] which the trustees took. It was I know the fruit of their generosity and the President's compassion, but much as I rejoiced at this positive result, I remain uneasy about the obvious fact that the radical students whatever their motives, will count one more victory by Castro-ite revolutionary tactics which exploits the uneasy conscience of faculty and students about racial and other injustice, the terrible, futile and now endless war in Viet Nam and the spiritual and moral emptiness of a culture which can boast only technical achievements and affluence.

I am an old man, conscious of the "generation gap." But I am cheered that in essentials a young Professor, Ronald Stone, agrees with me.

Affectionately yours
Reiniebuhr

14. Letter to the editor, *New York Times*, July 21, 1969, 7.

> R. is still very frail and not too well. This fall episode knocked out quite a bit, I fear, but his mind & voice is there. Elisabeth and Sam aged 2 years, 11 months are here for a brief weekend. Tony is too busy winding up a legal term; it was he who put Wolfson behind bars.[15]

RECONCILING WITH CATHOLICISM

The Christian Century's request for a contribution to its series "How My Mind Has Changed," inspired an essay on "Toward Intra-Christian Endeavors."[16] It was his third contribution to the series, with each essay a decade apart. He did not repeat changes since his previous essay in 1959. He had already published on those developments in *Man's Nature and His Communities* (1965). In the light of the disastrous anti-Communist war in Vietnam he backed off his criticism of Karl Barth's "Neutralism" regarding the suppression of the 1956 Hungarian Revolution. He also thought his anti-Catholicism of 1959 had been too strong. Now, given Vatican II, he called on both Protestantism and Catholicism to reform their negative attitudes toward human sexuality.

He particularly praised the Jesuits' reforming, liberal contributions to the church. He pointed out the Catholic critiques of Pope Paul VI's *Humanae Vitae.* The pope had tried to suppress the reports of his advisors while *The National Catholic Reporter* published the alternative reports. He affirmed Jesuit critiques of the pope's strong attempt to prohibit birth control. Sexuality was a human affair and not just an animal response for procreation. The humanity of it could lead to exploitation or to beautiful erotic love between trusting partners with human choices. Catholic women also joined in criticizing the encyclical's excesses.

The movements in the church for liberty permitted both Catholicism and Protestantism to be regarded as two branches of the same Christianity. Protestants could use more order and Catholics more liberty.

He went on to the main point of the essay—that both Protestants and Catholics need to affirm *eros* more fully than previously. *Eros* is intermingled with the *agape* of family life, and marriage should not be degraded as had both St. Paul and Martin Luther. He affirmed the superiority of the new Dutch Catechism recognizing the eros of conjugal union, which in Catholicism could be regarded as a sacrament. Here in his weakened health of old age he celebrated married eros and suggested that Chris-

15. Letter to Ronald Stone from Reinhold Niebuhr (May 17, 1969). Original in Niebuhr Papers, Library of Congress.

16. Reinhold Niebuhr, "Toward Intra-Christian Endeavors," *The Christian Century* 86, no. 53 (Dec. 31, 1969): 1662–67.

tianity needed to give up its negativity toward sexuality. By analogy he referred to the polemics of capitalists and socialists giving way to the newer dynamics of the modern welfare state. It was also characteristic of his most mature reflections that he referred to the mutual responsibility of Russia and the United States in maintaining the nuclear peace or détente.

Late in the first semester at Pittsburgh Theological Seminary, I overstated my disappointment in Pittsburgh in a letter to him. Now, I wonder if I was just missing him and friends. In any case I commented that the seminary was dull. He responded only with a brief, suggestive note. Ursula had more to say.

Yale Hill
Stockbridge, Massachusetts
Nov 12

Dear Ronald:

Thank you for your letter. I am sorry that you do not find the intellectual climate stimulating in Pittsburgh.

It would be a boon if you would return to Columbia and Union. Let me know whether a word from me to John Bennett would be of help.

Affectionately yours,
Reinie

P.S. Reinhold who is very frail, who has had many of those "little strokes," appreciated your note. Sorry Pittsburgh is dull. No place should be dull, yet theological and or religious institutions can be so dull. I have a theory that perhaps it is the Sin against the Holy Spirit. I had a very learned paper on the subject. Lots of endnotes and painful. 2nd Ecclesiastes: Despair and also the faith that Spirit = life—You might try a sermonette on it—but avoid pitfalls—esp: any leads from Vitalism—avoid all quotes from Bergson et al. Tillichisms—avoid like the devil. Romanticism—the very dangerous Nicene theology will be used vs. a (temporary) litmus test. Anyhow, one can vent one's resistance to Dullness this way. The Hymn to use is Veni Creator Spiritus in Latin—but print English esp. "Anoint and clean our soiled souls." What about no 2??

Love to you all![17]

17. Letter to Ronald Stone from Reinhold and Ursula Niebuhr (Nov. 12, 1969). Original in Niebuhr Papers, Library of Congress.

As 1968 concluded, the turbulent decade faded into the law-and-order administration of Richard Nixon and Spiro Agnew. The hopes of the new generation of John F. Kennedy had been broken. The Nixon administration would see the moon landing that Kennedy had initiated. The assassination of John F. Kennedy, Martin Luther King Jr., and Robert F. Kennedy released the rage of the Students for a Democratic Society, Black Muslims, college students, Chicago protestors, and groups of radicals who swung the country back to the right in Nixon's "Silent Majority" victory. The decade gave the country the music of Woodstock and new freedoms and heartaches with drugs and undisciplined sex. Underlying it all had been the My Lai atrocities of 1968 and the horror of the US destruction in Vietnam. It was less turbulent than the 1860s, which had erupted in civil war, but it marked and marred the republic in fundamental ways. It had been a decisive decade. Niebuhr would comment on it in the next year. Throughout the decade he had argued as he had in the 1940s for democracy and moderately progressive policies. His dual foci were on rights for the minority of black citizens and the avoidance of nuclear war. His support for Johnson and Humphrey's social policies was deeply consistent with his political philosophy, and Johnson's presidency was staffed by supporters of Niebuhr's thought inasmuch as they understood it. Kennedy too, not an expert on Niebuhr, had consulted him and was drawn to his realism. They failed to grasp his critique of their Vietnam commitments. On civil rights Humphrey had been the closest to grasping the urgency of the situation, but Vietnam ended his career too. The younger generation could not understand Niebuhr, and many faulted him for the war as they sought utopian solutions and radical politics.

Now enjoying our first Christmas in Pittsburgh, we heard from the Niebuhrs in Stockbridge with a note about expected death.

Yale Hill
Stockbridge, Massachusetts
Dec 27

Dear Ronald and Mrs. Stone:

Thank you so much for your Christmas gift of those luscious assorted cheeses. We enjoyed Christmas as we know you did. Our daughter Elisabeth Sifton gave birth on Dec. 20th so they could not be with us; but our son, Chris is wooing a charming young lady on Yale Hill. So he is with us as much as his romance will allow; and we have no quarrel with him since we don't approve of a long bachelorhood and very much approve, as a happily married couple does, of the "Honorable Estate" of matrimony.

We hope you will be again enjoying Union. John Bennett called up to say that he is retiring and will be teaching at the Pacific School of Religion. Thus all things change, except, thank God, old friends. We appreciate your friendship and partnership so dearly.

My health remains frail as I am 77 years old. "Time you old bogey man, will you not stay, will you not pitch your tent, just for one day?" But the longing for longevity of mortal man is one of the most foolish of dreams.

But fortunately that truth does not preclude the wish for a long and happy life, with its obvious promise of creative joy for both of you.

Happy New Year!

Affectionately yours,
Reiniebuhr

Your delightful & unexpected gift added to the extra occasions that holidays always bring of snacks and odd cups of coffee and tea or drinks. So they are going fast, the cheeses—I mean. All the best, especially a safe New Year . . .
Ursula[18]

18. Letter to Ronald and Joan Stone from Reinhold Niebuhr; note from Ursula Niebuhr (Dec. 27, 1969). Original in Niebuhr Papers, Library of Congress.

14.

Decline, 1970–71

> Nothing that is worth doing can be accomplished in a lifetime; therefore we must be saved by hope. Nothing which is true or beautiful or good makes complete sense in any immediate context of history; therefore we must be saved by faith. Nothing we do, however virtuous, can be accomplished alone. Therefore we must be saved by love.

Niebuhr was still cheered by visitors in his last year and a half, and he kept up a vital correspondence. His confinement to Stockbridge, of course, lessened the visitors and his contacts. I made a couple of trips, once with Bob Stivers. Reinhold wrote to John Bennett about our visit and our conversations. John had retired from the presidency and gone out to the Pacific School of Religion to teach. Reinhold's writing declined. Edward Long Jr. and Robert Handy published a *Festschrift* in honor of Bennett, but Niebuhr's short essay of five pages failed to add anything new to the distinguished authors of the rest of the volume. His praise for Bennett's fair, nonpolemical style and balanced judgments was accurate, but hardly novel for one with whom he had worked for so long.

Sentences warning about the ecological crisis and the need for a cleaner environment crept into his writing in these last few months. However, his memorandum of March 10, 1970 stressed a new priority. He sent a short memo to the Bicentennial Commission preparing for the 1976 celebration. Rather than encouraging them in self-satisfaction over America, he urged them to include addressing three problems in the American republic. The three were: the management of the nuclear weapons dangers; the winning of justice for African Americans, the correction of the age-old debt to these people; and the ecological crisis. He had not produced major arguments or essays on the ecological crisis, but his students particularly Roger Shinn, Paul Abrecht, and Robert Stivers were writing on the issues. A later student, Larry Rasmussen, would become an outstanding contributor to the theology of ecological issues.

We kept working on publications. He rejected one editor collecting essays and urged me to have nothing to do with him. He also wrote several times about a projected biography by a Mr. Turnbull whom Scribner's was negotiating with, and he asked me to cooperate with him. I was having trouble with Mr. Seaver of Braziller, as I only wanted to write an intellectual study of Niebuhr from my dissertation and the publisher was encouraging a much more intimate account, which, of course, I would not attempt. Before I broke with Braziller and turned to Abingdon Press, Reinhold wrote:

Yale Hill
Stockbridge, Massachusetts
May 30, 1971

Dear Ronald,

Thank you so much for your letter and your rather prodigious bibliography. If Seaver wants you to include biographical detail, perhaps on your visit to us in June, I could tell you something of my childhood—my father and mother and my education in Eden Theological Seminary, and, of course, Yale University.

Ursula is at the moment in Cambridge. We will be delighted to see you and Joan on the 6th or 7th of June. Perhaps you could phone Ursula about the most convenient hour for you and for us.

With affectionate regards, yours sincerely,

Reinbuhr

Was [away] for two days. Shall be for two days in New York. June 1–4, perhaps. Shall be delighted to see you next weekend. R. not too well. Rather weak & a bit distraught.

Love—U.M.N.

Niebuhr sent me an essay in the spring of 1970 titled the "Student Strike against War and Our National Self-Discovery." I responded, gently suggesting he not publish it, because his information on the student strikes was secondhand and often furnished by the older generation. He certainly had published enough against the war, and his writings on correcting injustices toward the black minority were sufficient without this piece coming down hard on extreme Black Power movements as they resorted to violence. On June 1, 1970, he sent the eleven-page essay to Daniel Schwarz, Sunday Editor of the *New York Times*. He summarized it as an analysis of the "student strike against the war in Indo-China." He contrasted the current protest to the rebellions of the 1930s, which in cooperation with a strong democracy resulted in the New Deal and the beginnings of the welfare state. He thought the violence in the current protests rendered them irrelevant to improving the current state of affairs in the American republic. He concluded: "I end with the rather negative conclusion that it is not a cure, but a symptom of the disease."[1]

He revised it in a shorter form and sent his essay "Indicting Two Generations" to *The New Leader*.[2] It was still too critical of the radical students as a whole. At least in *The New Leader* radical students would not read it and be further alienated from his type of thought. Of course, he was correct that the moralism, outrage, and political naïveté of the students and their allies had helped elect "Law and Order" Richard Nixon and Spiro Agnew. He compared the students to the laboring-class radicals of the 1930s, finding them to be quite different. Whether they were Black Panthers or Students for a Democratic Society, he regarded their violence as futile, growing out of their rage rather than out of political maturity. He thought their disparate grievances probably grew out of "moral uneasiness" with the culture. He came down particularly hard on the violence associated with both groups. Obviously, bombings, lead pipes, bank robberies, and ejections of students and administrations from college buildings were not politically useful, but neither were they "Stalinist" nor "Maoist." He had not talked with the radicals, and I'm certain he had not discussed the occupation of Union Theological Seminary with the students there. The students he had known well were either active politically or just studying for their vocations. The essay I had seen and advised against had much more critique of the older generation than the version published in the magazine. It had possessed more balance. However, he had been criticizing the establishment's racism and militarism for so long that either he or more likely the editors excised that part of the essay for *The New Leader*. Some of the indictment of the older

1. Reinhold Niebuhr, "John Coleman Bennett: Theologian, Churchman, and Educator," in *Theology and Church in Time of Change*, ed. Edward Leroy Long Jr. and Robert T. Handy (Philadelphia: Westminster, 1970), 233–36.

2. Letter to Daniel Schwarz from Reinhold Niebuhr (June 1, 1970) in author's possession. "The Student Strike against War and Our National Self-Discovery," unpublished manuscript in author's possession.

generation's policies appeared in *Christianity and Crisis* the same year as "The Presidency and the Irony of American History."[3]

"THE PRESIDENCY AND THE IRONY OF AMERICAN HISTORY"

Presidential decisions on the war in Vietnam led Niebuhr to conclude that the president was too strong. If the president succumbed to pride of power and assumed the righteousness of his own policies, it was nearly impossible to dislodge him from unwanted wars. "Our elected monarchs have become despots." The words of the president tended toward deification. Our abundance of wealth granted the president the power to hang onto an undeclared, unwinnable war. By 1970, the analyst and defender of democracy saw the failure in the system of presidential monarchy in foreign policy. The writers of the Constitution had been wise to keep the power of war making shared with Senate. But now, even the Supreme Court supported the president in an undeclared war and enforced the draft in its decision.

In his last essay for *Christianity and Crisis* he recognized more readily than in *The Democratic Experience* the dangers of strong presidencies to democratic decision making. Still, he noted how charismatic presidents like De Gaulle and F. D. Roosevelt had led their nations to responsible action. In the De Gaulle case it had been, at last, prudent withdrawal from unwinnable conflicts that won praise. The themes of irony, tragedy, fortune, pride, and failed presidential leadership could have balanced the "Indictment of Two-Generations" essay by really indicting the war makers as well as irresponsible actions in protest.

Niebuhr's last essay was published in 1971.[4] It was his longest work on religious toleration. By the time of its publication in 1971 it had been heavily edited, interjecting formal discussions, biblical quotations, and words that were not natural to Reinhold. In its very length it reveals that it was not produced solely by him in these last years when he was only capable of much shorter pieces. Previous pieces on Catholicism and Judaism were much more personal, anecdotal, and immediately historically relevant to Vatican Councils and the fate of Israel in its wars and nationhood.[5] Still, it represents his thought in these later years and

3. Reinhold Niebuhr, "Indicting Two Generations," *The New Leader* 53, no. 14 (Oct. 5, 1970): 13–14.

4. Reinhold Niebuhr, "The Presidency and the Irony of American History," *Christianity and Crisis* 30, no. 6 (Apr. 13, 1970): 70–72.

5. Reinhold Niebuhr, "Mission and Opportunity: Religion in a Pluralistic Culture," in *Social*

bears suggestions of an anamnesis who knew his thought intimately. Along with the earlier project on "Religious Freedom" undertaken for Franklin D. Roosevelt, the books on democracy and the essays on equality and freedom, it presents a complete political philosophy for American understanding. The three great religions, recognized at the time, all evolved from particular historical consciousness that gave them their particular shapes. They were particularly apt at cooperating on most moral issues to inform America of its moral responsibilities. They had non-negotiable aspects from their respective histories. Jews could not be expected to accept the Christological formulations of the major faith. The symbol of a suffering messiah was strange to most of Judaism, and Niebuhr regarded the symbol of a future messianic age as impossible. Christianity's universal claims were in tension with the Jewish particularity of a national religion. Protestants would never accept the pope and papal claims, and Catholics could not appreciate Protestant pluralism and disunity.

His final short essay in the *New York Times*[6] returned to a standard Niebuhr theme of criticizing the American president for self-righteousness. His target was Richard Nixon, who had pretended the American Armada in the Mediterranean Sea was a major force for peace in the world. He pled for an end to American pretenses of innocence and spelled out the three major issues of ecological destruction, the threat of nuclear war, and our unfulfilled promises to the black minority. Between the critique of the president and his priorities for action he surveyed a few of the great American presidents who had also repeated the myths of American superiority and innocence.[7] By this point in his illness and pain, he was not writing new material, but publishing on older themes for political purposes in criticizing President Nixon. Often his political-historical essays had been intended to shape the national thinking or national myth. He continued to work with the strength he could muster.

His final letter to me, typed by another hand, was written on April 27th in response to a letter I had mailed from the Washington, DC, jail:

Responsibility in an Age of Revolution, ed. Louis Finkelstein (New York: Jewish Theological Seminary, 1971), 177–211. Note from Ursula Niebuhr on the copy she sent me: "Asked for in 1966, written in bits and snatches, 1967 & declined in 1967, held by Rabbi Finkelstein until 1970, published in 1971." There is high internal evidence of Ursula's contribution to the essay.

6. Reinhold Niebuhr, *Pious and Secular America* and *Man's Nature and His Communities*.

7. Reinhold Niebuhr, "Redeemer Nation to Super Power," *New York Times*, Dec. 4, 1970, 47.

Yale Hill
Stockbridge, Massachusetts 01262
April 27, 1971

Dear Ron,

Thank you so much for your letter about your prison experience. And your lobbying in Washington, D.C. about this futile war. I am proud of that common editorial in the four papers, Protestant and Catholic. And even more proud of your non-violent demonstration, even though a minor law ordained your jailing. I am glad you found my *Reflections on the End of an Era* relevant. Let us hope we have arrived at an age of maturity. My book incidentally was too much influenced by the Marxist apocalypse. My affectionate regards to you. God bless you.

Reinie[8]

He had come home from the hospital, as he was too weak for further treatment. In April he would weaken and then regain some strength. Ursula continued to care for him, reading to him during the last days from among others her friend's book *Geography of Faith*, a dialogue between Robert Coles and Daniel Berrigan. The end drew near in May, and on June 1 a few weeks short of his seventy-ninth birthday he died peacefully in his sleep. I learned that the family had phoned me at the seminary and at the home of John Raines in Philadelphia. Joan, Randy, and I had been on a monthlong camping trip around the South and we spent our last night in Philadelphia with John and Bonnie. On June 2, on our way from Philadelphia to Pittsburgh we heard of the nation's loss over the radio. Randy, for the first time, observed his father's crying as he drove that long road.

8. Letter to Ronald Stone from Reinhold Niebuhr (Apr. 27, 1971). Previously published in Ronald Stone, *Professor Reinhold Niebuhr* (Louisville: Westminster John Knox, 1992), 26–25.

15.

Legacy

> If we live we live unto the Lord and if we die, we die unto the Lord, so then whether we live or whether we die we are the Lord's.

On June 4, 1971, Bob Miller drove Abraham and Susan Heschel and me to Stockbridge, Massachusetts for the funeral in Jonathan Edwards's old church. There were two others in the station wagon, but I can't remember whom. Susan and I, as the youngest, sat in the rear seat and gazed out the back window as we progressed over the beautiful Taconic Parkway and the connecting rural roads to Stockbridge. Stockbridge seemed too normal, as if it refused to acknowledge the moment of the sorrowful day. I said hello briefly to Ursula, Christopher, and Elisabeth at their beautiful white house on Yale Hill. Richard Niebuhr greeted me, and then we were off to the church. Across from the church was the cemetery where years later I would visit Reinhold's grave. The relatively stark Congregational Church reflected the New England Puritan heritage indebted to the Great Awakening under Edwards's leadership enriched by the tradition of his ministering to the surviving Native Americans of western Massachusetts.

The hymns and the 67th Psalm were the ones of their wedding in Winchester Cathedral on December 21, 1931. Having worshipped at evensong in Winchester, I could dimly hear the choir there joining in the church here in a town that had once been the American frontier. We sang:

Lord, who hast made us for thine own, Hear as we sing before thy throne, Alleluia! Alleluia!
Accept Thy children's rev'rent praise For all thy wondrous works and ways . . .
Dear living things that work his will, Teach us your children to fulfill. Our good is only through His grace, Our woe the hiding of His face.
Alleluia, etc.

We read together Psalm 67:

God be merciful unto us: and shew us the light of his countenance, and be merciful unto us;
That thy way may be known upon earth: thy saving health among all nations.
Let the people praise thee, O God: yea, let all the people praise thee.
O let the nations rejoice and be glad: for thou shalt judge the folk righteously, and govern the nations upon earth.
Let the people praise thee, O God: let all the people praise thee.
Then shall the earth bring forth her increase: and God, even our own God, shall give us his blessing.
God shall bless us: and all the ends of world shall fear him.

The prayer by Rabbi Abraham Heschel and the sermon by the Reverend Mr. T. Guthrie Spears were obscured by my grief, and nearly fifty years later I do not remember the words.

We closed with the hymn by George Herbert:

The God of Love my shepherd is,
and he that doth me feed,
While he is mine and I am his,
What can I want or need?
Surely thy sweet and wondrous love
Shall measure all my days;
And as it never shall remove,
So neither shall my praise.

The new president of Union Seminary, Bishop Brooke Mosley, pronounced the benediction. Leaving the church, Will Scarlett shook my hand, and we spoke of God's blessing to us in our loving friendship with Reinhold. As it was Friday, the rabbi and his daughter caught a plane back to New York City before the Sabbath began. For fifty years following, when in New York to speak at Union or Columbia, I would walk on Riverside Drive where in walks with him my mind was formed.

QUEST FOR JUSTICE

I recorded my sense of the major theme of his work under the title "Reinhold Niebuhr: A Quest for Justice" at the request of Americans for Democratic Action during the summer following the Stockbridge service in an essay for *American Report*. I realize now, which I did not then, its Don Quixote character. It is part of my understanding of his legacy:

> Reinhold Niebuhr wrestled with the problem of death from his 1915 Master of Arts thesis at Yale to the personal correspondence of his final weeks. He was ready to die as a Christian and yet he struggled for more strength with which to fight for justice. He knew man was finite, but he also felt within himself the urge to complete unfinished tasks. He taught that justice could only be approximated in human society, and yet he relentlessly pushed for a more perfect justice. The limitations upon man including death, did not make faith in God impossible, but rather made faith in God necessary for full life.
>
> He expressed his impatience with the limits his illness placed upon him in late April to a young friend. The young professor had written Dr. Niebuhr from the Washington jail in which he was incarcerated during Holy Week for protesting against the war in front of the White House. Dr. Niebuhr expressed his enthusiasm for the joint Roman Catholic/Protestant nonviolent protest and for their joint editorial published by religious organizations. He expressed his regret that his illness and weakness confined his contribution in such events to participation through friends.
>
> In the 1930s, 40s, and 50s, Reinhold Niebuhr thoroughly dominated the American theological scene and provided a greatly disproportional amount of social wisdom. In the 1960s he defined the emerging problems of technology, race, new cultural and family styles of life, the armaments race, and shed light in his declining health upon all these issues. He counseled statesmen and churchmen, and taught thousands how to live lives of responsible action. He argued brilliantly and polemically for a faith that stood humbly before the mystery of God but which was credible to modern man. No American theologian to date has provided as cogent and critical an interpretation of the life of man before God as has Reinhold Niebuhr. In political life, his eyes never left the goal of a greater justice while holding firmly to the understanding that the struggle for power would continually produce realities only ironically or dialectically related to human ideals.
>
> In his writing on economics over half a century, support can be found for both socialism and modified forms of capitalism, but there is no support for the greed of individuals or the concentrations of power that support totalitarian tendencies. His actions and initiatives in race relations can provide support for tacticians of both militant and nonviolent strategies of social change, but there is no toleration of those who would rationalize white racism or caution blacks to push slowly. His polemics in international

politics have been directed against both globalist and isolationist policies of the United States. He urged the responsible use of American power and attacked its misuse. He will be remembered primarily as an actor and theorist who continually sought ways to win in all areas of human life the maximum degree of freedom. Human freedom is rooted in transcendence and therein rested the agony and glory of human life. His political life was a continual struggle to realize a political order that would grant the greatest possibilities of freedom to the people.

The death of Reinhold Niebuhr is an awesome loss to the nation, the church, and mankind, but the measure of the loss and depth of our grief is a witness to the greatness of the gift we were given.[1]

Ursula wrote in July 1971:

Dear Ronald,

Your warm and sympathetic letter has been sitting on my desk for many too many weeks. Thank you so much for it. I have been reading it often.

Your column in *American Report* was a splendid summary, I thought. I found myself regretting that Reinhold, himself, could not read some of these pieces about him. None that I have seen have been sentimental or conventional . . . this in itself seems to be a tribute.

Christopher and I are glad and grateful that you are doing what you are—with your book and in your general studies to carry on the "tradition." Reinhold, as I, welcomed your independence of thought and outlook, and I find myself, perhaps sinfully, proud that Reinhold did not collect disciples, but had friends such as you, who sympathized with and understood his work, and developed your thought independently.

Meanwhile, I hope you have a good summer and some chance for rest and recreation. Do you carry on a double assignment next year at Pittsburgh and at Union? Let me know some time.

I was planning to leave this month for England and then Israel, but my tiresome back has postponed my plans. I shall be in New York, at least during the week, for the rest of July having intensive treatment with Hans Kraus, the back man. Then hopefully, [I will go to] England in August and Israel in September.

Love to you both,

Yours sincerely,
Ursula M. Niebuhr

1. Ronald Stone, *The American Report* (Summer 1971). Niebuhr Papers, Library of Congress.

P. S. I hear you are in Russia—Splendid—I shall expect to see some write-up.

P.S.S. Is there another copy available of your column, that we could send to the Library of Congress with other papers of Reinhold's, or should we have a Xerox copy made?[2]

RIVERSIDE CHURCH MEMORIAL

Richard Fox concluded his biography with the June 4, 1971 service at Stockbridge. Charles Brown carried his biography to the November 1, 1971 memorial service at Riverside Church. Bishop Mosley, president of Union Theological Seminary, phoned me and asked me about hymns and prayers for the service at Riverside. He also asked me to speak following Arthur Schlesinger Jr. Rabbi Abraham Heschel would have a role in the service, as would the former president, John C. Bennett. In the request he said something about needing a former student of Dr. Niebuhr's and a young voice in the service. Brown concludes his book with Bennett's prayer. Niebuhr's longtime colleague and close friend thanked God for Niebuhr's friendship, his sense of humor and laughter that enriched all encounters. He was thankful for Niebuhr's deep sense of justice, which led him to fight for the dispossessed. He thanked the divine for Niebuhr's deep commitment to the seminary and his work and loyalty for it. The gift that came to us was the light of his mind, and he prayed that we would keep the faith as Reinhold had in the words he so often used: "If we live we live unto the Lord and if we die, we die unto the Lord, so then whether we live or whether we die we are the Lord's."[3]

Brown emphasized Arthur Schlesinger Jr.'s address. Schlesinger portrayed Niebuhr as a "Prophet for a Secular Age." His synthesis of William

2. Letter from Ursula M. Niebuhr to Ronald Stone (July 12, 1971). Letter in author's possession. We continued to write to each other for another two decades. We sometimes agreed on our interpretations of Reinhold and we sometimes disagreed. She thought my sermon for his memorial at Riverside Church on November 1, 1971, was too political for the occasion. She regarded my paper on the Zionism of Reinhold Niebuhr and Paul Tillich as inadequately appreciative of Reinhold's early Zionism. She appreciated my book *Reinhold Niebuhr: Prophet to Politicians* (1972) and ordered extra copies for her friends. She commended me on the bibliography we published. She was not appreciative of *Professor Reinhold Niebuhr* (2012). Her late-life misunderstanding of the significance of the occasion led her to be very critical of my lecture at Union, "Reinhold Niebuhr on Books." Union faculty members, on the other hand, were very appreciative and used it in class. Her ire led her to write a valuable paper on "The Niebuhr Library," which is available in the Reinhold Niebuhr papers in the Library of Congress. Most of the three dozen pieces of communication I have retained from her are affectionate, and I have always held her in high esteem. I was surprised when my six-year-old son, Randall, asked me why Mrs. Niebuhr and I fought so much after one of our delightful visits. He had his observations from our disagreements over my criticism of Israel's foreign policy and conquests.

3. Letter from John C. Bennett to author (December 1971). Original in author's possession.

James and Augustine combined with an intuitive grasp of politics allowed him to speak a word from the Christian tradition to illumine modern realities. His modern criticism rendered Christian faith relevant even to the nonbeliever. In his revision of modernity and Christianity he produced the most impressive synthesis to illumine the realities that Schlesinger, as a historian, faced. He, of course, referenced White's tale of the academics organizing "an atheists for Niebuhr group." The dropping of this old chestnut into the evening forced me to relate the story of my Jewish atheist friend who told me of having to make a reverse leap of faith to keep from becoming Christian after reading Niebuhr. As a child of the religious Midwest I was never as certain as Schlesinger or Niebuhr that we were living in a secular age.

I processed into the sanctuary with Roger Shinn. He in his wonderful way chided me that the program listed me as Professor Ronald Stone while I had not earned that distinction yet. To my mind, of course, Roger Shinn or John Bennett should be giving the address. As we entered the sanctuary, I noticed off to the right four men in work clothes. They were my old friends from the night cleaning crew at Riverside Church. I had met them while I served as watchman for the church to earn funds for our first trip to Europe. With them standing as sentries in the rear I overcame my anxiety and Roger's teasing to know that all was well. Another unrecognized guest at the church was a student from my seminar in Pittsburgh who had hitchhiked through the rain to attend the service. While the hymn "God's Grace and God's Glory" rolled on in the magnificent gothic structure, Bishop Mosley asked me for the correct form of the Serenity Prayer and I whispered it in his ear. As Schlesinger spoke, I realized that the historical-political character of his address probably should have been complemented by a more theological-ethical address on my part. But I had what I had prepared, and except for adding the reference to my friend's reverse leap of faith I stayed with my manuscript. The eulogy, titled "The Responsibility of the Saints,"[4] was focused on the meaning of the times, which I assumed to be the civil rights struggle and the war in Vietnam in the context of theological education. The talk was quite political, as I assumed our problems were political. We seemed secure in our faith, and the problematic was the political. Likewise Niebuhr had never doubted his faith and it was its application that he worked upon.

I described him as a "laughing lion" that had lived among us. His role was different for each of us, and I could not impose my perspective, but

4. Original manuscript of homily in author's possession. Revised version published in *The Christian Century* 90, no. 32 (Sept. 12, 1973): 881–83.

only admit that I knew him in the quieter period of his life when he worked as a suffering cripple. I remembered the friend who walked with me for two years of Friday afternoons on Riverside Drive, rather than the creator of a theological school or the advisor to statesmen. But on those walks more happened to my mind than in the preceding five days of graduate study at Columbia. In his own way of anecdote, debate, reason, and cajoling he would leave my mind full and my presuppositions in tatters after each conversation. His dialectics spared neither his previous positions nor my recent study.

I described how students in Pittsburgh chose vocations in urban ministry and in graduate study in ethics under the influence of Niebuhr. They also took his opposition to the Vietnam War seriously, risking their careers by painting anti-war statements on the new chapel's walls. They went to jail in Washington, DC, attempting to take Niebuhr's books in with them. He knew he was dying, but his regret was that he did not have more strength to oppose the war. A few weeks after the service Donald Jones, a teacher in the religion department at Drew University, wrote me appreciatively saying his students reacted correspondingly to reading Niebuhr. He is gone now, but I've often wondered, as Don was Hillary Rodham's Methodist youth counselor, how much of Niebuhr she received from Don Jones.

I argued that the themes of most of the socially radical theologies appeared in several of Niebuhr's writings. He tried to hold the elements in balance, and to relate them all to relevance and responsibility. The balance was subjected to the norm of love and its expression in justice. I argued that the authority for such a norm rested in the priority of love in the ethics of Jesus and Paul and their heirs in the tradition. The love was understood to demand the actual good of the neighbor and just social arrangements in society. It also meant the overcoming of self and group interests in life. Though in society, those interests were limited by balancing each other in the power arrangements. For many of us, love understood in the context of a world loved by God is a more responsible and a more radical notion than permanent revolution, for loving the neighbor as oneself prohibits satisfaction even with permanent revolution.

In race relations his emphasis had been on justice. As he reminded James Baldwin, the races would not love another, but more justice must be achieved between them. Respecting the need for a power base in the black churches, he had no patience for Christians not pursuing the rearrangement of power in society between the races. Moral arguments were not enough, but justice demanded stronger sources of power for African Americans than boycotts and demonstrations. He had no patience for those who obfuscated the justice issue between the races. The moral issue was clear and needed to be forced to be heeded.

Our service was held on All Saints' Day whereas the next day, All Souls' Day, might have been more appropriate for a reformer like Niebuhr. In any case using the term "Saint" for Reinhold was in the context of Pauline realism, and referred to Christians as remaining sinners, but forgiven sinners. Reinhold would never exclude his Jewish brothers and sisters in the faith from the purview of the term. For him, the power to act responsibly and to qualify his pride came from Christ, but he was not fussy as to where others found the power, and he reflected often on the grace of our common life.

I reviewed his criticism of three administrations on their Vietnam policies. The focus concluded with his essay on the misuse of religion by President Nixon in justifying Vietnam policy, "The King's Chapel and the King's Court." The use of Amos and Martin Luther King Jr. to attack the pretensions of J. Edgar Hoover and Richard M. Nixon was Niebuhr at his most authentic.

Then the talk turned toward Niebuhr's analysis of religion being used to justify cruel policies and foolish wars. The need for repentance and forgiveness was echoed. The country needed to be led away from self-righteousness toward a change of direction and the ending of the war. This needed to produce forgiveness for both those who committed crimes in Vietnam and for those who were arrested or harassed for opposing the war. Some of the argument John Raines and I had developed and published advocating a general amnesty was woven into the remarks. It went beyond advocating general amnesty to recommending that the church rethink its provision of chaplains for Vietnam, and either abandon the practice or find ways to enable them to serve with the freedom of their consciences regarding the war, while preserving service to the warriors themselves. Keeping in mind Ursula's reading of Daniel Berrigan and Robert Coles at Reinhold's final bedside, I urged Union Theological Seminary to replace the John Foster Dulles–Reinhold Niebuhr dialogue with a Daniel Berrigan–Niebuhr dialogue. Union asked Daniel Berrigan to teach there in the following years after his release from prison.

Rereading the homily nearly forty years later, I find that its political stridency could have been reduced. However, I had chosen Reinhold to teach me politics, and he had. I reviewed some of his theological themes, but on our walks the searching conversations had been about the politics of the 1960s in theological perspective, and I brought this agenda to the occasion.

In speaking with Bishop Mosley about the service, I had insisted we conclude with the singing of "For All the Saints." I, of course, always remember Reinhold whenever the hymn is sung. On that "All Saints' Day," singing it in that recessional concluded our living friendship.

1. For all the saints who from their labors rest.
   Who Thee by faith before the world confessed.
   Thy name O Jesus be forever blest.
   Alleluia! Alleluia!
2. Thou wast their rock, their fortress and their might;
   Thou, Lord their captain in the well-fought fight;
   Yet Thou in the darkness drear, their one true light,
   Alleluia! Alleluia!
3. And when the strife is fierce, the warfare long,
   Steals on the ear the distant triumph song,
   And hearts are brave again, and arms are strong,
   Alleluia! Alleluia!
4. O blest communion fellowship divine!
   We feebly struggle, they in glory shine;
   Yet all are one in thee, for all are Thine.
   Alleluia! Alleluia!

RELEVANCE FOR THE TWENTY-FIRST CENTURY

The issues of Niebuhr's last decade project their trajectories into the twenty-first century. Some of the problems require new emphases and a reforming of strategies and tactics. Other causes need to be fueled by more passion than he could muster in his weakened condition.

His detailed political reflections and advice to policy formulators were consistently on the practical progressive side. He was concerned about forming progressive organizations that could push toward practical political gains. He understood the results would be compromises between a progressive Christian ethic influenced by European socialism and the more conservative American realities grounded in a deeper individualism than our European predecessors. He was particularly well received by the British Labour Party, but his closest allies were reforming Democrats and his cohorts in the Liberal Party of New York. Though he left the Socialist Party in the United States because of its tendencies toward pacifism and isolationism, he consistently worked to strengthen governmental support for the workers and the poor. His theory of democracy required an understanding of compromise and prudence, which he practiced in a progressive direction. Late in life he would still define his liberal politics in terms of his role as one of the founders of Americans for Democratic Action.

On economics, the gains for the working class and his allies in the union movements lulled him into satisfaction. The New Deal reforms were expanded by Democrats and accepted by President Nixon who expanded health rights. He became satisfied and relaxed his demands for more equity. The following fifty years of globalization, union decline, and technological development reduced the power of workers. Academic and populist rhetoric has demanded greater equity and bemoaned the decline of the worker's share of the economic rewards. The restoring of the regulative principle of equality as critique of present economics would be Niebuhrian in spirit. Thomas Piketty and Joseph Stiglitz's works indicate the right direction.

On race, the progress toward equity corresponded to Niebuhr's worries. The establishment's resistance grounded in popular support resisted real black empowerment. White backlash to black militancy for justice overwhelmed the optimistic hopes of many in the 1970s. James Cone criticized Niebuhr's lack of passion for racial change on the one hand. Elsewhere he recognized his contribution to racial justice as greater than other white church leaders.[5] As one who heard Malcolm X and James Baldwin speak in the 1960s, his rhetoric on racial justice could not match theirs, and Niebuhr knew it.

His approach to improving race relations was multifaceted. Early in his career, as chair of the Detroit race relations commission in the 1920s, he utilized a massive social research project to make detailed recommendations for policy changes in Detroit. Throughout his life he prodded government to effect change. He funded social action movements, founded organizations, supported demonstrations and boycotts. He urged voter registration and celebrated African Americans winning places in government. As early as 1932 he advocated in the spirit of Gandhi for massive, nonviolent civil disobedience. His preface to the *Mississippi Black Paper* and his foreword to Martin Luther King's Vietnam address were among his strongest statements near the end of his life. His 1968 discussion of the Kerner Commission Report had the most detailed policy recommendations of his late career based on the Commission's findings. The most recent book on Niebuhr decries his diminution of publications on race relations in the 1950s.[6] I count eigh-

5. James Cone, *The Cross and the Lynching Tree* (Maryknoll, NY: Orbis, 2011), 57.

6. Jeremy L. Sabella, *An American Conscience: The Reinhold Niebuhr Story* (Grand Rapids: Eerdmans, 2017), 129–30.

teen publications urging racial justice in the 1950s, which is not bad for a one-handed invalid. Since Brunner's complaint in the 1952 volume on Niebuhr's thought,[7] several careful scholars have noted his failure to support particular policies. I suspect Brunner had not read all the material advocating particular policies and specific candidates in the American literature. But the Americans should have read it before recording their criticisms.

The time for advancing racial justice through massive nonviolent demonstrations may have passed. However, winning justice through specific regulations and reforms supported by social science is potentially crucial and requires renewed political will and progressive victories. Sabella's recent book suggests that Niebuhr lacked a structural analysis in response to racism. He hints that Gary Dorrien provided this insight. Dorrien knows that Niebuhr, following the National Advisory Commission's report on urban violence, addressed issues of black poverty, unemployment, white prejudice, the Negative Income Tax, college scholarships for black youth, and government participation in overcoming oppression of the minority in housing and civil rights. Certainly these are structural factors. This is particularly true when the history of racism in the Constitution, the abolition of slavery, and the white suppression of voting is detailed. Sabella rightly points out that Niebuhr never used the term "white privilege." I don't know if anyone in the white part of the civil rights movement followed James Baldwin's introduction of the term that early. Maybe Sabella's real point follows the lack of structural considerations argument:

> We cannot address these structural dimensions of racism by calibrating the present structure of checks and balances. Instead, we must fundamentally restructure the way the system operates.[8]

Sabella does not suggest how the government passes fair housing legislation while ignoring checks and balances in counting votes and flails away at changing the whole system. At this unfortunate point Sabella's realism fails him. His quote of Dorrien restores the balance: noting the "immense passion that he has invested in this subject," Dorrien adds, "Just the fact that he is the white American theologian that cares about this

7. Emil Brunner, "Some Remarks on Reinhold Niebuhr's Work as a Christian Thinker," in *Reinhold Niebuhr: His Religious, Social, and Political Thought*, ed. Charles W. Kegley and Robert W. Bretall (New York: Macmillan, 1961), 30–31. Harlan Beckley, *Passion for Justice* (Louisville: Westminster John Knox, 1992), 340–41, 367.

8. Sabella, *An American Conscience*, 131.

really more than any of his peers, it's easy to miss. And many people have."[9]

Andrew Young has acknowledged Martin Luther King Jr.'s utilization of Niebuhr's thought in the race struggle. King detailed this use in his published writings and in his seminary research papers. Niebuhr's successors in the Reinhold Niebuhr Chair at Union Seminary have all acknowledged that Niebuhr's criticisms of the powerful did not usually contain recommendations for the oppressed becoming stronger. While there is a note of truth in his friends' critique, his use of Gandhi's tactics for the civil rights struggle in the 1930s should not be neglected. The recommendations of self-improvement of African Americans in 1925 and his 1968 essay "The Fate of the Negro Minority in a Self-righteous Nation" are full of strategies for overcoming racism. His advice and sponsorship of unionization of workers was also a strategy for overcoming poverty. Even the organizational support for refugee organizations, farm workers, and coal miners were all specific tactics for empowering the weak. Maybe his successors surrendered his legacy at positions they were not required to abandon.

Even his very early argument with his friend Archbishop Temple over the rights of women to be ordained was support for a vulnerable group for their self-development in the church. Feminist critique of his male language for the deity or in a generic sense to refer to all of humanity is in order, and I in most cases, but not all, correct his usage. Prior to his death, though, significant feminists followed the fashions of the day with similar usage, including Rosemary Radford Ruether. More significant is the Judith Plaskow, Susan Nelson tradition of criticizing his anthropology. However, their adoption of one of Doris Lessing's images of woman from one of her novels is inadequate. She changed as a person and writer, as did her images of women in various books. Lessing herself rejected overly simple models of women's experience and rejected feminists' use of her characters. The success of the women's liberation movement has certainly been more profound than Niebuhr could have seen by 1971. Both his wife and daughter enjoyed these positive movements, and he sought opportunities to empower both of them.

ON INTERNATIONAL RELATIONS

His warnings about the future for democracy in *The Democratic Experience* seem, fifty years later, to be appropriate. Liberation theology for Latin America had only begun to emerge in his last three years, and he

9. Sabella, *An American Conscience*, 132.

did not respond to it. *Christianity and Crisis* published critiques posthumously of his work from that perspective. My study of liberation theology with Gonzalo Castillo in 1990 in Peru, Central America, Mexico, Brazil, and Argentina revealed its suppression by the United States, the Roman Catholic Church, and local governments. Gutiérrez's hopes of seizing power with socialist regimes failed. The Roman Catholic Church declined more than it changed sides to join the liberation struggles.

The surprising advances in the Global South toward increasing social gains were found in India and China as Hindu and post-Communist China civilizations increased human welfare with capitalist, globalist reforms. Niebuhr had not seen those gains coming though he had hoped for democracy in India.

Of course, his philosophy was limited by his social context and time. He was not a liberation theologian. The changes in gender and sexual relationships date many of his remarks. Some of his comments on African Americans seem quaint even when uttered by one engaged in the struggle for social justice.

Despite his hopes for human progress, he was not as hopeful as the leaders of liberation theology or movements. Unfortunately his realistic tempering of many hopes has proven to be historically truer than their hopes. The resistance of the establishment has been furious. The results of the 2016 American election indicate how deep the resistance in the American people is toward science, reforming religion, feminism, immigration, Native Americans, and African Americans.

His insistence on managing well the nuclear deterrent still remains a number one priority for world leaders. He never would have agreed with me that the Christian ethicist must denounce the reliance on nuclear deterrence, assuming massive use of it if it fails. Niebuhr, Bennett, and Shinn, my teachers, all accepted the tragic reliance on deterrence. I insisted, as did the Presbyterian Church under the leadership of Dana Wilbanks and me, that nuclear deterrence was essentially immoral and that alternatives must be extraordinarily sought. Niebuhr's moral position was that no first use of nuclear weapons was possible. The US policy is that it cannot renounce first use of nuclear weapons. In many cases the United States has threatened to use nuclear weapons to bolster its position. His argument for no first use of nuclear weapons would have limited the overreach of the United States, if adopted. Of course, the United States has already demonstrated the only actual use of them. Daniel Ellsberg's argument that "no first use" should be the beginning of dismantling the Doomsday Machines of the United States and Russia shows how far ahead of US policy Niebuhr was, though he knew nothing of the science of "nuclear winter."[10] He accepted the permanence of Communism in both China and Russia. He suggested it might last as long as seven hundred years or about as long as the Islamic militancy. He was certainly mistaken in these judgments. Earlier he had hoped for a quicker demise of Communism due to some of its internal contradictions. His conclusion was that resistance to Communist expansion was necessary, and he advocated the use of soft diplomacy and aid for development to thwart its encroachments in the non-Communist world. While accepting nuclear deterrence as a tragic reality, he rejected the actual use of nuclear weapons unless the allies were subject to nuclear attack. In his opinion, deterrence stabilized the world and protected the peace between the superpowers, and there must be no nuclear war.[11] In the same review he distanced himself a little from John Bennett, who was more sanguine about the role of Marxist influence in the Global South.

Niebuhr's urging of the use of boycotts, divestment, sanctions, diplomacy, foreign aid for development, and the United Nations rather than normally relying on military force were all contributions toward peacemaking. President Obama's speech for the Nobel Prize and Hillary Clinton's advocacy of soft power both reflected their appreciation of Niebuhr's approach to maintaining some peace in an often-violent world.

The last decade of Niebuhr's reflection emphasized the contribution of political philosophy, history, and normative theory to the foreign policies of the United States. A central goal was the avoidance of the catastrophe of nuclear war and hoping for the transformation of US opponents in the Cold War. He labored on the ideological basis of the nations and empires interacting with power in the present system. Earlier he worked practically on transforming the international system through advocating for the United Nations and working in the formation of the United Nations Educational, Scientific and Cultural Council.

His perspective was much more complex than that attributed to him by the neorealist Kenneth Waltz.[12] It contained the revisions of realism suggested by Alexander Wendt's *Social Theory of International Politics*,[13] of utilizing normative theory and political philosophy. More importantly it connected directly to US policy in practice and perspective and refused to remain isolated from politics. Its perspective is grounded both in

10. Daniel Ellsberg, *The Doomsday Machine* (New York: Bloomsbury, 2017).

11. Reinhold Niebuhr, "Nuclear Dilemma," *Union Seminary Quarterly Review* 17 (Mar. 1962): 239–42.

12. Kenneth Waltz, *Man, the State and War* (New York: Columbia University Press, 1959).

13. Alexander Wendt, *A Social Theory of International Politics* (Cambridge: Cambridge University Press, 1999), 76.

ontology and national myths, indicating the historical development of national interest. Additionally it incorporates into foreign policy interpretations of world religions, which are an important part of world politics. Immediate gains in rejecting the overly secular interpretations of the Kennedy administration and the neoconservative perspective of the Bush administration would have been realized if religious questions had been asked. What is the cost of imposing a Catholic regime of French allies on a Buddhist peasant culture freed by Communist revolutionaries? How wise is it to destroy a Sunni regime and empower a Shia regime in a wrecked nation-state bordered by an aggressive revolutionary Shia regime?

While practically involved as a writer for Franklin D. Roosevelt, a UNESCO delegate for Harry Truman, and a State Department consultant for George Kennan, he is correctly thought of as a teacher and writer of political philosophy. Though he wrote on structure in *The Structure of Nations and Empires*, he needs to be remembered not as a theorist of international relations but as a philosopher of US foreign relations in a time of war.

He has been credited as the founder of the realist school of political thought about US foreign policy. George Kennan, Hans J. Morgenthau, John C. Bennett, and Samuel Huntingdon have all credited him as the Father of the school. His was a moderate realism trying to preserve the peace. Robert Kaplan in 2018 defined the school: "Realism is about the ultimate moral ambition in foreign policy: the avoidance of war through a favorable balance of power."[14] Kaplan's definition fits Niebuhr particularly well in the nuclear age. In our own time as we become more aware of the total destruction of "nuclear winter," we need to dismantle the Doomsday Machine which can be unleashed by accident, mad rulers, or miscalculation.

As a philosopher he informed the critical reflection of the Protestant churches on US foreign-imperial policy. The church thinking on international relations and foreign policy has a normative element that is ignored by international relations commentators at the nation's peril. The perspective of many other communities is needed also. The ignorance of the normative perspectives of the organized religious communities with their international reflections of other religious communities is potentially blinding to the United States.

If Alexander Wendt[15] is correct that international relations theory requires ontology, the foundations of ontology in various theologies are

14. Robert D. Kaplan, *The Return of Marco Polo's World* (New York: Random House, 2018).
15. Wendt, *A Social Theory of International Politics*, 370–79.

needed. Even beyond understanding theology or the logic of reflection upon the ultimate, as Niebuhr wrote in *The Annals of the Political Science Association*, an understanding of myth is required.

In a previous work, *Politics and Faith*, I devoted forty pages to responding to feminists, liberation theologians, socialists, and pacifists.[16] Often Niebuhr has been subject to an "Ideal Type Critique" in which he is criticized for not being more like a feminist or a liberation theorist, or a European-type political theologian. His own ideal type was that of Jesus as he understood him through critical New Testament studies, especially by Albert Schweitzer and W. D. Davies, but that "ideal type" was not achievable. These types of critics often reveal more about themselves than they do of Niebuhr's thought and action. Beyond his writings, his organizations like the Americans for Democratic Action, the Delta Cooperative Farm, the Highlander Schools, the Fellowship of Socialist Christians, and the dozens of organizations he worked with were all compromises between his perception of reality, the social good they could accomplish, and his Christian faith. As Ursula said: "He did pretty well."

The agenda for the twenty-first century is much as he suggested for the 1976 Bicentennial Commission. Manage the nuclear umbrella. Save the environment. Achieve justice for the African Americans and other minorities in America. Other less crucial agenda items he advocated on behalf of were justice for the Arabs while protecting Israel, justice for women in American society, universal healthcare, and greater financial equity in America and in the world. All of the above were taught in his final years of social ethics classes and in his writing. They all require realistic-democratic political action here and international cooperation abroad.

16. Reinhold Niebuhr, *Faith and Politics: A Commentary on Religious, Social, and Political Thought in a Technological Age* (New York: George Braziller, 1968), 364–402.

Index